SO YOU WANT TO BE A FIGHTER

PROFILES IN FORTITUDE, RESILIENCE, AND ACCEPTANCE—INSIDE AND OUTSIDE THE RING

O YOU WANT TO BE IGHTER

PROFILES IN FORTITUDE, RESILIENCE, AND ACCEPTANCE—INSIDE AND OUTSIDE THE RING

CHRIS ALGIERI

Publisher Mike Sanders
Editor Christopher Stolle
Design Director William Thomas
Contributing Writer Renee Wilmeth
Book Designer Rebecca Batchelor
Compositor Ayanna Lacey
Proofreaders Lisa Himes & Matthew Crowley
Indexer Beverlee Day

First American Edition, 2022
Published in the United States by DK Publishing
6081 E. 82nd St., Suite 400, Indianapolis, IN 46250

Copyright © 2022 by Chris Algieri
DK, a division of Penguin Random House LLC
22 23 24 25 26   10 9 8 7 6 5 4 3 2 1
001-325197-MAY2022

Note: This publication contains the opinions and ideas of its author(s). It is intended to provide
helpful and informative material on the subject matter covered. It is sold with the understanding
that the author(s) and publisher are not engaged in rendering professional services in the book.
If the reader requires personal assistance or advice, a competent professional should be
consulted. The author(s) and publisher specifically disclaim any responsibility for any liability,
loss, or risk, personal or otherwise, which is incurred as a consequence, directly or indirectly,
of the use and application of any of the contents of this book.

Trademarks: All terms mentioned in this book that are known to be or are suspected of being
trademarks or service marks have been appropriately capitalized. Alpha Books, DK, and Penguin
Random House LLC cannot attest to the accuracy of this information. Use of a term in this book
should not be regarded as affecting the validity of any trademark or service mark.

ISBN 978-0-7440-4255-9
Library of Congress Catalog Number: 2022931020

DK books are available at special discounts when purchased in bulk
for sales promotions, premiums, fundraising, or educational use. For details, contact:
DK Publishing Special Markets, 1450 Broadway, Suite 801, New York, NY 10018
SpecialSales@dk.com

Printed and bound in the UK

Cover photo © Daniel Newman
Photograph on page 10 and back cover © Chris Algieri
All other images © Dorling Kindersley Limited
For further information see: www.dkimages.com

A world of ideas:
see all there is to know

www.dk.com

DEDICATION

In memory of Patrick Day

A champion in life and a warrior in the ring

Patrick was one of the rare good guys in the boxing world. You'd be hard pressed to find someone who didn't like him. You'd be a liar if you said you outworked him in the gym. Always respectful and always busting his ass.

A gentleman and warrior at the same time

What a champion is supposed to be

If there was someone who truly embodied the Champion Lifestyle through and through, it was Pat. He lived and breathed boxing, he loved the craft, and he made it his everything.

I think I speak for all who knew you: I miss you, Champ.

Rest in Power

"All Day"

10-16-19

CONTENTS

FOREWORD

Whether it began as a formal sport in ancient Egypt circa 3000 BC or among the Minoans in 1500 BC, boxing might be deemed one of the world's oldest and certainly toughest sports. As an ardent boxing fan, a layman practitioner, and sport science and sport psychology researcher, I've long contended that the sweet science of boxing is the world's fiercest sport. Foremost, while most sports regard incidental or intentional contact to an opponent's head as illegal, a penalty, or a reason for ejection from competition, direct contact to the head with an effort to injure is the first and principal objective of pugilism.

The primary goal in boxing is to damage one's brain—the very resource which enables an athlete to plan, predict, calculate, navigate, and apply the physical and mental skills that have taken years to master. Moreover, the force created by an elite boxer when attacking the body is enough to relocate one's organs within the chest cavity. Couple these factors with two highly conditioned and exceptionally fast athletes launching strikes at each other at 25mph within a 30-inch range—and this while instantaneously applying offensive and defensive maneuvers. Herein are only a few of the numerous reasons boxing might be the world's hardest sport and observations one must accept before deciding with absolute certainty that they want to be a fighter.

Chris Algieri is a former all-state wrestler, former WKA and ISKA kickboxing champion, former WBO junior welterweight world champion, and college-educated sport scientist and nutritionist. Such experience and credentials afford Chris the requisite abilities to elucidate the complexities of boxing and support the contention that it very well might be the world's toughest sport. Just consider the way Chris achieved his WBO world title in 2014: boxing 11½ rounds with a broken nose and an orbital bone fractured in three places.

In this book, Chris shares his personal journey and interviews some of the world's greatest combat sport fighters as well as coaches, trainers, and broadcasters, providing novel insights into the mental and physical challenges of this highly demanding sport. Chris and the athletes who share their insights and experiences afford us the opportunity to see, hear, feel, and live through the fights in the first person.

If you're a boxing or mixed martial arts fan, coach, trainer, analyst, or elite-level fighter, *So You Want to Be a Fighter* presents combat sports in a context that's long overdue. Chris and the great athletes who've been interviewed show us that while these sports are an art—and ones that require more than the highest levels of physical conditioning—they also demand rare abilities in mental intellect, acuity, confidence, discipline, and resiliency. This book isn't just an excellent read. It's an organic experience in fighting.

TONY RICCI (Ed.D, MS, FISSN, CSCS, PES, CES, CNS)
assistant professor of exercise physiology and nutrition
at Long Island University in Brooklyn, New York

INTRODUCTION

A couple years ago, I posted a photo to my Instagram of what a boxer looks like after a winning bout. My face was swollen, the bruises were dark purple, and the blood was dried. It looked like it hurt a ton, but my expression was calm and I had the start of sly smile on my face. That photo perfectly captures the mentality it takes to be a fighter: If you want to experience the thrill of victory, you've got to be willing to go through hell. And it's gonna hurt.

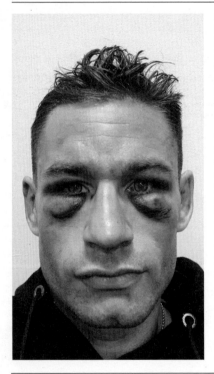

So you want to be a fighter...are you sure? People "want" to be a lot things but they have no idea what it takes to get there. I've heard the same story countless times from those around me over the years- "I'm going to do this...and I'm going to be that... then after I do that, I'm going to do this...". Cool, now go try and come back to me and let's see if you have that same energy.

Winning is fun. Success isn't winning. Success is making a habit of winning and winning when the odds are stacked against you. Success hurts. The road to success hurts even more. On the way you will fail, over and over...and over. The successful, the Champions, have endurance- not physical endurance- spiritual endurance. The spirit and the will that doesn't fade. The act of showing up and the ability to keep showing up goes a long way. You never truly fail till you give up.

Bruises fade, cuts heal, scars become distant reminders...make sure the results match the effort and the effort is worth the pain. If you want to truly be successful- it's gonna fuckin' hurt. #success #boxing #will #skill #motivation #win #champion

In 2019, I wrote my first book, *The Fighter's Kitchen*, a cookbook with healthy recipes. But I had a new idea brewing in my mind—something I'd been thinking about for a long time and which I called the "Champion Lifestyle." As I've met so many fighters and trained as a professional fighter for years, I've learned that being a champion is much more than just defeating the person in front of you. Every champion I've ever met had something special about them, an aura, an energy. It's about the mindset, the attitude, the preparation, the professionalism, and a deep understanding of the sport.

Over the past few years, I've interviewed countless champions. I've written articles, called fights, and joined podcasts—all delving into the mindset and spirit of a fighter. Everyone has ideas. And as we follow our favorite fighters, we get fragments of stories but never really the full picture about the drive to win. We talk about the victory, but we don't talk about what makes a fighter get up off the mat when they've been knocked down.

With the stories in this book, I wanted to get to the heart of what it really takes to be a champion and see if there was a consistent message. I wanted to collect thoughts from the most successful people in some of the hardest fighting professions in the world and find out what sets champions apart. What I got was an amazing outpouring of experiences from fighters at every level and a wealth of knowledge for those looking for the secrets to winning.

As a commentator and boxing analyst—as well as a professional boxer— I've made incredible connections with people I've watched and studied for years. Having access to these brilliant athletes isn't something I take for granted. A big part of doing this book was just taking the time to speak with and interview my favorite fighters. Long before I was champion of the world, I was a fan—and that won't be changing anytime soon.

I've written this book to shed some light on how difficult the journey to a championship truly is. The fans only see the tip of the iceberg when it comes to the making of a champion. We live in a world where social media makes everyone believe they can do anything. Social media posts from athletes and fans make it look like everyone has their own personally curated highlight reel for the world to see. It makes it look like anyone can do it. It's not reality. The stories shared in this book are the opposite of easy. They're the cold, hard truth that being successful takes a lot of pain, sacrifice, and failure.

It's ironic that it was a viral social media post of my own brutalized face after a fight that became the catalyst to make this book a reality. "So You Want to Be a Fighter" is sparking a movement around the idea that the path to success, to being a champion, is about more than meets the eye.

In this book are profiles of combat sports champions who share their personal experiences. They talk about their struggles, victories, motivations, and how they ultimately overcame obstacles. The unifying themes that come up in each and every interview are extremely eye-opening. It certainly makes one think that some people are just meant to be champions. No matter what insurmountable odds are in front of them, they'll find a way.

I wrote this book from a fan perspective first and I hope it's obvious as one reads through these pages. I've taken great care to be true to the champions who chose to share their stories—many of whom showed incredible bravery and vulnerability during our discussions.

I hope that by reading these amazing stories of drive, discipline, and perseverance that you're able to take as much away as I did while writing it.

CHRIS ALGIERI
Boca Raton, Florida
January 2022

ONE MORE ROUND

"Fight one more round. When your feet are so tired that you have to shuffle back to the center of the ring, fight one more round. When your arms are so tired that you can hardly lift your hands to come on guard, fight one more round. When your nose is bleeding and your eyes are black and you are so tired you wish your opponent would crack you one on the jaw and put you to sleep, fight one more round—remembering that the man who always fights one more round is never whipped."

–"Gentleman Jim" Corbett

My fight to win a world championship didn't follow the storybook route I had in mind. It was a brutal life-and-death struggle with ebbs, flows—and plenty of drama. I'll be honest: It hurt. It wasn't the kind of pain that professional athletes in soccer or baseball talk about. It was a visceral, soul-searching type of pain—the kind only fighters know about. The pain of being hit over and over again. The pain of trying to see through blood and around swelling. The pain of getting hit and losing time, waking up moments later in a different place. But I won. I'm forever a champion—and I don't regret a moment of the journey.

Movies, media, and novels all romanticize boxing. It's the sweet science—a sport that incorporates the best elements of nearly every other athletic endeavor: speed, endurance, power, fluidity, timing, footwork, strategy, and training. So much training. But it's also brutal and damaging. It takes a different level of commitment than other sports. You don't "play" boxing. What truly separates the champions is that ability to dig deep in those key moments and tap into that spark, that drive, that something deep inside. It's the ability to just keep going, to do whatever it takes.

Call it what you want: the will to win, drive, competitiveness, grit, never-say-die attitude—combat sport athletes all have names for it—but ultimately, it's what makes a champion. It's the difference between holding that belt in the air at the end of a fight—no matter how bruised and bloody you are—and going home to analyze what went wrong. My own championship bout was no exception.

ON THE TITLE SHOT

The lead-up to the fight felt more like the lamb headed to slaughter than a matchup for the ages. When the fight was announced, I was listed as a 15-1 underdog to unseat the reigning WBO junior welterweight champion. Ruslan "The Siberian Rocky" Provodnikov had fought in the Fight of the Year against future Hall of Famer Tim Bradley and now he'd fight me. At the time, he was considered the bogeyman of the division—one of the most violent and devastating champions. I was 19-0 but relatively unknown on the world stage and had just broken the top 10 in the rankings.

During fight week, Provodnikov told a reporter he was "willing to die in the ring" and that he didn't think I had the same level of commitment. When reporters asked for my response, I laughed and said, "No one has to die. This is a boxing match. I'm going to outbox him." Little did I know …

ON ROUND 1

I'm circling the ring and subtly feeling the canvas beneath my feet. I'm testing the ropes to see how tight or loose they are at various points around the ring. I'm getting accustomed to the space my opponent and I will share for the next 36 minutes—or less. I know I have time. The plan has always been to box smart early and avoid the brutal power-punches of the defending champion. A classic boxer-versus-brawler matchup.

The strategy is simple: Be the matador. Use lateral movement, avoid the bull's horns, use your darts to weaken the bull, take the bull late when he's tired, and get ready for the *coup de grâce*. I've done it countless times through rounds in camp, practicing on every sparring partner, session after session, week after week. Rinse, repeat, focus, refocus.

It's a minute into the first round and everything's going perfectly. I'm moving, boxing, sticking the jab, making the champion miss wildly. I'm curious and decide to see if what they say about this guy is true: that he's a brutal puncher. I've been hearing he's been laying sparring partners out cold in the gym even with big gloves and headgear. He sends a wild sweeping right hook aimed for my ribs. I take it on the left elbow as I'm moving away to absorb and deflect some of the impact. BANG. Okay. So everything they said is true. The punch lands on my left elbow and reverberates through my body. I feel it all the way on my right side.

The blow is just another reminder to stick to the game plan and play it safe early on. It's funny how focused you can be in the middle of the action. It's amazing how much goes through your mind in such a short period of time. You can have a full conversation in your head in the time it takes to throw a jab.

"Man, we really have a great game plan," I think.

I get caught on the ropes for just a second and immediately step off with a no-look Hail Mary uppercut, never expecting it to reach its target, but …

CRACK!

It lands squarely under the chin of the champion. "Man," I think. "Everything is working." And then I think, "Maybe we can fast-forward the game plan a few rounds … ."

See, now, this is where I made the mistake. Good old hubris almost took me down. I plant my feet and throw a right uppercut, followed by a left hook, but the champion was already set in his stance and threw his left hook at the same time. Mine lands. His lands bigger.

And just like that, in an instant, my world is upside down—literally. I do a somersault when I get hit. The next thing I know, I'm on the canvas for an official knockdown. Not my first in fight sports but the first in my pro boxing career. In my professional kickboxing career, I'd been knocked down. I know I just need to take my time and assess the damage.

I get up right away, a little rattled but nothing I've not experienced in my long pro fight career. But something's different this time. Something's wrong. It feels like … like … a piece of my face is caved in. There's an intense pressure behind my right eye and a sharp blade-like pain shooting down my face to my upper teeth. I can no longer feel my upper lip or part of my upper gums. It's a weird combination of sharp, searing pain and tingling numbness. Probably why it feels like a hole has been punched in my skull.

The boxing match I'd planned on has turned into a life-or-death struggle with a relentless opponent. In that moment, I'm thinking, "Maybe I was wrong—maybe I do have to be willing to die to win."

That one punch cost me a very important point in the scoring of the round as well as the use of my right eye. I get up pretty quickly and take my first standing eight count from the referee. My legs feel strong, my head is clear, but my eyes aren't working. I can't focus even with my one good eye. All I can see are blurry figures: first the referee right in front of me, then the shadowy figure of my opponent as he closes the distance. I make the decision that before taking any more damage in a defenseless state, I'll take a knee to give my eyes time to clear up.

My tactic proves to be a pivotal point. As I'm on my knee receiving my second standing eight count, my eyesight suddenly comes back. I can see the referee and my opponent. I think, "Okay. If I can see, I can fight."

ON THE EMOTION

People always wonder what's going through a fighter's mind when they're in the middle of a fight. They usually assume that time speeds up. In reality, time slows down—and it slows down enough to let you process and recognize your emotions in real time. The secret is getting them under control and harnessing their power.

My first emotion was anger. I was angry I'd made the mistake because it was grounded in greed and impatience. I was too busy relishing the fact that the plan was working and that I'd be world champion by the end of the night. When you make mistakes with world-class competitors, they let you know immediately—with hostility and violence.

My next emotion was fear—not for my own safety but that I was going to lose my chance to be world champion. Fear I was going let down my team and my family. I'd worked so hard and sacrificed so long. I'd convinced everyone around me that I could do this and that tonight was the night my dream would come true. What had taken decades to manifest was about to be gone in an instant.

It's funny how your mind prioritizes your thoughts during times of crisis. I had the referee giving me a standing eight count positioned between me and a seething Siberian across the ring looking to finish me off. All I could think about is who I was letting down. All the sacrifices my family has made, the struggles they've watched, and the help they've given me along the way. All the times they'd asked when I was going to be done with "this fighting thing."

This was my chance to prove everyone wrong: My dreams were in reach, and all the hard work and suffering were worth it. And I was blowing it. But these thoughts disappeared very quickly as I got back into the fray. The referee cleans off my gloves and yells "BOX!"

No time to think. Time to fight.

ON ADVICE: "YOU STILL GOT YOUR LEAD EYE."

The bell rang to close the first round. It was the round that felt like an eternity and it's finally over. My nose is a faucet, my eyes are blurry, I can't feel my upper teeth. I can feel my eye swelling as my heart pumps. I feel the tender flesh of my eyelids stretching.

I sit on the stool in my corner feeling panic and hectic energy. The doctor is fighting to get in first to see the damage, saying, "Hey, Chris, how are you? Can you see?"

I vividly remember watching countless fights where a boxer is asked this question and they'll either hesitate or say they can't see. If that happens, the doctor must stop the fight in order to protect the fighter. If you can't see, you can't protect yourself. If you can't protect yourself, you can't fight.

"Yes, Doc. I'm good."

In comes the cutman—the man I trust to pull this situation out of the fire. He skips the ice to reduce swelling and goes right to the enswell. An enswell is a heavy piece of metal placed in ice so it becomes cold. The cutman presses it against the bruise to move the swelling away from the eye. As one might imagine, it's incredibly painful because it damages tender fascia. The skin literally tears away to accommodate the swelling. He gets to work. I sense he's frustrated, but I see the resignation on his face. Now my panic is real. My stubborn competitiveness takes a major blow and I start to think all is lost.

"Hey, baby! You still got your lead eye. We're good!"

My head trainer, Tim Lane, whom I've known since I was 16 years old, gave me that small and specific piece of information. I've still got my lead eye. I can still see my opponent's right hand and I can protect my damaged right eye with my right glove. I've lost an eye, but I've still got two hands and two legs.

It's a brilliant coaching tactic at a vital point in time. It's all I need to hear. I anchor my will in the facts. I focus on what I still have, not what I've lost. I'm prepared enough to win this fight, even at a deficit.

One of the things I love most about boxing is there's no hiding what you are and what you've done. If you don't do the extra roadwork, your cardio will suffer late in a fight. If you don't follow a strict diet, the weigh-in will reveal it. If you don't believe in yourself, your opponent will capitalize on it.

I've done my homework and I've prepared my body for this moment. There's no confidence booster like preparation. I have an unshakable confidence in my skills, my training, and my ability to stick to the game plan.

ON BECOMING WORLD CHAMPION

As history writes it, I got off the deck twice to outbox the champion to take a split decision win after 12 rounds. The fight was later named Upset of the Year by *The Ring* magazine because I boxed 11½ rounds with a grotesquely swollen eye. I had to go through hell to finally hear my mantra come true.

"And the *new* champion of the world …"

If there was ever a single moment that made all the hard work and sacrifice worth it, this was the one. All the long hours in the gym, the pain, the sweat, the blood, the tears. All the missed experiences, vacations, weddings, and nights out. It was all worth it in that moment.

The feeling was more of a relief than anything. The weight of all the promises I'd made along the way had been lifted. I told everyone I'd be champion one day and that I was going to win the big one when it came my way. There were many times I watched my friends and family roll their eyes or placate my delusions of grandeur.

Leading up to the fight, a boxing pundit said I was either "a genius or crazy" for taking this fight. Afterward, I looked more like the former than the latter—but with a plum-sized hematoma for an eye.

ON MY MOMENT

My team and I are escorted back to the dressing room, surrounded by microphones and recorders in the hands of reporters, who are bombarding us with questions. It's a tornado of frenzied energy and excitement.

I overhear my coach, Keith Trimble, tell a reporter, "Day one, we knew this would happen. With Chris, it's all in his head. It's all mental. If he sets his mind to it, he'll figure out a way to win."

I do a few quick interviews, then my matchmaker, Ron Katz, the guy who arranged many of the fights leading up to this moment—someone I credit with helping me be ready for a fight this difficult—grabs me to say I have to go to the hospital. To which I retort, "The hell I am! I'm going to my press conference." I've always dreamed of presiding over the post-fight presser as the champion of the world. This is my moment.

Even though everyone is pressing me to go to the hospital right away, I shower up and put on the outfit I'd brought for this specific reason, along with some dark sunglasses to hide my badly swollen eye. They try to get me to skip the presser one final time and go to the ambulance.

"Nope. Where's the presser? I'm ready."

I get to the dais with the WBO super lightweight world championship belt draped over my shoulder. Reporters are hurling a flurry of questions my way. One of the organizers tells everyone to relax and wait their turn.

The first question: "Chris, can we see the eye?"

My promoter, Joe DeGuardia, cuts in. "No, no. Chris, you don't have to."

I say it's fine and I slide my dark shades up. The lip of my sunglasses has caused a few droplets of blood to pool up. As the glasses go up, a single "tear" of blood dramatically rolls down my face as the crowd gasps at my horrific-looking eye. I field a handful of questions and then it's time to go. The swelling is causing me a tremendous amount of pain at this point. There isn't any more room for my eye to swell, so it's started to swell into my skull, which is causing a splitting headache.

I finally allow them to take me to the hospital to see what the damage truly is. I get in the back of the ambulance. I've got my championship belt over my waist, my protein shake in my hand, and a smile on my face.

My lawyer, Eric Melzer, says, "You did it, kid. You should be proud. … Does it hurt?"

"A lot," I say. Pain never felt so good.

CHAPTER 2

THE CHAMPION LIFESTYLE

"I am the greatest.
I said that even before I knew I was."

–Muhammad Ali

"To be champion, you have to believe
in yourself when no one else will."

–Sugar Ray Robinson

BANG! POP! BANG BANG POP!

I'm in the back of a small room, warming up with my coach by hitting pads. It's cramped. It's humid. It feels like the walls of the room are closing in as the minutes pass. Only my head coach, his assistant, and the cutman are there. They're cheering me on as I blast the pads with laser precision.

BANG! BANG! POP! POP! BANG!

I'm dialed in. I'm feeling it. I don't want to stop. I wish I could fast-forward to the middle of the first round. There's something about that seemingly never-ending walk to the ring. That moment when your name's being announced while you stare at your opponent across the ring like a caged tiger is painfully long. That first bell. That first contact. That roar of the crowd. It's all a sensory overload at first. Then suddenly, you're there. You're finally present. You're home. You feel every moment like never before. Time moves slower and it's like you're seeing things before they even happen.

I've finished with my warm-up when I hear someone yell, "Okay! Let's go! You're up!" No matter how ready you think you are, you panic. "Okay. Where's my robe? Are my shoes tied? Is my music going to play? I need water. Wait, my glove feels funny. ...' It doesn't matter. There's no time to think anymore. This is it. It's go time.

My team says a quick prayer and has a group hug. I know this is it. They know this is it. Nothing left to do. In what feels like an eternity, I'm walking to the ring with my music, Eric B. and Rakim's "Don't Sweat the Technique," blasting in a small event hall deep in Nassau County, Long Island. Friends and family in earshot chanting my name: "Al-gier-i, Al-gier-i, Al-gier-i ... ."

On the outside, I'm ice-cold. Looking in my eyes, you'll see a killer with a chilling gaze and lasers for eyes. On the inside, I'm a wet noodle. The doubts and the negative talk race through my mind: "What are you even doing here? Why are you here? You don't belong here. You haven't trained long enough. What are thinking? Take your beating and go home. No one cares. It's okay. You tried. It's not for you, kid."

Before I have the chance to contemplate any of that, I hear "ding, ding."

Round 1.

Well. This is it. Time to do what you trained for.

That first contact—whether it's you landing or getting hit—is everything. The niceties are over and this person in front of you is there to destroy you. The choice is now out of your hands. The time is now.

And just like that, the room goes silent and I'm right where I need to be. All the doubts, all the negative thoughts are gone. I'm home. I'm firing and sliding. Snaking the jab through my opponent's guard, finding my range, analyzing his movements, assessing and assimilating his rhythm. I'm in it already. This is where I belong. ...

At the end of the second round, I feint a jab to the body and switch to a left hook to the head. The hook lands clean to the side of the upper part of my opponent's head. As soon as the connection was made, my third metacarpal bone snaps. It felt like my middle finger's knucklebone literally came off my fist. The bell rings to end the round shortly after.

Does it hurt? Hell yes it does. Excruciating pain like white-hot fire shoots up my arm and I feel it with each pump of my rapid heart rate, making my glove tighter. But pain during a fight is different. You experience it more than feel it. You acknowledge the pain and then assess. How hurt are you? Can you go on? It'll go numb after a bit, then I'll be able to use it again. This is all going through my head in the short moment it takes me to walk to my corner.

I don't show it on my face at all. I don't tell my corner because what's the point? I'm not gonna quit. They don't need to know. I'll figure it out in there. I'm used to things falling on me to figure out. This is nothing new.

ON WINNING WITH HONOR

Growing up, I wanted to be a champion. As a kid, I was wickedly competitive, obsessing over wins and losses in anything from checkers to fistfights. I also grew up watching kung fu movies and practicing martial arts, so I had a deep appreciation for the ideals of honor, discipline, and respect. I was willing to do anything to win, but I had to achieve it the right way. Truly, winning didn't just mean getting a higher score. It meant winning with principles I put on a pedestal throughout my young life.

I was also a boxing fan and enamored with the great champions, like Sugar Ray Robinson, Gene Tunney, Willie Pep, Alexis Arguello, and Sugar Ray Leonard. Aside from their obvious talent and accomplishments, these men all carried themselves with great character outside the ring. They were men with class—expert warriors who wore fine suits and acted like gentlemen. Arguello was especially known to help lift his defeated opponent off the canvas after he knocked him out. Robinson tried to pull out of a fight because he had a dream the night before that he killed his opponent.

Their stories taught me that a person of honor doesn't need to hate their opponent in order to destroy them in the ring. In my mind, a champion in the ring was a champion in life. If you lived and competed with honor, discipline, and respect, you lived that way outside the ring too.

Maybe I was naïve when I was a kid. But as I became a professional fighter, I began to understand there was a difference between those fighters who were successful and respected as honorable competitors and those who, well, weren't. As I formed my own philosophy on my way to becoming a champion, I learned so much more.

ON THE CHAMPION LIFESTYLE

Over time, I began to formulate the whole body/mind approach I call the "Champion Lifestyle." It's more than just a finely tuned training plan. It's the entire mindset of a champion. Champions know how to fine-tune their craft. They know how to set goals and hit milestones, but true champions have something more. They have drive, discipline, and an ability to live their lives with the knowledge they have what it takes deep inside.

Being a champion is more than simply having a title. It's not a binary state—it's a transient state. A champion is a champion before they win or after they lose. The title might be fleeting, but the achievement of having won it will always be with a champion.

I often tell young fighters at the gym, "However hard you think it is to win a title, it's much harder." Some of them interpret it as solely pushing themselves past their physical limits, but I have to explain that it's about more. It's about making your plan for training to fine-tune your body, but it's also about creating a routine to optimize what your mind can do. It's about setting goals and milestones as well as creating a strategy to meet them, even if you need to do some research or get some help. It's about finding what mental exercises work to help you ground yourself and visualize success. It might be yoga, meditation, or even Bible study, but developing a mental training regimen is just as important as your time in the gym. Planning can include a strategy to win but should also include a plan if you lose. Most importantly, it's about defining your core ideals for living like a champion.

Some fighters think combat sports are purely physical. They equate winning solely with how hard they physically train. But pushing yourself beyond your limits in the gym day in and day out is only part of the process. Before becoming world champion, you have to believe, act, and train like a champion. You must have the mindset that no matter what, you'll achieve your goals. That there's no obstacle that could deter you. That you've done everything to earn it. And that you'll never quit. If you don't believe in yourself and your ability, it will show in the ring on fight night.

Under the lights in the ring, every fighter is naked. All inner thoughts about yourself are on display. Everything that you did or didn't do in training will be exposed on the world stage. There are no shortcuts. Competition is the ultimate proving ground for your belief in yourself, your skills, and your preparation. Sometimes you can do everything right and still lose, but if you didn't do the work and your mind isn't present to execute the plan, then defeat is almost guaranteed.

ON THE CORE PRINCIPLES OF BEING A CHAMPION

My professional life has two aspects: one as a professional fighter and the other as a professional broadcaster and boxing analyst. Both aspects help me find a balance in my relationship with boxing and both give me the opportunity to meet current, past, and future champions nearly every day. In conducting these interviews, I've begun to see some common themes that have added to my own thoughts on what it takes to live the champion lifestyle. I want to explore what it really takes to win—in the ring and in life.

Here are the four main principles of the Champion Lifestyle:

- Drive (Why)
- Mindset (Who)
- Conviction (How)
- Execution (What)

This list might not be complete. It might grow and evolve. It might even be different for you. In the following explanations, I also incorporated some key factors to success, like creating a strong team, knowing the business, and understanding how to transition to the next stage of your career.

ON DRIVE (THE WHY)

In psychology, the concept of "drive" in sports refers to an increase in arousal and internal motivation to reach a particular goal. In clinical psychology terms, "arousal" means "vigilance" and "alertness." It's mental sharpness and wakefulness, not sexual arousal, and when it comes to boxing, it's directly related to a fighter's performance in the ring. If a fighter has a low level of arousal prior to a fight, their reaction time and concentration levels will suffer. A fighter with a high arousal level is primed and locked into the task ahead of them and will likely perform at a high level. Every fighter can attest to this: On sparring days, you've either got it or you don't.

Whether it's about performing in the gym on sparring day or in the ring for a fight, internal motivation coincides with training for what we call "preparation." A highly motivated fighter will put in the extra hours in the gym, do the extra reps, and run the extra miles. Their motivation? Being prepared. Drive is the fighter's level of desire to push themselves forward to reach new levels of fitness and readiness.

Having drive without preparation can spell disaster. A fighter who's in great shape but not prepared to face an equally matched or more talented foe will likely lose. A fighter who's highly dialed in but out of shape also runs the risk of defeat or, worse, serious injury. Champions know how to master the ability to consistently tap into their internal motivation to prepare properly as well as to lock in on fight night when it's time to perform.

A phrase I've always heard at the gym: "Hard work beats talent when talent doesn't work hard." In other words, even if you're not naturally talented, you can get pretty far down the road with hard work and preparation. That takes drive. That takes an internal motivation to keep going. And to the contrary, the most talented athlete will suffer at the higher levels if they aren't driven to work hard.

How does an athlete tap into the amazing tool that is drive? Ultimately, it comes down to finding your "Why?" Many of the champions I've spoken to have very specific goals, like escaping poverty, proving people wrong, providing for their family, or simply the feeling of "I want to be great."

Understanding and acknowledging what motivates you—and what you really want—can be a hard path but one that's ultimately worth it. You'll probably take the twists and turns along the way, with a few near misses, surprising opportunities, and total failures. But you'll get to your destination, even if it's not quite the way you thought you would.

ON MINDSET (THE WHO)

In *The Art of War*, Chinese general Sun Tzu writes that you need to know the enemy as you know yourself: "If you know yourself but not the enemy, for every victory gained, you will also suffer a defeat. If you know neither the enemy nor yourself, you will succumb in every battle."

I've always loved this quote because it speaks to so many aspects of the champion lifestyle. Knowing about your task is important. Knowing yourself is important too. Having one without the other makes success nearly impossible. Having true knowledge of both makes tasks much easier. This quote speaks to yet another element that removes the doubt of failure even during the most difficult and painful times: your mindset.

For many fighters and coaches, knowing your opponent is a matter of research. You can watch fights and analyze technique, find certain mistakes your opponent makes, or read their tells and telegraphed movements. But knowing yourself can be more difficult in many ways. I've found over the years that the best way to know yourself—or anything for that matter—is self-analysis. I often refer to this as "homework."

You need to know your intentions, goals, and level of spiritual endurance. How far are you willing to go to achieve what you want to accomplish? If the answer isn't "To hell and back," then you might need to reassess. Knowing who you are and what you can do might be the hardest part about any endeavor, especially one as risky and as dangerous as a combat sport.

You also need to know your "enemy" (or task). This takes homework and research. Be obsessed and devour all the information you can about what you want to achieve. Having knowledge of yourself and the knowledge of the journey to achieve your goals gives you tremendous power.

Mantras and visualization are two techniques that have helped me to not only know myself but to also understand the task in front of me. Both are forms of meditation and can be powerful tools in preparation for any task. A mantra is a word, thought, or idea you repeat over and over again. It can be repeated in your mind or out loud or written repeatedly on paper.

Leading up to winning the world title, my mantra was 'I, Chris Algieri, will defeat Ruslan Provodnikov on June 14, 2014, at the Barclays Center in Brooklyn, New York, to become WBO super lightweight champion of the world." I wrote this on a sticky note and put it on my bathroom mirror so it would be the first thing I saw in the morning and the last thing I saw at night before bed as I brushed my teeth.

I've also used visualization to deal with anxiety related to the unknown. When there's anything I have to do that gives me anxious feelings, I run through it over and over again in my mind. I walk through every detail as I prepare to accomplish the task that's making me uncomfortable.

Think about the first time you drove a car: You were excited and nervous. After a few years of driving consistently, it became second nature. Now you probably try to do too many things while behind the wheel. I feel the same way about being in the ring. Even though I haven't physically done what I'm visualizing, I've accomplished it in my mind countless times. I've seen my hand raised 10,000 times before I ever step in the ring.

There are other techniques you might have tried or that work for you. Whatever it is, find it and do it! And don't be afraid to learn something and adapt a technique from other athletes. You might be surprised that a calming technique for a world champion gymnast or tennis player works for you too.

One last note on knowing yourself: Don't be afraid to talk to a professional. Many of the fighters I've talked to over the years have sought professional help for everything from overcoming a training hurdle to dealing with defeat. Some have endured the deaths of children, the breakup of marriages, or even addiction. Many have close relationships with their pastors. Every step forward you make with self-exploration is another step toward knowing yourself that much better.

ON CONVICTION (THE HOW)

Conviction is a strongly held belief or opinion. It's the state of mind of someone who's absolutely sure of what they believe in. Conviction is an essential element to winning. It's the belief you can win. All those naysayers? Those people telling you to quit, to give up on your dreams? That doubting negative self-talk that creeps into your mind? All are silenced by conviction.

Closely related to conviction is "courage." It takes bravery to stand up for what you believe in. It takes courage to get in the ring or cage. It takes courage to believe in yourself and your abilities to accomplish greatness.

As a principle of the Champion Lifestyle, conviction works closely with the principle of drive. Drive—the motivation—is how you realize conviction: your belief in your dream. Without it, people might see successful fighters and say, "Why not me?" or "That was easy." The funny thing about success is that you see only the triumphs. You don't always see every failure and struggle along the way. To be good at anything difficult, you must be all-in. Your time, your thoughts, your hopes, your dreams—all have to be part of a singular focus that's all encompassing. You must be open to the possibility of failure. Failure is never failure until you quit.

Conviction is what a fighter needs in order to stay disciplined through the pain and rigors of training and competing. I often call this "spiritual endurance." Physical endurance is vital, but to have the spirit to push through the pain and find that extra gear is what separates the top performers from everyone else.

ON EXECUTION (THE WHAT)

Watching two highly trained human weapons fighting with their lives, livelihoods, and legacies on the line is a powerful event. From a 4-round bout to a 12-round championship fight, that moment is central to that individual's very being. Every time I watch a fight, I'm there with them in the ring, feeling what each fighter is going through. If you're a true fan of the sweet science, it's always worth it to take a moment before the first bell rings to absorb the reality of what you're about to witness.

For a fighter, the moment is bigger. It includes the technical ("Look for when he drops his left hand after he jabs"; "Go to the body after the cross"). It includes the strategy ("He gets tired after the sixth round, so wear him down"). And it includes the moment ("The arena is full, the fans are loud"). While fighters talk about time slowing down in the moment, they still have a plan to execute. Execution is following the plan on autopilot. It's the result of preparation so the body can perform while the mind reacts and responds.

During my title-winning effort versus Provodnikov, I didn't have time to think about my damaged eye because I was too busy thinking about how to win. Losing an eye early in a fight might seem like a disaster, but in the heat of it all, it was just a distant thought. I was 100% focused on what I needed to do to win. Champions find ways to win—no matter the circumstance.

When it comes to executing the game plan, use all four principles together. Focus on what matters and leave negative thoughts behind. Execution is all about being in the moment.

ON YOUR TEAM

Boxing is the loneliest sport on the planet. But a fighter will never get to the elite levels without a team of supportive individuals who can help them perform as close to their potential as possible. A fighter's team works tirelessly in the shadows of the gym and on the street. Your team doesn't throw blows with you in the ring, but they're battling alongside you. Your corner is with you in the gym and on fight night.

Then there are those who wage the battles outside the ring and understand the pitfalls of the business side of boxing. These include your team members who know how to prioritize media obligations and have the legal chops to deal with any contract issues. Lastly, your team must know what to say to motivate, how to celebrate success, and how to have hard conversations.

One of the biggest advantages a fighter can have in today's elite world of fight sports is a knowledge of the business. In the world of professional fighting, it's always hard to know who to trust, but by assembling a good cadre of reputable managers, attorneys, and agents, champions can ensure they're making smart decisions out of the ring. And while a college degree isn't a necessity for fighters today, an ability to communicate, present yourself, and act professionally is. How you present your story to the world is important, regardless of your ability to knock out an opponent.

A strong team that communicates well and works together effortlessly can make each member feel like they're part of a championship endeavor. They'll unselfishly give their professional skills and personal time to a real champion. While good teams make good money, their dedication makes it seem more like a labor of love than a profitable endeavor.

Your team can also make or break your training camp and gym sessions. The culture of a gym is critically important for the mental and emotional health of a fighter. Training camps are hard. Between your conditioning, sparring, making weight, being away from your family, and media obligations, the psychological stress surrounding a big fight is immense. Having coaches and team members around you whom you trust and rely on is often an overlooked aspect to camp. And if you're in a gym or camp where you don't feel your team members are supporting you, communicate with them. Open discussions about problems, concerns, and worries are critical to success.

It's up to an athlete to perform and get the win. But a coach's instructions in the corner can pull a fighter away from the brink of defeat. Think of the famous line from Angelo Dundee to Sugar Ray Leonard versus Thomas Hearns in 1981: "You're blowin' it, kid!" As history tells it, Leonard was behind on points and roared back to stop The Hitman in the 14th round of one of the best fights of that generation.

ON WHAT'S NEXT

The champion lifestyle is a path of success that permeates everything you do in life. Just like the classic fighters who were gentlemen inside the ring and out, modern fighters are equally successful in boxing and in life. It takes a lot of hard work (and the occasional lucky break), but champions have what it takes to perform time and time again—whether in the ring or a cage, with a microphone in their hand, as a CEO, or as a parent.

It's imperative that athletes understand that a professional fight career won't last forever. A fighter's career, especially at the elite level, has one of the shortest lifespans of any sport. Having the self-awareness to accept this fact and having the forethought to set yourself up to transition to the next victory in life are critical.

Fighters often attach their identities to fighting, which makes it difficult to move on after they hang up their gloves. But those who understand the champion lifestyle know how to move to the next level—whether it's as a successful gym owner or YouTube video personality. They know how to mourn their career, but they celebrate it, set new goals, prepare a plan, find that motivation, and execute. They know how to find the courage for the next stage. A champion isn't just a champion in the ring or the cage. They're a champion in life. Knowing you have the tools to be successful in all aspects of life is what the champion lifestyle is all about.

CHAPTER 3

LOVE & LOSS

"It's like being in love with a woman.
She can be unfaithful, she can be mean,
she can be cruel, but it doesn't matter.
If you love her, you want her, even though
she can do you all kinds of harm.
It's the same with me and boxing. It can
do me all kinds of harm, but I love it."

–Floyd Patterson

Many fight fans today won't remember Floyd Patterson unless they're into old-school fighters from the 1950s and 1960s, but he was a champion. He was the youngest heavyweight to hold the world title and he was the first heavyweight to ever lose the title and then regain it. He understood the struggle every fighter faces. No quote better encapsulates the internal battle that plagues every fighter on the planet.

There's no question that fighting for a living is bad for you. The harsh reality is none of us end our careers the same way we started them. There's inherent danger in training, competing, and fighting. The scars, internal and external, build up over time. But enduring that pain isn't the struggle; the struggle is that we all know the quest is bad for us. We know it's going to leave those scars, but we don't care. The important thing is that as we encounter each injury—spiritual or physical—we let it heal. We accept it and we understand that we'll learn from it and become a better fighter, a better person, and a better champion.

"Do you like getting hit?" I've been asked this countless times throughout my two decades as a fighter. It's a fan question that every fighter's heard—and one that seems to have an obvious answer. Mine is and will always be the same: "No. I hate it actually. But I love hitting people more than I hate getting hit." Fight sports can be a mystery to people who don't understand that they aren't so much about hitting as they are about winning and losing. Champions want to win and they're willing to risk humiliating defeat in order to achieve glorious victory.

ON THE CHAMPION MINDSET

Fighters are different. I liken a fighter to a race car driver. That "need for speed" is there but in a different way. Drivers and fighters are willing to risk their lives to be victorious. But to succeed in either sport, you have to be wired differently. You have to feed off the intense physical and mental focus while performing at an elite level. For fighters, the thrill of victory following pitched physical combat might be one of the most powerfully addictive drugs known to humankind. There's something about the one-on-one fight, the physical endurance, the pain, the power shots, even the fight inside your own mind. It's a feeling only fighters who've been in the ring can understand.

Some outsiders—and even some fans—will never understand the appeal. Some love the strategy of the matchups and psychological battles. Others feed off the visceral appeal of combat. But the fact is that most ordinary people will do anything to avoid a fight.

It's nearly impossible for a normal, average sports fan, onlooker, family member, spouse, boyfriend, or girlfriend to wrap their head around why someone would put themselves through the rigorous training programs, nutritional routines, and physical pain that fighters endure. It's hard for outsiders to understand the mindset of a champion—and *why* they'd sacrifice and struggle for the chance to win. Why they'd risk everything for a chance to know sweet victory.

Fighters know that the pain of defeat and the mental scars associated with loss can do as much, if not more, damage than the punches to the skull or ribs. Wounds scar over and bruises fade, but the psychological damage can persist for much longer. Modern medicine and time can heal most injuries, but it takes a different kind of treatment to heal the wounds you can't see.

To be a professional in combat sports is a job that, quite simply put, you have to love in order to do successfully. It's a cruel and unforgiving endeavor that can bring you to the highest highs when you win and the lowest lows when you lose. Especially when you lose. And while most people think of fighting as strictly a sport of one-on-one combat, the battle of the fighter against their own self is the harder fight. It will strip you of everything you are and leave you a broken-down shell of your former self if you let it.

So why do so many continue to pursue their dreams even when losing is so hard? They carry with them passion, desire, and a willingness to sacrifice. They know the process will seem intolerable at times, but they also know that with this drive, the journey will all be worth it. Those who succeed are the ones who took the biggest risks and who ultimately know that "the juice is worth the squeeze." Win, lose, or draw.

ON LOSING

Entire books have been written on winning. The victories, the fights, the wins no matter the cost. But there aren't any road maps for loss. No one tells a fighter how to process a knockout or a loss by a close decision. Fighters have to figure out for themselves how to mentally handle injuries, media backlash, and decisions on when their professional fight career is over. Life is always a battle and no one wins every time. And for fighters, losing is an inevitable part of competition, especially at the highest levels. So how does one deal with a loss?

When I was a younger fighter, losing a fight was never part of the equation. I feared it, but it didn't seem possible. It was like the bogeyman, always out there but never a realistic ending to a bout. I spent so much time visualizing and preparing to win that the idea of losing wasn't tangible. I lived and acted like a champion even before I was one, and in my mind, champions *always* win.

So the first time I experienced a big loss, I realized that while I'd obsessively prepared for everything when it came to winning, I was completely unprepared for losing. I was mentally, emotionally, and psychologically destroyed. Suffering my first real professional loss was the hardest moment of my life—almost the exact opposite of how winning a title was the best. I'd always dreamed of and envisioned winning a world championship, but I'd never spent any time envisioning loss. I had to regroup. I had to go back to what always got my mind right: my homework.

As I looked for answers, I went back to the history of fighting. I studied the legendary champions of the past, the ones I idolized—all of whom had lost. And aside from how they dealt with professional hardships, I started to see how they became champions. They all had a mindset that allowed for winning—and losing. They'd all had to figure it out. I learned that understanding loss was just as much a part of the champion mindset as the drive to win. That's when I had to acknowledge that losing was a part of the sport—and made winning all the sweeter. For me, as a professional, that knowledge raised the stakes and made me want to win even more.

My first loss was in the biggest fight of my career versus the legendary Manny Pacquiao. I was 20-0 and the WBO super lightweight champion of the world. I moved up in weight class to fight Pacquiao for the welterweight world championship in Macau. I had in my mind that I'd be an undefeated two-division world champion and beat a living legend. The sky was the limit.

Not only did I lose, but I was outclassed over all 12 rounds, losing a unanimous decision. I was devastated. Many people gave me credit for going the distance and lasting 12 rounds with a great like Pacquiao, but I didn't want to hear it. Once losing became tangible to me, I realized I had to *learn* to lose. It didn't mean I had to be good at losing, but I had to understand how to move past it. Losing is no easy task and, honestly, it's something every fighter struggles with. Every loss hurts, as it should. When it stops hurting, when it stops ripping your guts out, you probably shouldn't be fighting anymore. Until that first defeat, it never occurred to me that part of being a champion, part of the preparation and training to win, included an understanding—and healthy respect for—loss.

After my fight with Pacquiao, Paulie Malignaggi told me, "In boxing, you got to have thick skin and a short memory." His words hit home on so many levels for me. You have to have a thick skin to deal with the ridicule and the trolls as well as a short memory in order to move on in your career and return to championship form.

ON CHAMPION ACCOUNTABILITY

Just like Floyd Patterson says, "If you love her, you want her, even though she can do you all kinds of harm." That harm is real. That love is real too, but you need to be realistic about what you can do and what you're risking. I've always seen myself as a champion, but the day I can't compete at the championship level, I won't be in the ring any longer. Some might call it ego, but ultimately, for champions, it's about accountability.

Champions don't lament failed quests for glory—whether it's a loss in a championship fight or retiring from a professional fight career. The acknowledgment that the end might come is just as important as understanding losing versus winning.

Champions learn from their mistakes. They look for the opportunities those mistakes offer them and they capitalize on them. Most champions will tell you a loss is a failure to execute. It's because they know they made a mistake. We train day in and day out to not make mistakes because we understand it only takes one mistake at the highest level to affect the result.

However, it also means champions know how to analyze loss and capitalize on the lessons. Those lessons might be technical, like adjusting your foot position or refining a specific combination. They might be strategic, like executing a game plan or changing your strength and conditioning program. Or they might include life lessons—the most important lessons of all—like letting go of bitterness and anger or moving on to the next chapter of your career and, possibly, your life.

Fighters at the highest levels are there for a reason. They want the biggest challenges in front of them because they believe in themselves. They believe they can find a way to win. The greater the self-belief, the greater the risk they're willing to take because they know that with the risk comes the glory. But these high performers also operate on the precipice of failure day in and day out because that's where the biggest improvements happen.

Stepping into the ring takes an amazing amount of desire, courage, and heart. If maintaining the dedication and drive to train at a championship level were easy, then everyone would do it. If the act of fighting another highly trained combatant were easy, a lot more people would be world-class fighters. The highs and the lows of fight sports might be the wildest swings of any endeavor. You consistently live on the brink of being a hero or being labeled a "bum."

ON PUBLIC BACKLASH

Any professional athlete has to deal with the media and fans. It's just part of the game and some are better at it than others. It's never easy to be under public scrutiny and hear criticism from unknown sources—on a daily basis—for months at a time. Daring to be in the public eye leaves you open to the anger and critiques of those watching. I've seen it break fighters down, while others have seemed to never be bothered.

Social media doesn't make this any easier. More than ever before, fans have direct access to the athletes they watch fight. They feel they have an ownership in that fighter's success or failure, and they feel very comfortable offering their negative opinions. Public responses can affect a fighter to varying levels, but no one is completely immune. Moments of weakness hit everyone, even your favorite fighter. Champions learn over time to deal with public opinion and personal pressures triggered by fans and haters.

The athletes of today also deal with career pressures related to news coverage, social media, and public perception. We live in a transactional world. Fans and promoters want to know, "What have you done for me lately?" No one cares about anything but your last fight result. The good thing about the lightning-quick news minute is you can overturn poor public opinion easily with a good win. But it also means if you're overcoming an injury or aren't at the top of your game, you might be in for a long layoff.

There can be two additional outcomes. Some fighters end up fighting for longer than they should. They're seeking those last one or two good wins, and they hope that combined with name recognition, they can be back in contention for a title and earning potential. Others end their careers in obscurity, out of sight, and out of mind, serving as fodder for the next generation of hungry lions coming up through the ranks.

Ultimately, champions must understand that public sentiment isn't a weapon aimed directly at them. It's a tool they can use to build excitement when they need it. Some fighters spend their entire careers figuring this out. Others are crippled by the ill will backlash can foster. And while public opinion is important, it doesn't have be positive for it to be beneficial.

Floyd Mayweather perfected using a negative public image to advance his career. "Pretty Boy" Floyd—his early persona as a boxer—was a young, handsome, undefeated champion who was blisteringly fast and a brutal finisher at the lighter weights. He was a nice guy but didn't get as much recognition as he did once he evolved into Floyd "Money" Mayweather. Mayweather's later career persona was a loudmouthed, fast-talking, money-flashing defensive wizard who dominated the sport in the early 2000s. He's a perfect 50-0 and is the highest-paid boxer of all time. Ask him if he cares if the public likes him or not.

ON A CHAMPION'S ACCEPTANCE

A champion owns their wins and loses. Fighters don't choose to fight—they're born to fight. No excuses and no one to blame. All the glory and all the pain. Champions are the ones who take meaning from their wins and losses to hone their perspective. A champion is an ever-evolving organism that understands not only its surroundings but looks inward. Self-reflection is a skill that comes only with wisdom and experience. It's not the fear of losing that drives a champion to push themselves beyond the limit. It's the thrill of victory and the feeling of accomplishment that come with the win. There's always been a romanticism around warriors: gladiators, boxers, soldiers. There's a reason great writers have devoted stories, songs, and legends to the warrior spirit. We live in a way people can only dream of. We look fear, doubt, and death in the face for the chance to be great.

"It is not the critic who counts; not the man who points out how the strong man stumbles, or where the doer of deeds could have done them better. The credit belongs to the man who is actually in the arena, whose face is marred by dust and sweat and blood; who strives valiantly; who errs, who comes short again and again, because there is no effort without error and shortcoming; but who does actually strive to do the deeds; who knows great enthusiasms, the great devotions; who spends himself in a worthy cause; who at the best knows in the end the triumph of high achievement, and who at the worst, if he fails, at least fails while daring greatly, so that his place shall never be with those cold and timid souls who neither know victory nor defeat."

–Theodore Roosevelt, "The Man in the Arena"

JAMEL HERRING

Boxer
Status: Active
Weight class: Junior lightweight
Ring name: Semper Fi
Hometown: Long Island, New York

CHAMPIONSHIPS
- WBO junior lightweight title (2019)
- USBA junior lightweight title (2018)

HIGHLIGHTS
- World Military Games silver medalist (2010)
- US National Amateur Championships gold medalist (2011)
- US Armed Forces Championships gold medalist (2011, 2012)
- Olympic Games Team USA co-captain (2012)

Madison Square Garden is the Mecca of boxing—and fighters from all over the world dream of fighting there. It's no different for native New Yorkers. And while we've always heard that tough guys come from Brooklyn, Jamel Herring and a few others now form an elite group of world champion boxers hailing from Long Island.

For a long time, Jamel and I unknowingly traveled in the same boxing circles around the Long Island and New York areas. He was a decorated amateur and I was a late starter coming from kickboxing. We just missed each other in training and competing. When I finally met him, I knew we were kindred spirits. We're just a couple nice guys, doing the work, coming out of Suffolk, Long Island—or, as we call it, "Strong Island."

Jamel's story is a powerful one, taking him from the boxing rings of New York to the deserts of Iraq. He's suffered from PTSD (post-traumatic stress disorder) and he's tragically lost a child from SIDS (sudden infant death syndrome). Other athletes would've left boxing behind, but Jamel has a unique drive that's kept him going. He's a boxer, a father, and a mentor, and he's recently stepped into a media role as an expert broadcaster and boxing analyst. I sat down with him to ask him about his thoughts on being a champion and what motivates him to succeed.

ON THE DRIVE

We talk about his first memories of boxing and how he discovered his love of the sport. Jamel says he was always into sports, but when it came to making the basketball team, he says, "I missed the cutoff on grades, so I couldn't play." Jamel was driven to stay busy. "I was never into hanging out in the streets, so a friend of mine, Ashantie Hendrickson, invited me down to the gym, where his father was a trainer."

When he got into the "mix of it," he could see that boxing involved discipline and smarts. It changed his attitude about school. "You have to be smart in the ring and outside the ring as well. I just fell in love with it," he says. He credits boxing with motivating him to get serious about academics. By the time he graduated, he was on the honor roll, "looking at the bigger picture of moving ahead in life."

For Jamel, the mental discipline of boxing is one of the most important things he loves about the sport. It's helped him overcome some difficult aspects of his life. "There are times you get in there and start doubting yourself, but I believe in the whole aspect that boxing is 80% mental and 20% physical," he says.

Jamel discovered how to harness the mental aspects of the sport early and used them to push through difficult situations. "I was always the underdog, even in life. People thought I was never going to make it out of Long Island. My friends and my circle never really got out and people just assume you're never going to make it out either." He loved proving people wrong. And he loves using his story to motivate his own kids, of which he has five.

ON BOXING CULTURE

As a young boxer, Jamel came up watching some greats, like Buddy McGirt, Pernell Whitaker, Oscar De La Hoya, Érik Morales, and Bernard Hopkins. They were the fighters he wanted to model himself after. They were fighters who showed him that this was what he wanted to do.

"Floyd [Mayweather], the great [Sugar] Ray Robinson, the list goes on," he says, listing them on his fingers. Jamel approached boxing as a student, studying the best fighters in the US, UK, and Mexico. "I didn't just follow African American fighters or even just American fighters," he says. "I gravitate toward everyone who's doing something great in their own way."

Jamel has had lots of opportunities to build relationships with boxers from every background, using his experiences in the World Military Games, Armed Forces Championships, and the Olympics. Those relationships have helped him become a student of the sport, learning something from each of them and marveling at how they're all interconnected.

His first amateur loss was to Danny Jacobs, who went on to become middleweight world champion. Their fight was at the famous Gleason's Gym. ("Nothing but history in that gym," he says.) Throughout his amateur career, he came across a lot of good people whom he still knows now. "I think I'm actually more happy to see guys I came across and see them achieve success in their careers. It's just good to see good people living out their dreams."

ON BEING A MARINE

During his senior year of high school, Jamel was big into boxing and wanted to try out for the Olympics. But it was also 2001, the year of the 9/11 attacks on the World Trade Center. For many New Yorkers and Americans, the world changed. Everyone in the surrounding New York City area lost friends or family when the towers fell that day. Jamel says he felt called to find more in his life. He recalls thinking, "I've got to do something with more of a purpose. I looked at it as putting others in front and not just thinking about me."

He decided to enlist as a Marine at 17. He'd end up serving two tours in Iraq. "I had my 18th birthday in boot camp, so I was just a kid myself." He had to become an adult "real quick and in a hurry."

He was 19 when he deployed, having never been out of the country and not old enough to drink. When he saw the reality of how others live and what it was like in the Middle East, he came home with a new appreciation for the most basic things in life. He marveled at green grass, working plumbing, and clean water. "I came back more grateful for what I was given, for what I had in life. I don't take anything for granted," he says. "It's definitely kept me humble."

ON THE DARK TIMES

Jamel focuses on the good times and his successes, like excelling in school, joining the Marines, and fighting through the amateur ranks. But along with his success came some dark times too. In 2004, he lost his best friend, who encouraged him to enlist in the Marines, to cancer. In 2009, his two-month-old daughter died from SIDS.

He says it was his drive inside the ring that taught him lessons he used to fight through these adversities. "I always had those moments when people said, 'I don't know how he does it. I don't know why he doesn't give up.'"

His daughter's death was devastating. "[The loss of] my daughter hit me the hardest. I'd never experienced anything like that in my life," he says. "As a Marine, you experience war, but when it comes to your own children, it hits the hardest."

He describes a three-week "funk" when he didn't leave his room, didn't eat, and thought his life was over. But he credits his family and his fellow Marines with helping him work through it. Afterward, he discovered a principle he lives by today: how to turn a negative into a positive.

When he fights, he always has his daughter's name on his trunks and uses it for motivation. He wants to live up to the standard of making her proud. "She's my guardian angel," he says. "I've been in a lot of tough fights where I'm the underdog, but I always use the motivation of what I'm fighting for."

Jamel takes his motivation out of the ring too, using it to live his daily life and teaching others how to do the same. "I'm in control of my own story. I'm not going to let anyone—the media or the negativity—get to me. As long as I wake up every day and have the chance to do what I love, I can't be stopped."

ON THE COMEBACK

Boxers are famous for staying in their comfort zones. Changing trainers, weight classes, and career strategies take courage. It's a risky move. So by 2018, Jamel decided to do something bold. After two losses in three fights, he moved down to a new weight class, switched trainers, moved his family to a new city, and changed to a new promoter. It was a move that reflected his deep drive to win and his ability to write his own story. "In boxing, it's easy to just become that stepping-stone, that journeyman," he says. "I could not see myself going that route."

He wanted more and he knew he had to make some changes to get it. "I knew what's in me and I still had something to prove." He had to make the circumstances right to "get it out of me." Once again, he decided to control the narrative. "Man, I was scared," he says. "But I had to take the reins on my career and my story."

His career strategy paid off. In 2019, he unseated Masayuki Ito as WBO junior lightweight world champion. Jamel, who went in as the underdog, worked hard, kept his head down, and focused on the changes he made in his career to get there. It was a tough fight. "Even as I would go back to my corner, I'd think, 'All right, I got that round.' But I knew I still had to be careful. Ito kept getting up every round and coming out trying to win."

He's a believer that the obstacles you overcome early on affect your decisions later. And that it's all about the timing—of when you encounter those hardships and of the lessons you learn. "But I wouldn't change it," he says. "It's those moments early on that made me who I am today."

ON MEDIA BACKLASH

When it comes to controlling your own story, it's hard for fighters when the media gets involved. Every writer, editor, blogger, and commenter has an opinion. Social media only makes it worse. Fighters are more accessible to fans than ever before, but it's a double-edged sword. Online, everyone's a critic when it comes to comments and commentary.

In September 2020, Jamel defended his WBO junior lightweight title against Jonathan Oquendo. Oquendo was disqualified after the eighth round for an illegal headbutt, which opened a cut under Jamel's eye. He couldn't see. Officials stopped the fight. (Later, doctors had to confirm his orbital bone wasn't fractured.) It was a win—but an ugly one—and the media had a field day. The comments were vicious. Jamel had been on the ropes too much, they said. It was just Oquendo's aggressive style that led to the headbutt. The backlash was negative and intense.

Before the fight, Jamel had battled COVID-19 for the entire summer. He struggled with the aftereffects of the virus and worried that his body might never be the same. Once confronted with the negative media pressure, he wondered if he'd ever box again at the same level. Things were so bad with the media, the critics, and the lingering effects of COVID-19 that he considered retirement.

"I really questioned whether I was going to continue with my career after that. We *are* human and that negativity affects us. I'm thinking, 'I'm a world champion—but are you *really* a world champion?'" he says. "You start doubting yourself."

But he wasn't done yet. Jamel says he ultimately thought about his legacy and how much he wanted to box—and win. He didn't want to retire not having been the best. "If I can't get through the Oquendos of the world, how can I say I'm the best in my division?" He decided to stick with it, and with support from his family—and staying off social media for a while—he let the negativity go.

As he watched other fights, he knew his passion was still in boxing. He found his drive. "As a fighter, you can be gone for as long as you want, but there's always that hunger that creeps up and brings you back. And I'm thinking, 'I can't just go out like that.'" He was determined to rewrite his story again. "I remember thinking, 'That's not going to be the last memory they're going to have of me.'" He used that negativity as fuel for his fight against Carl Frampton in April 2021.

Many analysts were questioning if Jamel would be able to perform— physically or mentally. He was an underdog again but kept his head down and kept training. He was a little in awe of Frampton. "I remember when he was *Ring* magazine's 2016 Fighter of the Year," he says. But in boxing, fortunes change. "If a younger me had ever dreamed I'd fight him—let alone knock him out—no one would have believed it." It's another example of why he believes you can control your own destiny if you make good decisions. "You have to acknowledge the mistakes you make along the way," he says. "A lot of fighters out there won't take that constructive criticism."

ON WINNING

Nothing could better demonstrate the heart of a champion than the rush of emotion every boxer gets when their hand is raised in victory. It's even more intense to win a championship belt and hear the ring announcer proclaim them as "the *new* champion."

Jamel notes the feeling of relief he experiences in every fight when the last bell rings. Up until then, every fighter has doubts. "You're thinking, 'Am I worthy? Do I belong here?' But you play it smart and you fight your fight," he says. It's his winning strategy. "I have to believe in myself, keep my cool, and just fight my fight."

"Getting your hand raised is always one of the best feelings in the world." And when he won his world title, in that moment, he reflected on how much he'd been through with his life, family, and career change. But it was all worth it in the end. "I believe those obstacles in my life early on along the way made me who I am now. I appreciate it much more because I worked for it," he says.

ON ADVICE TO HIS YOUNGER SELF

I ask him what advice he'd have for a younger Jamel even though he feels the obstacles made him who he is today. "When I was young, I had a lot of self-esteem issues. I was afraid a lot. I was around a lot of negative people," he says. He heard "You can't do this" or "You can't do that" every day. And while he learned to set goals and achieve them despite the negativity, he says, "I would encourage myself to believe in myself a *lot* more. It took me until later in my life to believe I was really going to be able to do this."

Even as he worked his way up, he struggled with his self-confidence. Every fighter does when they arrive at a tournament and see who they'll have to beat to come out on top. "I didn't even think I was going to make it to the Olympic team," he says. "I was just glad to be there. It was literally that week in the Olympic trials when I was winning fight after fight that I thought, 'Maybe I can do this.'"

While he'd started the trials simply feeling glad to be there, he finished them with the hunger to be an Olympian. Not only that, but he was also the captain for Team USA at the 2012 London Olympics.

"If I could go back in the past, I would tell my younger self to always believe in who I could be," he says. "I always dreamed of being something big, something more, but I had those thoughts in my head that I couldn't do it. I would say, 'Keep pushing and believing in you.'"

He reminds his own kids that success takes hard work and belief in yourself. "I tell them, 'You think I just woke up one day and decided to do this?'" he says, laughing. "You never know how far you can go unless you try."

"In life, you're going to have setbacks," Jamel says. "You can look at them as failures or life lessons. If you learn from it and you get back up, you may be successful or you may be just a little bit better. You can go far in life, but you got to believe in yourself first."

"I always tell my kids, 'You're in control of your own destiny.' People can give you all the tools and put you on the right path, but it's up to you to continue that journey," he says. He hopes the next generation can see how to succeed and be better than they dreamed. "I want them to see I come from *this*, but that didn't stop me from getting to where I am now."

HEATHER HARDY

Boxer, mixed martial artist
Status: Active
Weight classes: Featherweight, bantamweight
Ring name: The Heat
Hometown: Brooklyn, New York

CHAMPIONSHIPS
· WBA featherweight title (2018)
· NABF featherweight title (2018)
· WBC international super bantamweight title (2014)
· UBF international super bantamweight title (2013)

HIGHLIGHTS
· Won MMA debut by TKO (June 2017)
· Golden Gloves featherweight title (2012)
· Fought in the second female boxing match in HBO history
· Known as the "First Lady of Brooklyn Boxing"

I've known Heather Hardy for 18 years. My first and lasting memory of meeting her was on the New York City amateur kickboxing scene. I'll always remember her blonde cornrows and Irish flag accents on her fight trunks. She was always full of smiles, but her demeanor on fight night meant business. She might look sweet and angelic, but her poker face is one of the best in fight sports.

I tell her I've been following her career over the years. And she jokes that she's been following me too—only following in my footsteps as we made our way through kickboxing and, later, boxing. She was even on some of my undercards from kickboxing all the way up to the top of the boxing world at Barclays Center.

She's a fellow New Yorker, a Brooklyn girl, a single mom, and a tough adversary in the ring, and I've long been interested in what makes her a champion. Heather has the soul of an old-school Brooklyn trainer in the body of a modern woman who looks as if she could be just as comfortable behind a desk instead of a boxing ring. With a college degree in criminalistics, Heather is something of an anomaly. Underneath a tough exterior and thick Brooklyn accent, there's a deep understanding of life and intelligence that can be extremely disarming.

Today, Heather is a persistent voice advocating for equal pay in women's fights sports. She's also a risk-taker known for making smart choices in the boxing world, including her crossover to MMA.

Heather got a late start in her fighting career, learning martial arts and boxing at the age of 28. As a single mom, Heather and her sister were living together and raising their kids. Her sister gave her a gift card for a karate studio a few blocks from their place. "'Get a life,' she said." Heather laughs, but she won her first fight after only three weeks of training. It was a game-changer for her.

"Wow," she remembers thinking. "I'm actually good at this. I knew that night I never didn't want to fight."

There's an old fighter's adage that you should fight like a lion was just dropped into the ring and only one of you will get out alive. Heather's style is just this—and she agrees. It's something she says she thinks about after such a late start to her career.

"I was 28 when I started and I was learning on the job," Heather says. "I'm not the most technical fighter. I'm not the strongest puncher or the prettiest to look at, but I got something you can't learn in the gym. I always brought that as my strength into the ring."

ON WOMEN'S BOXING

Many fans see only the glamour of the big-name fights, but for the average club fighter, getting to the ring isn't so easy. These fighters are often required to sell tickets to their own fights to help fund the bout for the promoter, pay the way for their opponent, and, ultimately, fund their own purse. It requires dedication and courage.

Heather came up through the ranks selling tickets and managing life as a single mom at the same time, but she was willing to do it because she wanted to fight. That drive became part of her personal brand—and personal branding is everything for a boxer. The better known you are, the more eyes are on you. And the more butts you put in seats, the easier it is to get fights.

Heather emphasizes that when she started her career, women weren't fighting in network-televised fights and pay-per-view events. Women's boxing wasn't made an Olympic sport until 2012. While Heather is modest about her role, she was a big part in driving that change.

"It's thanks to a lot of women. I refuse to take credit for that," she says. "There were a lot of pioneers that opened a lot of doors for women like me."

What it means today is that promoters are now signing women, giving them more chances to compete, and Heather has been a major force in increasing this visibility for female fighters. To make it happen, she had to know the business of boxing to maximize her opportunities.

"I had to hustle. I had to get creative," she says. And she had to work around the barriers.

"Many networks would literally say, 'We refuse to air women's fights,'" she says. Which means promoters had to take a chance. And when she did get a fight, she had to produce results.

"I had to get creative and sell out the show because I was a short-term investment for my promoter. I had to do every interview, guest bartending spots, everything I could to get myself out there. I was a full-time boxer, a full-time trainer, and a full-time ticket seller." And a full-time single mom.

"I always get goose bumps," Heather says when I ask her about the women who came before her. Her callouts? Alicia Ashley, Melissa Hernández, and Ronica Jeffrey. "Not only did I have girls to look up to, but I realized these are some of the best fighters in the gym, male or female. You had these incredible fighters that nobody knew." Her philosophy was simple: "I didn't want to just win a world title. I wanted people to know who I am."

"Even right now, I don't consider myself as good," she says when she talks about the women she fights and trains with on most days. Heather's drive to win a title was never to be better than the women who went before her. "I just wanted people to know I was doing this. Not just for me but for little girls. How many little girls didn't know that they could be a world champion just because they liked to box?"

Heather says was a total tomboy and played baseball when she was a kid, noting she was "really good" at it, but she wasn't allowed to play Little League. "I had to play softball because I was a girl." In her heart, she just wanted to play. That heart translated to boxing. She remembers thinking, "How come everything I'm good at I'm not allowed to do?"

As a mother, she thought, "What about the little girls who feel like that? It was 2010 and I'm thinking, 'How we are still saying this?'" That heart is what she credits for launching her career as a female boxer and as an advocate for the sport and the girls coming up.

ON THE AHA MOMENT

For many fighters, there's a specific moment when they realize they have what it takes to be a world champion. For some, it comes early in their careers, and for others, it happens in the ring. I ask Heather about hers.

"I was boxing this girl in the Aviator Arena [in Brooklyn] and a lot of people didn't think I could beat her. She was really good and could box. And I beat her and I made it easy. I realized then I was actually good. That was when I realized, 'Yeah, okay, I can do this. I'm not just getting tough. I'm getting good at this!'"

After that moment, she knew she was staying in boxing for the long haul.

ON DRIVE

Heather credits her mom for the source of her drive. Both of her parents worked full time, so she helped raise her younger brother and sister. "I lived a life before I got to live a life," she says. "I made mistakes. I learned lessons raising my brother and sister, being the one in charge of them. The mistakes I made 'parenting' them shaped me into an adult who already 'adulted' by the time I had my daughter."

Heather's mother was tough on her children, and Heather preached hard work, dedication, and discipline to her brother and sister. For her, the drive continued with the birth of her own daughter.

"I was solely responsible not just for her safety but for her success and her exposure to things," she says. But she also knew there was a business side to her drive—one that would allow her to give her daughter things she never had growing up.

Today, she's a passionate advocate for athletes having a college degree. While it's not necessarily the key to success, she believes it's important to have exposure to subjects like psychology and business. For her, a degree was also an important way to learn how to communicate and express herself professionally. She believes it's an essential way to learn about life.

"It's important to learn how to deal with people, how to speak properly—things that come with boxing that people don't associate with boxing," Heather says. "You can be a great athlete, but if you don't have the smarts to navigate the business side of it, to keep the right people in your corner, pick the right management—all of those things are so important."

ON DOUBT

Every fighter experiences doubt. For Heather, it was after her 2019 loss to Amanda Serrano, a remarkable boxer with championships in seven different divisions. Heather knew she was an underdog going into the fight, but her fighting spirit kept her in it. "I was always known as a tough fighter, not full of technique, but I'm a fighter and I believed I could do it. I had a shot," she says. "But I know the business, and I knew [that] after a loss, the future was not going to be bright for me. No one would be looking out for me after that."

Boxing doesn't give fighters many opportunities to come back after losses or even draws. There's a growing obsession, a public aura around the "0." Certain fighters can transcend a loss and still make top dollar, but more commonly, a fighter's earning potential diminishes dramatically after their first loss. It plummets exponentially after another. The pressure for a boxer to remain undefeated is unlike any known in sports today.

> **"The defeat of one man is the triumph of another: But we are apt to read this 'triumph' as merely temporary and provisional. Only the defeat is permanent."**
>
> **–Joyce Carol Oates, *On Boxing***

Heather admits that after her loss to Serrano, she questioned why she was working so hard or why she was doing this at all. Something drags all champions back—often tooth and nail—and for Heather, the COVID-19 pandemic helped her get past the loss—and back to being a mom. The pandemic came so soon after the loss that she says she didn't really have time to "sit with the sadness. I'm a single mom. I had to think of survival."

At the height of the pandemic, she started hustling, relying on that now-famous creativity. "I totally switched gears and started teaching boxing. The same way I hustled my boxing career. I would take my mitts and jump rope, and I was hustling lessons in the park. Handing out business cards. We built a little makeshift boxing gym out in the park where we'd sit on benches and the clients would come."

She gets a little emotional. "If you can survive in a pandemic, you can survive anything. I'm turning down short money fights now because I know I am good. I can survive."

ON ADVICE TO HER YOUNGER SELF

I like to ask boxers what advice they might give to themselves if they could time travel to the past. No one wants to discourage their youthful excitement, but age sometimes brings a few insights. What would her advice be today to a young Heather Hardy? "Know your role in the business," she says immediately, referring to the ability to understand how the fight business works and where she fits in that equation. "Boxers are put on a path based on their training and amateur pedigree," she says, which puts her at a disadvantage because she didn't start fighting until she was 28.

"If you don't have that background, you have a hard road ahead of you. Learn the business and surround yourself with good people who are looking out for you," she says. "And be smart. It's not always about being good. It's who you know." And if she could say anything to her younger self? "Honey, it ain't gonna get much better."

We laugh, but she wants to explain. Fighters pay their dues, but for women, it's even harder. It's a well-known fact that women are paid much less than their male counterparts. Heather has been on the front lines as an advocate of eliminating the gender-based pay gap in fight sports. Women, she says, work hard—maybe even harder—for the same job.

"There is a thought that if you just work a little harder, just try a little more, just market yourself a little better that your pay will go up, your worth and opportunities will go up. I spent my whole career chasing that," she says.

However, as she fought for bigger titles, the pay was still low. In 2018, Heather fought the WBO world featherweight championship fight at Madison Square Garden, which was only the second female fight ever aired on HBO Sports. She beat Shelly Vincent for the title and earned only $20,000. Her male counterparts would've earned 10 times that. Today, she still finds herself being offered the same amount of money to fight for world titles, but she has the wisdom to say "No" when it's not worth it.

"I would still work hard, but I wouldn't let disappointment affect me," she says. "I'd say, 'Relax, have fun, but don't kill yourself, Heather. Box, have fun, but don't think it's going to get better.'"

She remains a passionate voice for women in the sport and isn't afraid to push boundaries in asking for equal treatment and equal pay. And she's not afraid to break through the old boxing stigmas. Some fighters feel she shouldn't complain because she's just lucky to have the opportunity to box professionally, but Heather feels she's earned the right to speak out.

ON CROSSING OVER TO MMA

MMA and boxing fall under the umbrella term "fight sports," but they're as different as church and state when it comes to business. The UFC provides women an opportunity to earn a decent annual income as full-time fighters by receiving appearance fees and win bonuses. But female MMA fighters still suffer a significant wage gap compared with their male counterparts.

In 2017, Heather fought Alice Yauger in her first MMA bout. "Bellator Fighting Championships offered me the fight," she says "and all I was thinking was, 'It's at Madison Square Garden. That's where Billy Joel plays his piano. Of course I'm going to do it!'"

But then the suffering began. The training regimen for MMA was grueling. On top of her job as a trainer, plus her own boxing training every day, she added a lengthy commute involving a car, a train, and a mile-long walk loaded down with gear. And after a long day, she'd head home to make dinner and check her daughter's homework.

The training for kickboxing is brutal. "Even drills hurt," Heather says. In addition to the long hours, she experienced the extreme stress MMA fighting took on her body during training and in the arena.

"I spent two months training, then the day comes and I look out from behind the curtain at the cage and say, 'What am I doing?'" She experienced a moment of panic when "Girl on Fire" played for her entrance. "I'm just looking around, saying 'I don't how to do this.'"

For all the physical abuse, MMA has its advantages, especially in the world of personal marketing and for Heather's advocacy work. Her reach on social media and with fans has increased and helped her build her brand.

In the end, she feels it was worth it to prove the naysayers wrong about women in the sport. And she felt MMA was more accepting in some ways than boxing was. "In the end, it was my proof that it wasn't me who wasn't marketing myself. It wasn't me who wasn't good enough for boxing. MMA took me in differently than boxing did."

While Heather is a humble champion, I see someone with incredible courage and the ability to take risks. To become a champion, she was willing to step out of her comfort zone, take a chance, and put herself on the chopping block. She didn't always come out on top, but she always came out with her chin held high and her spirit unbroken. More than anything, that's what separates her from her contemporaries. It's also why her fan base is doggedly loyal. Everyone loves an underdog, especially one who refuses to quit.

ON SUFFERING

So much of training is centered around suffering. But even after a full day of work and training, she still made it home for her daughter's bedtime. She remembers sobbing every day because she was so tired.

"Everyone saw the result: the incredible KO at Madison Square Garden [in my 2017 Bellator MMA debut]. What they didn't know is that I had to train on Long Island at 8 o'clock at night, taking the LIRR [Long Island Rail Road]. I was 36 years old, learning a new sport, getting beat up by white belts, with so many different injuries. My legs are black and blue from kicking. I came home every day sobbing and I remember asking myself, "Why do I have to do this? Why does my job have to hurt so bad?'"

She laughs as she remembers, but she emphasizes how awful it was. "I'd rather get kicked in the face than get kicked in the leg. I gag just thinking about the pain," she says.

ON RETIREMENT

Every fighter wonders how they'll know the time is right to hang up their gloves. Some go out dramatically with an injury, while others find themselves drawn to family or other opportunities. But others feel they have one more fight or one more championship still to finish. Heather is pleased with her accomplishments. She wants to be happy with the mark she's left on the sport—and happy with the marks the sport has left on her. "I'm already going through it mentally. I won't take a fight unless it makes sense to me to want to do this."

Ultimately, she'll make the decision with the same business smarts that have guided her career—with a healthy dose of calculated risk-taking. She feels she's past having to fight for opportunities to get something bigger down the line. "My worth is not based on what anyone else thinks. It's based on what I think my time is worth, what I think my health is worth, and what I think my body is worth. I have mentally come up with a number that is worth it for me to do this. If I don't hear that number, I'm fine not getting in the ring," she says.

TIM BRADLEY

Boxer, analyst
Status: Retired
Weight classes: Lightweight, welterweight
Ring name: Desert Storm
Hometown: Palm Springs, California

CHAMPIONSHIPS

- WBO welterweight title (2012, 2015)
- WBO junior welterweight title (2009)
- WBC super lightweight title (2008)

HIGHLIGHTS

- Fought Manny Pacquiao three times (one win, two losses)
- Ranked the #3 best pound for pound boxer
  by *The Ring* magazine (2013)

Tim and I had overlapping professional fight careers and have followed each other over the years. I turned pro just a few weeks before he won his first world title. Although we spent some time in the same weight class fighting at the highest level, we never had the chance to share the ring. Now we hurl jabs at one another across boardroom tables during meetings when we broadcast for ESPN. It's always fun to playfully spar about what would've happened had we crossed.

We've fought many of the same opponents—Ruslan Provodnikov and Manny Pacquiao come to mind—so I have respect for the work Tim has done as a boxer. The stats tell the story and show why he's ranked among the greats. Aside from his incredible accomplishments, knowing that his path was far from easy made him one of the first people I wanted to talk to about becoming a champion. He has an analytical mind and a high boxing IQ that make any conversation regarding the sweet science insightful and informative. (And his straightforward "I don't give a fuck" attitude always makes a chat that much more entertaining.)

Now that he's retired, he's had time to reflect on his attitude and look at how it's made his current career path as a boxing analyst clearer for him. His philosophy can be summed up simply: "You just gotta turn shit into gold."

"Life sometimes throws you curveballs, I always say, or throws you shit and so you just gotta make gold outta shit," he says. "I'm always looking to elevate my game. I believe that the ones that work hard, the ones [who are] constantly trying to grow in whatever area it is, I think you're going to do well in life."

Tim's perspective has served him well, as has his ability to rise above what anyone else has to say about his career, his boxing, or even his life. Letting go of the expectations and judgments from others has been a key factor to his happiness and success. "How you perceive things and how you take things, that's [important]. Like me, I just don't give a damn about what anybody thinks of me or says about me or whatever," he says with a laugh. "And I feel like, honestly, I've grown wings because I'm able to deal with that."

Tim's known for sometimes saying exactly what he's thinking, and while it's not always well received, he appreciates his ability to say it. "I feel like I can speak and say whatever I want to say. Freedom of speech is real in my household. I say what I want to say, I mean what I say, I wear my heart on my sleeve, but I also work my behind off, so I think that's the reason why I'm in the position I'm in now," he says. "It's just been hard work."

ON THE BEGINNING

Tim says that even though he's from Palm Springs, he grew up in a gritty urban environment. It was, as he says, a "tough neighborhood." "I never really thought about boxing," he says. "You wouldn't think being from Palm Springs there's a tough neighborhood, but there's an urban area in every city you go into. I don't care, there's poverty, there's a lower level of living."

"Growing up in North Palm Springs around gangs, violence, drugs" was how he learned "grit and toughness." "It was the neighborhood I grew up in. It kind of grew me into who I am today."

His parents were a hardworking dad and a stay-at-home mom, but he credits his father with teaching him to stand up for himself. But Tim's competitive nature was with him from the start. "My father [was] always telling me never allow somebody to bully you. Always stand up for yourself," he says. "So I got those principles from my father. But that competitive nature, I've always had it since I was a kid."

He notes how critical that innate competitive nature is for a champion. "I feel that's nothing you can teach. You either have it or you don't. You can give somebody rules or say you shouldn't act that way or be that way, but ultimately, at the end of the day, they're going to be who they are inside and what they feel," he says.

For Tim, it was an internal desire to win, no matter what sport—football, basketball, or, eventually, boxing. "I started boxing at 10 years old," he says, but before that, he was having a hard time channeling his energy. "I got kicked out of two schools early on. In second grade, I got kicked out of school for fighting. Then in fourth grade, I got kicked out of school for fighting and they were going to expel me out of the entire district."

Because his father worked for the school district as a security guard, they gave him some "grace" to go to school close to home. "They wanted me to fail," he says, noting that many of his buddies in the neighborhood had parents who ran in a gang or sold drugs. "It wasn't the greatest environment, but I made the most of it."

A childhood friend had started boxing, and at 10 years old, Tim asked his father to take him to the boxing gym. "I begged my dad for about two months to take me to the gym because my buddy Julio was boxing. He had been boxing for six months and he kept telling me go down to the gym."

His dad was skeptical but made a bargain with his son. "He finally took me," Tim says, "He said, 'All right, son, I got to deal with you. If you go in there and you like it, you can't quit.'" Tim agreed and they went to the gym. "I just remember walking into the gym. I remember that day."

A big guy named OJ with "Coke bottle glasses and a big ol' belly" handed them a clipboard, and despite Tim's dirty, torn shirt, OJ noticed something about a young Tim Bradley. "My dad filled out the information, and as I was walking to the scales, OJ stopped me. He put his hand on my chest and he said, 'I see something in you, kid. You're different.'"

Tim laughs as he tells the story. "My dad is looking at him, saying, 'What are you talking about?' and he says, 'You're gonna be a champion.' And my dad was like, 'Man, get the hell out of here!'" Tim's dad thought he was getting a hard sell. "'My son wants to box. You ain't gotta boost him up. Stop playing.' And he's like, 'No, I see something in his eyes. There's something in them.'"

Whether it was the early confidence boost or Tim's weight training with his father, he'd already developed a work ethic—or, as he puts it, "a nature about me." From that point on, he was a regular at the gym.

"It was heaven. I'm serious. It was heaven on Earth, man. I remember walking in the gym and seeing all these pictures all over the walls of champions, and they all had this green belt. Muhammad Ali, these pictures on the walls, like, these guys had worked and been in the ring with the best. They had trained the best guys out there," he says.

Tim's new trainer was Russell Rodriguez, who'd worked the hand pads with Ali. "These guys were throwback, going way back. They're in their 60s and 70s already when I met them, so they were an older group of guys."

"I learned how to jab and that was it. Footwork and jab." Which didn't prepare him for his first sparring match with his friend Julio a few days later. "He beat my behind, dude. And it's crazy because I learned something that day," he says. "The madder I got, the more I got hit. The more aggressive I got, I left myself open. And I could hear Russell saying, 'Hey, relax. Don't get mad. Control your temper. Control your temper.'"

"The more I would rev it up, the more I would get hit," Tim says. "I remember sitting on the outside of the ring after the sparring session. My neck was hurting. I had a headache. You know, my nose is busted. It just felt like my face was hot from the leather I was getting hit with. It was my first time ever being in the ring, so I fought back as hard as I could. I mean, I only knew how to jab." It was a lesson he still remembers to this day.

He was sitting on the edge of the ring when his dad came up to him. "'See? I told you this was hard,'" his dad told him. "'Are you ready to get in the car? Let's go.'"

But young Tim Bradley realized that thing inside him was a competitive drive and he wasn't going to be able to walk away. He told his dad he wasn't going anywhere and he wasn't quitting. "That's my competitive nature in me. I said, 'I gotta get him back, I gotta get him back!' and he was like, 'You know what we got to do then?' I said, 'Whatever it takes, whatever it takes, Dad. I got to get him back.'"

And just like that, at 10 years old, Tim was motivated to win. "From that point on, at 5 a.m., my dad would wake me up in the morning, knock on my door, and I'd already have my shoes on ready to hit the roadwork," he says.

ON DRIVE

I talk with him a little about where that drive comes from and how every champion I've talked to understood they had that drive—often early on. For many, it helps them know how to dig down into those dark places when things seem too tough.

"People can argue this, but when a lion is born, he doesn't realize he's a lion. As he gets older, his nature is there. It's naturally there. It's what God gave him," Tim says as an unsurprisingly philosophical answer. He's a thoughtful guy and I knew he'd have an answer for this particular question. He believes competitive drive is innate.

"I was born with that nature, man. I just have that competitive nature in me already and that's what fueled me. That's the reason why a lot of people when I would fight, they would see it. You know, they would see the hunger, they would see the determination, they would see the will to win. But that just comes from within," he says.

He adds another reason: family. "You gotta put family in there, of course," he says. "I fought for my family. My kids, my wife, my mother, my father, my trainer, everybody that was attached to me, man. I really went in the ring with that on my conscience as well." He doesn't leave out his fans that supported him along the way.

He also appreciates that in addition to the drive, he set some goals early on and they pushed him along the way. He trained in a gym with a legacy of WBC titles—the winners who wear that famous green belt. And he knew what it meant—to him as a fighter and, in a broader sense, to the sport.

"What motivated me was that green belt, getting to that championship, seeing that green belt on the wall in the gym at a young age. And feeling that if I can accomplish that green belt that I've accomplished something in boxing and just trying to be doing something greater than myself," Tim says.

He acknowledges the appeal of excelling at boxing because it's not something everyone can do. He laughs. "If I wanted to, I could go to school and get the degree, but there's a lot of people getting those degrees, bro! There's not a lot of people winning world championships in the hardest sport in the world—boxing! There's not!"

He didn't just want to be good—he wanted to be great. And his father instilled the motivation in him at a young age, teaching him the value of hard work and making him earn everything he wanted along the way. "So it was like, 'You want that motorcycle for the Christmas? I need 100 push-ups and 100 sit-ups every day for a year straight. Once you can do that, then you get the motorcycle and that tells me that you're strong enough for that motorcycle,'" Tim says about his dad's requirements.

His dad knew how to feed his competitive nature, constantly pushing him as he got in better shape. When he was running, his father would say, "'Oh, you gonna let them run harder than you? Just 'cuz you the only one out here don't mean that somebody on the other side of the planet ain't out here doing the same thing you're doing.'" His father would plant the seed in his mind and Tim would work harder and longer to compete.

"He puts that in my mind and I run another mile. It was three miles a day and now I run four miles, so then it just carries on as you get older." The result was what made Tim a champion. "I learned how to motivate myself. I didn't need someone to get me up at five in the morning and go run. I didn't need someone to tell me how to get myself in shape," he says. "And as I paid more and more attention to my body, I just got better and better at it, and I knew what it took eventually to get to where I was at tip-top shape. I knew, but that's just from experience and drilling and learning along the way."

Tim also learned how to set goals—and achieve them. The goals helped motivate him as he tapped into his own competitive nature. "I just wanted to be great at something."

When it came to setting goals, he designated milestones along the way. The first was winning a world championship in four years. (He did it in three and a half.) Once he checked that box, he set his sights on becoming unified champion. "I would set little goals for myself and try to accomplish those goals." The only goal he set for himself that he didn't achieve was to become ranked #1 pound for pound in the world. (He was #3.)

"And the Hall of Fame," he says, laughing. "I haven't got it yet, but I know I'm going to get in there."

"I didn't do this just to be average. I did this to be considered one of the best. And that nature, I was born with it. Just like somebody is born with power. Just like somebody is born with speed. It's just there," he says.

ON WATCHING BOXING

I've learned that there seem to be two different types of fighters: Those who love the sport and absorb everything, watching every fight and fighter, and others who tend to stay away from watching other fights and instead focus on their own techniques and game. I ask him which category he fell into and the effect it had on him growing up.

"If you love something, you're going to watch it. I don't care what anybody says. If you love it, you're gonna watch it, no matter what. When there's boxing on TV, I'm watching. I'm watching on my phone. I can be at my kid's game. I got it on because that's my job, but most importantly, I want to see what else is out there," he says.

Tim takes boxing very seriously and he thinks it's important to know the history. "You got to know your history. If you're going to do a job and you don't know the history, I think that's a huge problem because you got to understand how did we get here? How did we get to this point in boxing? Where did it start?" he says.

And, naturally, he watched boxing with his father growing up. "I remember in the '90s, when the heavyweight division was hot. Evander Holyfield, Riddick Bowe, [Mike] Tyson was still there, Michael Moorer. There were a lot of top heavyweights. This is when the US had probably the best heavyweights in the world at the time. Roy Jones Jr. was there too." I agree that the '90s were the golden age of heavyweight boxing, with the US providing much of the top talent—a result of strong training programs for the 1980 and 1984 Olympics.

As Tim was coming up through the ranks, he watched all the videos he could of fighters who were just above and just below him, constantly formulating a game plan before he knew his opponent. Sizing up another fighter's strengths and weaknesses was something he learned as an amateur.

"Later in my career, I was about 18 years old, I went up to Marquette, Michigan, and trained with Al Mitchell, and he used to watch film," he says. "He taught me how to break down guys, but initially, it was just me watching guys' strengths." Tim didn't know how to watch for trends or the latest moves, but he got very good at "taking little bits and pieces from different fighters." He learned how to take the best of what he saw on film and incorporate it into his own style—"but still being myself."

ON FIGHTERS TODAY

We talk for a while about younger fighters today and the challenges they face. We've seen a lot of guys miss opportunities because they take the safe approach and focus on avoiding danger, ignoring the entertainment factor. We agree that boxers today have to be exciting if they're not power-punchers. Footwork, hand speed, and ring IQ all matter, but understanding that the game is a spectator sport and that you have to entertain makes a real difference between being a star or just being a good fighter.

As an amateur, he notes he was "a quick-fisted, in-and-out guy." But he also knew something that many younger boxers struggle with today. The reality is that to make it as a pro, you can't just be good—you have to be exciting to watch. Tim changed his style as he climbed up the ranks to be more exciting. "I wasn't a power-puncher, but I got more aggressive with my approach, which helped me win some more championships."

More importantly, he feels younger fighters still need a strong character to succeed. He spends a lot of time with youth today because he thinks it's important they build a strong foundation. "I think character is built at a young age," he says. "Of course, things happen in your life and it changes over time, little by little, either for the good or the bad. But it's important that they learn we all fail. The ones that get up and keep trying are the ones that always win. You've got to fail to be able to understand what you need to do to win."

He worries that young fighters might be losing the concept of searching out the best competition and instead opting for the easiest route to the biggest money. The allure of making big money, made famous by Floyd "Money" Mayweather, has many young fighters thinking that boxing can be the fast track to making millions. The reality is that it's a long, hard road, and even if you become champion, there are no guarantees for the big paydays. "I understand making money. I get it," he says, recognizing that money in boxing is a driving force. But he worries that too many fighters will believe they're the best because they make the most money. "I like the guy that fights the best fighters in the world. That's what I like," he says. "Because that's what competition is about."

ON TURNING PRO

I ask him about what it was like in his first professional fight in 2004. We laugh as Tim nearly screams with laughter at the memory. "Ooooooh, damn!" he says. "I WAS SCARED!" It wasn't like he was new to the sport. He had 145 amateur fights and had multiple amateur titles. He'd traveled internationally to fight in tournaments and beaten future professional world champions. But he laughs at his memories of his first fight without headgear and an amateur regulation tank top.

"You got a whole bunch of drunk people in the crowd, you know, and you got eight-ounce gloves on," he says of the frenzy of his first professional fight. "You gotta be straight lunatic to get inside the ring. Man, I don't care, I had experience. You gotta be crazy! I'm not gonna lie! I'm a little psycho. I'm a little crazy," he says, dissolving into laughter.

Even though he won that first professional bout, he says it still took six months to fully transition to a professional boxing style. His trainer had to work with him to change amateur fight techniques to meet professional boxing needs. "I remember being in the dressing room and I remember, man, my nerves are up," he says. "I'm thinking to myself, 'I can't get embarrassed out here. The pressure's on because I'm about to embark on something that is risky and my life's on the line. I can get completely embarrassed. I can get knocked out on TV,'" he says. "I would have to get as mad as hell. I would get extremely tense because I had a hard time dealing with the rage that I felt."

He learned to use fear as a motivator as part of his routine. "That fear drove me. It was either freakin' fold under pressure or go out there and just fight your ass off, fight your heart out. You have a choice, man: You can flee or you can fight."

Still, he admits how terrified he was in the ring—something that every fighter feels but few will admit. "I was scared as hell. I'm not going to lie to you, man. Scared. And it never left," he says. "I think I was able to cope with it as I continued to fight. I think for my first five fights, I had that rage and I would scream before the fight in the dressing room," he says. "But by my sixth fight, I started getting a bit under control. I started relaxing."

He says it helped to talk to other pros, who told him that if he relaxed, he'd think more clearly inside the ring instead of just fighting with pure aggression and anger. Still, Tim says his nerves were always there. He just learned to disguise them better. "Even in my biggest moments, I felt like that little boy."

ON FIGHTING JUNIOR WITTER

After a successful string of wins in the first four years of his pro career, Tim was ready for a title fight, which came against Junior "The Hitter" Witter, the defending WBC light welterweight champion. A fleet-footed Englishman, Witter was a stance-switching tricky fighter who had skills and power. With a record of 36-1-2 and 21 KOs, the defending champion was favored to win. Embracing the underdog role, Tim went to work, preparing for his first world title challenge. Ultimately, he put on a clinic, showing the value of preparation and technique.

"I studied Junior Witter for a year," he says, noting that he watched videos of all the former champions and learned what he could from their styles. Even before Witter was an opponent, Tim had done his homework. "I would study him. I would look at him every single night, looking for weaknesses."

He found that Witter tended to fade in the second half of the fight, and from there, he formed a game plan. He'd focus on body shots, then push the pace after the first six rounds.

Tim had international fight experience from his amateur days and wasn't worried about fighting on hostile territory. And despite problems with the hotel, healthy heckling from fans, and media coverage that said Witter would win, he knew he was ready. "I knew I was gonna win that fight. I don't know what it was, but I was extremely confident going over to England," he says. "I was supposed to lose, so not having that pressure on me, I'm like, 'Okay, all right, I'll show you guys.'"

He continued to do his homework, checking the altitude, the time of the fight, and his energy level, noting that they tend to fight late in the UK. "I stayed on West Coast time, United States time, [and it] worked out perfectly," he says. "When [Witter] got in the ring, I saw the bags under his eyes. He wasn't sleeping. I was energized, ready to go."

His game plan paid off and he upset Witter in a close split decision to win the WBC light welterweight title. "Planning is a big part of everything in life. You don't just put together a business without a plan and I was strategic about everything," he says.

Tim planned everything down to knowing his judges for each fight and their own judging styles. For the Witter fight, he knew there was a Mexican judge who'd favor Tim's aggression in the second half of the fight. His knowledge paid off, giving him critical points for the win from the Mexican judge after Tim made an aggressive move.

"Just the glory that came along with that [win], the gratification that I finally captured it, what I did," Tim says with a strong sense of gratitude. And there was the money "because my wife and I were broke." There's a famous story in boxing that Tim was down to his last few dollars going into the Witter fight. He confirms it's true. "Fourteen bucks, bro. Fourteen bucks in the account."

He tells the story of how his wife arrived in the UK the day of his fight. "When I saw her, she said, 'You have to win this fight. We only have $14 in my account. I spent our last $350 to get here.' And I said, 'Don't worry— I'm going to win.'"

But the financial issues put even more pressure on him to deliver. "I remember being in the dressing room and everybody's face was down before the fight. And I said, 'You motherfuckers, this isn't a fuckin' funeral. We going to win this fuckin' fight.' I'm hyping myself up and hyping my whole team up because everybody's walking around with sourpuss faces."

His energy worked. "I'm a guy that if you put my back against the wall, I'm gonna deliver. It carries me wherever I go." Tim is a gamer and it shows. And while he notes that he used to get "his ass whooped" in training all the time but that he'd still go out and win, there's more to it than that. There's heart, but there's also his intense preparation. The two combined are the innate values of a champion.

ON FIGHTING KENDALL HOLT

In his second defense of the WBC super lightweight title, Tim fought Kendall Holt, the reigning WBO junior welterweight champion. Hailing from Paterson, New Jersey, Holt was a vicious counterpuncher with considerable hand speed and devastating power. Tim was at a three-inch height disadvantage and gave up four inches in reach to the challenger.

Tim came out in the first round and immediately put pressure on Holt, closing the distance and ripping hooks and overhands. Holt met that aggression with power and speed, and he dropped Tim awkwardly to the canvas. Tim was hurt but prepared. He got up right away, but realizing he was still dazed, he took a knee and the referee gave him the full eight count. However, he came back to outwork Holt (despite a second knockdown) over 12 rounds to win a unanimous decision.

I ask him what he tapped into to keep going. "Let me tell you something about that fight, man," Tim says. "I knew I needed to break his will in that fight, and if you can break a guy's will, you got them. And I knew this is the only way I have to beat this guy because he's taller, he's longer, he's fast, if not faster than I am." Holt's style was as a powerful counterpuncher, so Tim had to work to form a plan. "The only way that I can beat this guy is that I have to push the pace, have to stay on him, and I just beat the fight out of him."

But getting knocked down in the first round wasn't part of the plan. "I had a talk with God for a minute," Tim says. "I said, 'This ain't the way it's supposed to be.' I remember taking that knee, and I'm looking around, and I'm just like, 'Man, it's not going like this. No way. No way.'"

He made it through the round and his trainer reminded him that they had a game plan. "He's saying, 'You got to go out here, and you still got to be aggressive, and let's go for it,'" he says. His philosophy was solid. "If I'm gonna go out, I'm gonna go out swinging. That's what made me, honestly, even more vicious after the knockdown. I wanted some get-back."

Nevertheless, the knockdown still stings in an otherwise solid win. "It embarrassed the hell out of me—to get knocked down on my ass like that," he says. "That was the first time I'd ever been down in my entire career. I never was dropped as an amateur. My first time ever!"

ON PACQUIAO & THE PRESSURE

After winning the WBC and WBO titles, Tim got the opportunity of a lifetime to challenge legendary WBO welterweight world champion Manny Pacquiao. In what turned out to be a fast-paced and hotly contested bout, Tim won a controversial split decision win over the Filipino legend.

A fighter's first exposure to the real pressure of a big media fight is a wake-up call. It's something champions have to learn how to handle, and for Tim, the big one was his first fight with Pacquiao in 2012. (He'd go on to fight Pacquiao twice more.) There isn't a much bigger event than fighting Manny Pacquiao and he talks about that experience.

"I mean, it was everything that I wanted to do," he says. "I got to the pinnacle, the top of boxing. It was on pay-per-view. I'm fighting the arguably #1 fighter in the world next to Floyd Mayweather." He was scared, but he also understood the importance of the opportunity. "I was like, 'I gotta seize this moment.' These are the moments that people live for. Champions, athletes, they live for these types of moments."

He remembers the added pressure of the media, especially just before the fight. "I'm not going to lie," he says. "The week of the fight, there was so much pressure, *so* much pressure." It was the first time he had that much media exposure and he found it draining.

"You're saying the same thing over and over and over again, answering the same question a thousand times, taking photos, and just the pressure alone, just that tension around to do this, just like it's magnified at that level. And you're trying to stay as calm, cool, and collected as you possibly can and stay relaxed, and it was new territory at the top level—at least it was for me."

ON PACQUIAO & THE CONTROVERSY

For Tim, the biggest triumph of his career turned into one of the biggest controversies in boxing. The decision had already been close, but the WBO questioned the judges and formed a special committee—unheard of before in boxing—to review the scores after the fact. The committee rescored the bout and called for an immediate rematch. Tim was champion and he'd beat the legend, but many fans and the boxing media didn't like it.

No one anticipated the loyalty and passion everyone in boxing had for Manny Pacquiao, a living legend, first-ballot Hall of Famer, and cultural icon. Tim was the new world champion but had no opportunity for celebration or recognition because of the backlash. It was a slap in the face for Tim, who'd worked so hard to get to the pinnacle of his sport.

"I don't know what death feels like, but it felt like death," Tim says. He's had time to reflect on what it meant to him, his family, and his career, and he speaks about it very seriously. "It felt like everything that I had ever done was a lie. I did everything right to get to this point. I fought the best fighters. I trained hard. I did everything I was supposed to do to get to this point. And instead of being uplifted for what I just did inside the ring, I was demonized, ridiculed in the media."

"I did everything right. I didn't do anything wrong, and I fought as hard as I possibly can, and I fought every minute of every single round. But, you know, I worked so hard since I was 10 years old to get to this place. It was a dream of mine to fight the best fighters in the world, and I got no respect for it and honestly felt like death."

The backlash was severe. Tim received death threats and had to hire extra security for his family. He even contemplated suicide. The idea that people he respected were questioning his achievement made him doubt himself. "I felt like, 'I'm a failure,'" he says. "People are telling me that I'm not the true champion. They're questioning who I am, what I believe in."

However, even with the harsh realities of fan and media criticism, he found some perspective. He leaned on his "strong wife" and "close-knit family." "I saw some people in the industry that I respected turn their back on me," he says. "And some people that I respect still today, they actually had my back, which I respect, and I love them for that."

But he really regained his perspective when he took a family trip to Hawaii—just to get away. He tells the story of driving back to his hotel when he cut off another driver. The guy honked his horn and it pissed Tim off. "You know, I was already kind of daydreaming about everything back at home and I'm waiting for this guy to pull up on a side of me." He was ready to have it out with this guy. "I'm rolling down my window, getting ready to give him the business—like, 'Do you want to fight?'" Somehow, this driver had become the focus of all his energy.

But as he sticks his head out the window, the other driver pulls up and gives him the Hawaiian shaka hand sign—the universal sign for "hang loose." It was as if he was saying, "No big deal—we're good." Tim looked at his wife and kids, who'd been ready for a blowup. "And I say to myself, I say, 'You know, there's still some good people in this world.'"

It was the beginning of a turnaround for Tim and his attitude. "I said, 'Damn, when I go home, I'm going to change some things.'" He decided to quit social media and take what happened as a learning experience. He decided to "turn shit into gold." His new philosophy was freeing. "I actually know who I am inside," he says. "What happened to me was a blessing, so whatever happens, I'm gonna turn shit into gold."

He decided that he'd come out of the situation stronger. And he did. "I thank Manny Pacquiao."

The idea of "turning shit into gold" has become part of his personal philosophy. He talks about how important it is to learn how to face challenges and turn them into opportunities. "Sometimes things happen in your life you can't control. But what you can control is how you perceive it," he says. "How you perceive what's going on and then how you react to what's going on, you know that's important."

ON FIGHTING
JUAN MANUEL MÁRQUEZ

In 2013, Tim would defend his title twice—the first against Ruslan Provodnikov, who knocked him down twice. Then he delivered a master class performance against Mexican legend Juan Manuel Márquez. Márquez was fresh off his amazing one-punch KO of Pacquiao and was favored to win.

Tim's fight against Márquez has always been my favorite performance of Tim's career and I wasn't surprised to hear it's also his. I ask him about that pivotal fight—one that some believe showed the world he was the champion he knew he was. He'd taken "an extreme amount of punishment" against Provodnikov, only to face Márquez, who'd just KO'd Pacquiao.

"I boxed circles around this guy," he says. "I have the best performance of my freakin' entire career against this guy. It was vindication! Vindication right here, bro," he says of his critics. "They saw the heart. They saw the will. They saw determination in the Provodnikov fight. They knew what I was about, and then after that, they saw a brilliant boxing lesson against one of the best counterpunches in the game."

He considers his win against Márquez to be one of the highlights of his career, especially after everything that had gone on with the Pacquiao fight. "I embrace it now more than ever because it's what built me, bro," he says. "It's honestly what built me. It's what turned me into who I am today."

KATLYN CHOOKAGIAN

Mixed martial artist
Status: Active
Weight class: Flyweight
Cage name: Blonde Fighter
Hometown: Quakertown, Pennsylvania

CHAMPIONSHIPS
· Cage Fury Fighting Championships flyweight title (2016)
· Cage Fury Fighting Championships bantamweight title (2016)

HIGHLIGHTS
· Earned a brown belt in jujitsu

A surprising number of people don't know Blonde Fighter by her real name. But that's not to say Katlyn Chookagian isn't a well-known athlete. In fact, she's one of the most active contenders in the UFC—male or female. She's also a consummate martial artist, competing in boxing, kickboxing, jujitsu, and mixed martial arts, on top of having a sense of humor. Of course, her trademark blonde hair and five-nine stature are hard to miss.

But as a professional athlete, she's much more than her nickname. Her champion mindset has made her one of the fastest-rising contenders in the UFC's featherweight division, willing to fight anyone at anytime. She has a very businesslike approach to her career and she knows that when she fights, good things happen. She's not scared to put herself out there and trusts not only her abilities but her preparation to get the job done—time and time again. She fights with a confident and methodical approach that speaks volumes to her lifelong dedication to the martial arts. Rarely do you see someone so at home battling another person in a cage the way Katlyn is while trading blows with the UFC elite.

ON THE BLONDE FIGHTER

I ask her about the name "Blonde Fighter" and how it became her alter ego. It was a bit of an accident—one she didn't think would become so popular.

"It's funny. I was in college when Instagram came out. My friends said I should get it, but you could only post one picture. I'm thinking this will never take off." She thought she'd post "something girly and something about fighting," so she took a quick photo, not thinking it was going to stick. But of course it did. Instagram took off.

"When I was fighting, people were asking my nickname," and by her second fight in the UFC, everyone was calling her "Blonde Fighter" and it just kind of stuck. "I'm in everyone's phones as Blonde Fighter and even my husband calls me Blonde Fighter," she says with a laugh.

ON THE BEGINNING

Katlyn has a long history in martial arts and began karate when she was only four years old. Her older brother took lessons and she describes being part of the "younger sisters" who were always in the lobby watching. "It was just me and my older brother growing up, and I always wanted to do what he did," she says.

She played other sports, but she excelled at karate. "But it just wasn't cool. We were just a little bit past the *Karate Kid* stage," she says, referencing the popular movie from the 1980s that set off a martial arts craze. When she got to middle school, she played other sports but always came back to karate because, as she says frankly, "I was really good at it."

By high school, she was competing in kickboxing matches, but there weren't many women in the sport at that time. Looking for an alternative, her instructor encouraged her to try boxing. There were more women competing in boxing than in kickboxing at the time, so Katlyn tried Golden Gloves. She'd never boxed, but her coaches, who really didn't know any better, just told her, "You'll do fine—just don't kick."

Katlyn won the Pennsylvania Golden Gloves women's division when she was just 16 years old. She was also playing field hockey at the time and discovered that one of her coaches was a former professional boxer. He became her trainer and she started to get serious about the sport. In college, she really wanted to do MMA, and she mixed it up with grappling, boxing, and kickboxing competitions. "I took a year off after college and just competed in jujitsu to kind of level it up."

It seemed as if she'd always known she wanted to be a professional fight sports athlete, but like many fighters just starting out, she wondered if she could earn a living. She'd known it was what she'd wanted to do since high school, she says, but didn't really think about what it meant to be a professional. She knew only a few professional boxers who made enough money to live on. She always figured she could teach kickboxing to kids but always assumed she'd compete "for fun."

But after college, she could see MMA fighters starting to break through to the mainstream. "Ronda Rousey started becoming popular and I could see that there were girls at that level. I kinda told myself, 'All right, if I'm not pro by the time I'm 25, then I'll just use my college degree and get a real job.'"

She started bartending on weekends, and at 25, she indeed turned pro. Which, as she notes, doesn't really mean anything if you're not fighting or earning money. Still, she said, "I think I can do this" and she gave herself another two years to make it.

ON TIMING

Timing was everything when it came to MMA and Katlyn's career. When compared with boxing, MMA as a fight sport is in its chronological infancy, but the growth and trajectory have been nothing short of meteoric. The first UFC match was in 1993, and in less than three decades, MMA has become a multibillion-dollar industry and the fastest-growing sport in the world. The expansion of the female divisions is even more recent. The first female fight in the UFC was in 2013. Katlyn's timing for her decision to turn pro couldn't have been better. If she'd been ready to turn pro even two years earlier, she isn't sure she'd have been able to make it a full-time commitment.

Women's MMA came into being in 2012, when Ronda Rousey became the first woman signed to fight with the UFC. She was a crossover star moving from combat sports to film and TV. She was also an accomplished mixed martial artist, winning the bronze medal in judo at the Beijing Olympics. Katlyn was one of the first rare breeds of female fighters who'd trained their entire lives for what would become MMA and made it into her career. "When I started [in MMA], a lot of girls were just starting their training," she says. The new sport saw a lot of women coming in as college athletes just getting started. By then, Katlyn had already been competing in fight sports for 10 years.

There were no girls on the fight cards as she came up, but she was less worried because "I wasn't trying support myself financially with fighting." She hadn't yet decided to make it a full-time career but still trained with some of the best.

"Frankie Edgar was a big influence for me," she says of the American MMA star. She'd see him in the gym, even though he was still getting ready for main event fights. "He would still help me after for no reason—just because he's a really nice guy." She took away some lessons from his openness and willingness to help a young fighter just starting out. "He was the first guy in there every day and, like, you'd never realize he was who he was. He'd have a crazy war [in the fight] and would come back as soon as possible to help his teammates. I always admired him," she says.

ON BEING A PROFESSIONAL

We talk about the thing she has inside of her that inspires her to get up every day and put in the work to win—that thing that motivates her to fight through hard fights. Katlyn credits a lifetime of training.

"I'm so used to training, my whole life, it's a part of who I am. I don't think it's necessarily cool what I do. I still think it's like I'm 13 and this is my after-school activity. I feel like I never grew out of that. I don't really know how to do anything else."

When it comes to competition, Katlyn says she still mentally approaches fight days just as she did when she was getting started. "Fight day doesn't feel any different than it did when I was boxing in high school. I don't get into the zone like some people where they're like, 'I'm going into a war' before a fight." She laughs. "Maybe I should get into that zone. Maybe it would help me."

But for Katlyn, the consummate professional, she doesn't need to change her steady attitude. "I'm used to thinking of it as a sport and what I do every day," she says. "Fight day is just a step up from sparring day. And sparring day is just a step up from hitting the heavy bag. At home, hitting the heavy bag, I use the same mentality as a fight bag. To me, it's all kind of the same."

Her calm, steady approach is what sets her apart in the ring. Known for her focus, she approaches each fight—and training session—as a professional endeavor, even though for her it still feels like an extracurricular activity.

"It's what I've always done. I don't know anything different."

ON THE TITLE FIGHT

She felt the same calm, steady routine when it came to her UFC title fight against Valentina Shevchenko, a surgical destroyer and dominant UFC champion. She lost that fight but still remains one of the most active and winningest female UFC fighters.

The life of a contender is a tough one. Generally, you work your way up the ranks, knocking off hungry fighters ranked above you in order to earn your shot at the title. Katlyn had been fighting at a very high level in the UFC and winning, beating most of the women in the top 10, so it wasn't a surprise when she got a call for the championship fight.

She fought Valentina Shevchenko in February 2020 and lost by TKO when she was caught in a crucifix position, unable to defend herself. Until that point, she fought on relatively even terms, trading strikes in the middle of the cage. Even in defeat, she left the cage that night with her head held high because she never looked out of her depth. She showed she belonged with the elite fighters and that a title could very well be in the near future.

Shevchenko was a step up in skill, but Katlyn never felt she was outmatched because she'd fought so many good opponents over the years. "I spar so much and I spar with really good people all the time, so I'm not scared of anyone. Even if someone is going to be a little bit better than me, I'm confident enough in myself that I don't feel like I'm really going to get in trouble. No girl is that much better than me."

Her loss to Shevchenko was a high-profile setback, especially because Katlyn was finished in the third round of their five-round contest. Still, she was mentally fine, noting it was the first time she'd fought someone better than she was. "It happens, but going into that fight, everyone was scared of her, but I wasn't. If I was that scared of her, I wouldn't have taken the fight."

On losing, Katlyn takes a professional, matter-of-fact approach. "Obviously, it sucks. But I know if I fought her again, I'd have that unknown factor. It was the first time I'd fought anyone better than me. Getting in there and getting it out helps a lot." She hopes a rematch will come in time. And she keeps winning, so it could happen soon.

Because she's more of a tactical counterstriker, critics love to call her out for her technical style, which yields results without the flair of a KO striker in the cage. Katlyn is a dynamic fighter, but her strategy-first style tends to shut her opponents' offense down. "I get criticized that my style is boring, but if I keep winning, well, for me, it's the ultimate 'Yeah, whatever.'"

ON BEING THE UNDERDOG

Even with her skill, somehow Katlyn always seems to be the underdog in her fights. Some of that impression has to do with her high-profile loss. But she also cites her technique-driven style, which pits her experience-driven skills against tough, aggressive, flamboyant opponents.

Plus, she thinks there was some confusion around her second Shevchenko fight—this one with Valentina's sister, Antonina. "I fought her sister on short notice. I was considered the underdog in that fight, which was odd because she was the lowest-ranked and most unknown fighter I've fought in the UFC." She beat that particular Shevchenko sister.

"I think because I don't score KOs and finishes that I get looked over when it comes to the odds. I have such an advantage in the striking department that I neutralize girls and make them look bad. People think they're going to come in and finish me right away," she says.

ON BEING THE BUSIEST

Katlyn is one of the busiest fighters in the business. "I think it's because I'll fight anyone," she says. In 2020, she fought five times in 13 months, replacing fighters who couldn't travel or train because of COVID-19. But sometimes the timing doesn't work.

A few years ago, her manager called to offer her a short-notice title fight, which happened to be on the day of her wedding. "I told them and the UFC said, 'Well, okay, can you let us know by the end of the day?'" She laughs at how ludicrous the situation was. She turned it down.

By turning it down, she knew she'd have to fight another one or two more opponents to get another shot at the title fight, but she was up for it. "If your goal is to be #1, why would you say 'No' to anyone? If you can't beat the other contenders, how are you going to beat the champion?"

She also takes fights on short notice because she knows that for top-ranked female fighters, the opportunities to fight don't come up very often. And after a shoulder injury in 2019, she realized that if she wasn't fighting, she wasn't earning. "It was my first injury and it made me realize you can get hurt. And when you're not fighting, you don't make money."

"And it was really scary, especially for me. I'm a girl. I'm kind of running out of time. But I was thinking, 'I need to fight as much as I can.'"

ON THE BLONDE MOM (SOMEDAY)

The general feeling is that women can compete in fight sports longer than men at the elite levels. I ask Katlyn if she's had thoughts about when this train ends. What will be the mindset that brings her to that decision?

"In my last five fights, I've been in the locker room before, thinking this might be my last time doing this. I don't think about it a lot during fight week, but when I'm cutting weight, I'm thinking, 'Ugh, this sucks, but this might be the last time I have to do this.' And, of course, then I get an extra jolt of energy."

And like every fighter, two weeks after a fight, she's wondering when the next one is coming. "I take it fight by fight." There's only one thing that would drive a decision for her to stop. While she has respect for the women with kids who fight, it's not something she necessarily wants to do.

"The only reason I think that I would stop is because I want to have kids. For me personally, I don't see myself fighting after having kids. I just don't see myself being a mother and a fighter because I know how much time I put into training, and I know that if I had a kid, I wouldn't be the same," she says.

She sees herself as an obsessive trainer, but as with all things in Katlyn's style, her training is measured, purposeful, and planned. She calls her training, preparation, and schedule "super obsessed." But with kids, in that next chapter of life, things will change. "I'll still train, probably all the time," she says of her idea of mom life. "I'll be the crazy old lady at the gym telling the young girls, 'Oh, in my day, we used to … .'"

She worries a bit about what the stress of fighting and cutting weight a few times a year might do to her body. "I would hate to put it off and then when it's time to have kids, you think, 'Oh, maybe I should have started trying when I was younger.'"

Still, she doesn't see herself leaving the sport anytime soon. She's not ready to retire or stop "because I'm having so much fun, and in my training and my fighting, I'm improving so much. I'm so much better than I was six months ago."

ON ADVICE TO HER YOUNGER SELF

I ask her if she could go back and talk to a younger version of herself, what would her advice be? Her answer was surprising.

"To be confident in myself. I feel like I wasn't 100% confident in myself as a fighter and my abilities until recently. My coaches always told me I was good, but I always thought they were hyping me up. That's what they're supposed to do. And they would always talk very highly of my skills, of my abilities, and not that I didn't believe them, but I always kind of had the feeling they were thinking I was good for a girl."

Part of her lack of confidence might have been that she was always younger than the other girls she was fighting. She says she always thought everyone was better than she was because she was the young one coming up. And in the UFC, she always assumed that girls with more fights were better. Now she can see the difference and recognize she really does have abilities.

"I didn't get my confidence or my swag until the last year (2020), but I had over 10 UFC fights in that time, so now I'm one of those girls with all the experience."

What would Katlyn say to young girls trying to find their own confidence? "Spar with as many girls as you can." She's surprised when she runs into fighters—even those in the UFC—who are scared to spar. "And I'm thinking, 'Wait, but you're going to fight?'"

She notes that letting go of her ego was the real difference for her, especially when it comes to learning from everyone she can. For her, sparring is about learning, not about winning.

"To spar, you have to have no ego. I think that is when I got more confident and upped my level in the last two years. When I let it go because it's about not being scared. You have to put yourself out there and be vulnerable to get better."

But she does feel like she'd have a tough time being a parent of a son or daughter who wanted to train for fight sports. "I'd be into it, but I would want to be telling them how to train the whole time. If they were into another sport, I wouldn't know enough about it, so I wouldn't be able to help them train," she says.

SHAWN PORTER

Boxer
Status: Retired
Weight class: Welterweight
Ring name: Showtime
Hometown: Akron, Ohio

CHAMPIONSHIPS
· WBC welterweight title (2018)
· IBF welterweight title (2013)

HIGHLIGHTS
· Golden Gloves middleweight title (2007)
· Hosts *The Porter Way* podcast

When I talk with Shawn, the WBC had just ordered a title fight for him with current middleweight champion Terence Crawford. For Shawn, who's already won two world championships, the fight is a part of his ever-expanding legacy after a high-profile loss to Errol Spence Jr. in 2019.

I've known Shawn for years and remember when he visited me in 2014 as I was training to fight Ruslan Provodnikov for the WBO super lightweight world championship. Shawn and his father, Kenny Porter, stopped in one day to watch me spar and give me some words of encouragement as I was prepping for the biggest fight of my career to that point. That was when I learned how small the elite level of boxing is and how, as fighters, we all have eyes on those near our weight classes. Friend or foe, it's important to know your surroundings. Shawn and I spoke about how we ultimately watch and learn from each other—whether we know it or not.

Anyone who personally knows the Porters knows Shawn and his dad, who serves as his trainer and manager, are two of the most genuine, hardworking people in the sport. Shawn has a unique talent for observation, learning from everyone he sees fight. He's also known for his particularly aggressive fighting style, never letting up on the pressure, as well as his physical strength and high work rate. If you're fighting Shawn Porter, you're in for a hell of a battle!

Shawn is also a philosopher and consummate student of the sport, not to mention a superb analyst of his own motivations, drive to win, and heart. Talking to Shawn means a wealth of stories—and advice—especially from someone as adept as he is at learning from others.

When we talk, Shawn's waiting for the date of his title bout against Crawford. To schedule title fights, the boxing federation in charge of a title will call for the current champion to defend his title against a worthy opponent. Once the federation calls for the match, promoters, managers, and venues work out the details. He notes it's a relief to be able to put a face on his next opponent. Having a face and name to focus on is an important part of a fighter's mental preparation. Knowing his next fight is with Crawford provides extra fire. "When I work, the only person I see is him now," he says.

ON HIS FATHER AS MENTOR & MOTIVATOR

One thing Shawn is known for is his partnership with his father, Kenny. Everyone in the boxing world knows his father has motivated and inspired Shawn throughout his career. They form a strong team and together have created an attitude and training philosophy that other fighters now adopt, which they call "The Porter Way." But while Shawn remembers his father pushing him early on, he also sees his journey in boxing as a personal one.

Shawn started training at four years old, with his father teaching him the fundamentals. Shawn's memories of his first match are clear to him today.

"The first thing I remember is that my feet didn't touch the ground when I sat on the stool. I didn't know where to put my arms, so I remembered seeing on TV that the fighters put their arms on the ropes, so for no reason, I have my arms on the ropes," he says, grinning at the idea.

And because he was learning a disciplined regimen of the fundamentals, Shawn boxed his first match "just by the book." But his opponent wasn't so disciplined. "I'm really conventional, but the kid coming at me is just swinging at everything! My dad thought I might be losing the match, so in the last round, he said, 'Forget everything I taught you. When the bell rings, run across the ring and swing, and don't stop swinging until the bell rings.' And that's exactly what I did. I ran over there, and I swung and swung and swung. And I ended up winning the match."

While some might see the origins of his "never let up" style in that first match, he simply remembers the winning moment. "I'd always see people on TV win trophies and they always held them up," he says, gesturing like he's holding an imaginary trophy in both hands over his head. "But I remember getting this trophy that was half my size and getting to the ropes and holding it up."

Even though no one clapped or cheered for a kids match the way he was used to on TV, he still remembers how that first win felt. And since then, the cheering at his matches has gotten a little louder. The energy in the crowd is important to him, and he knew from a young age he wanted to be a fighter and fight in front of an audience.

"I remember watching the [Marvin] Hagler/[Thomas] Hearns fight [in 1985]. For me, it wasn't just the action in the ring. I was called to the sound of the crowd, to the reaction of the crowd during the fight," he says. "I remember thinking, 'I want to do that one day.' I wanted to make people scream and get excited that I was in the ring." To this day, he's always eager to see a full house. "One thing I always do when I come out, I'm looking around, it's got to be full."

He credits his father with his early training, including a wide variety of sports to broaden his skill levels for boxing.

"I think when my dad looked at me as a young kid that he saw a lot of himself and I think that he knew from an athletic standpoint what my potential was," he says. The young Shawn played football and basketball, ran track, "and even had a pool, bowling for hand-to-eye coordination, all of that—even badminton!"

It was all to improve his boxing. But apart from the athletics, Shawn fed on the energy in boxing. He describes the first time he went to a Floyd Mayweather fight years later and was up in the bleachers, where it was loud. "Something told me 'Close your eyes' and I could feel the crowd and the energy." In that moment, he describes soaking up the atmosphere and thinking, "If I want to beat the best, I need to know what it feels like when the moment happens. When it happens for me, I don't want it to be brand new."

ON BEING A CHAMPION

Shawn's a confident guy. He knows exactly what led to his success and he's not afraid to tell you. However, he also put in the time and the hard work. He's carefully managed his career and learned from others along the way.

He also says his natural competitive streak has played a role in his desire to win. For him, a lifetime of training and preparation could have only led to one place: the champion's title. "I think that everything I've become in the ring, it's almost like it couldn't have been avoided," he says about his boxing success. "I think becoming a world champion was almost unavoidable for me."

He also recognizes the responsibility of being a champion. He feels being at the top of his sport means he must also set an example for what it takes to get there. And he believes you can act and train like a champion before you ever win that match. "I think there's a way a champion should walk, should talk, should present himself, and I take it very seriously," Shawn says. "Once I became a champion, it was as if I've been acting like a champion, and now I am a champion and I have to be that champion."

But Shawn's championship journey hasn't always been easy. He talks at length about two pivotal fights that were key to his career in a positive way. As he ticks off the lessons and observations, you realize they were both losses: a close one to Keith Thurman 2016 and another against Errol Spence Jr. in 2019, where he came in as an underdog.

Rarely does a fighter speak about losses as positive points in their careers. In this era, a loss at any time can be all but career-ending or at least remove you from the elite conversation. The media would've called either loss "career ending" for another fighter but not Shawn, where they termed them "almost upsets." After his loss to Spence, he gained a lot of respect and the opportunity for big fights down the line.

As an ultracompetitive fighter, Shawn wages mental battles with his opponents as well as the physical ones in the ring. He learned early on to study his opponents with a focused intensity, watching them, observing their moves in the ring, and, with his hypercompetitive mindset, hating everything they stood for. He describes fighting Danny Jacobs, a frequent opponent during his amateur career and his longtime boxing rival. In their first match, he underestimated Jacobs, a talented boxer who came on strong and beat him. After that, Shawn says he focused his intensity on detesting Jacobs, even to the point he hated New York, where Jacobs is from. He'd tense up with anger every time he'd enter the city for a fight.

In the past few years, he's fought frequently at the Barclays Center in Brooklyn, where he found it hard to hold on to the past. "I only let my hatred of New York go recently," he says. He'd internalized the rivalry and needed to move past it. It was a lesson in how to let go of something because he loves the crowds in New York. "How can I hate a place that's giving me all this love? I had to let it go. Once I let that go, then I could let go of our rivalry."

ON OBSERVATION

I ask Shawn about his role models when he was growing up. I wanted to know which fighters he watched as a kid and idolized. He talks about not only his pat answer—the one he gives everyone—but also how he came to love the history of the sport and develop a keen eye for observation.

As a role model, "I held on to Marvin Hagler forever," he says. However, as a kid, outside of training and actually fighting, he distanced himself from the sport. It was almost as if he didn't want boxing to take over his identity.

"Looking back now, I think that I was engulfed in the sport and it was so much of the sport at home with my dad that when I wasn't doing it, I didn't want to be involved with it. When I wasn't doing it directly, I didn't want any piece of it." The result was that for a long time, he avoided watching boxing and the people who wanted to talk to him about it. He had some canned answers, but for the most part, he was always worried that someone would figure out he really didn't know much about the sport.

"When I got a little older and people started to try to talk to me about boxing, I didn't have any answers. I didn't know what to say," he says. "But there were a few guys who stuck out to me and I'd think, 'If anyone asks me, I'm going to say Sugar Shane Mosley is my favorite fighter.' He had it all. He was fast, he was explosive, a combination puncher, he was aggressive. Kind of like Marvin Hagler but with a little more speed and a little more flash."

When Shawn's professional career took off and he started to do interviews, he was increasingly worried about being called out as a fraud. So in classic Shawn Porter fashion, he started studying the greats. He began to learn about the sport in an entirely new way: watching old fights and forming new opinions on styles, techniques, and what it took to win.

"When someone asks who's your favorite fighter of all time, you always have to say 'Sugar Ray Leonard' or 'Muhammad Ali,'" Shawn says. But once he became a student studying fights, fighters, and the history of the sport, he feels he could easily name another 10 fighters who left an impression.

He still marvels that he nearly got caught. "I went through years of BS'ing the whole question." He laughs. "I didn't know they'd be so interested in my opinion on fights and fighters." Today, he does commentary on fights and he gets to ask the question of others. He appreciates their answers even more knowing the history.

ON HARD WORK & DISCIPLINE

Shawn is well known for his work ethic—and for being a fighter who isn't afraid of hard work and discipline. I ask him where he thinks this drive originated and how he finds it every day. Not surprisingly, he credits his dad for getting him in the ring, day in and day out.

"My dad, he pushed me at times where I didn't want to be pushed. He pushed me at times when I didn't even *understand* why I was being pushed. He practically forced me to work hard, even when I was young and didn't understand," he says of his father. Kenny's a highly disciplined man who demands ultimate discipline from his son. He also knew Shawn had to grow and mature on his own as a fighter—and as a man. They're a rare boxing father–son duo that's been incredibly successful.

Shawn says his father also got him through his immature days. "Today, I understand exactly what it takes for me to get in the ring and do what I've got to do, no problem," he says. "But at 23? Heck no. If my dad wasn't there, I probably would have done just enough to win a fight. I would have done just enough to be in shape. I would have done just enough to win. My dad took me from good to great because he knew what my potential was."

Shawn thinks it can be hard for younger fighters without a strong mentor to believe in themselves and in what they can do. "A lot of times, we don't know our potential because we are too young to realize it. We haven't had enough experiences for us to understand who we are and what we need to do. I was blessed enough to have my dad in that position."

Of course, he also knew that with his dad pushing him, it was sometimes easier to just do what needed to be done. "I was blessed enough to learn if you don't want him on your ass, you gotta do things the right way."

ON THE GLADIATOR MINDSET

When I think of Shawn's style, work ethic, and attitude as a professional, there's one word that comes to mind: gladiator. And like gladiators of the ancient world, he's learned how to size up an opponent and adapt quickly. His talent for observation has been a valuable part of how he's become such a successful boxer. "My dad has always taught me to pay attention to what's going on," Shawn says. "I've always paid attention to the way other fighters reacted to certain moments in fights and I always pulled from that," he says. His father taught him to look into a fighter's eyes and see the warrior inside. He learned how other fighters show heart. "If you don't display that kind of heart, you're not a true champion."

Today, as a modern-day gladiator, he's built a war chest of experience. He builds his armor by observing, learning, watching, and preparing. "I've pulled from so many other athletes and fighters, champions in their sport, I'm a big ball of everybody but trying to be the best version of all of those people."

> **"There is a fine line between self-confidence and wishful thinking— and opponents are usually very good about letting you know when that line is crossed."**
>
> **–unknown**

Additionally, he believes in preparation, always trying to experience "the moment" before it catches him by surprise. Whether it's soaking in the crowd noise or watching fights to catch an opponent's weakness, he does his homework. "People say [about fighters] 'Did the moment get to him?' and I was never going to let the moment get to me," he says. "Of course, God's given me the abilities," Shawn says. "My dad and I put it together, we get it in shape, we do the game planning, but when there's a tough moment in the ring, if it's not a moment I've experienced myself, I'm looking at an experience that I saw and I'm saying that's what you've got to be. There's so much to how I've become a champion and so many people out there in the world who contributed to it and didn't even know it."

ON THE TURNING POINT

I ask him how he digs deep to find that desire to win and how he finds a new gear when he's down in a fight. As he often does, he cites a fight he learned from. In this case, he talks about one of his first real step-up fights: his 2012 draw with Julio Díaz, a tough former champion. It was a fight inside a fight—Porter versus Porter—which yielded a revelation for him about his future in boxing. Shawn has a way of making a fight look easy and he'd discounted Díaz's experience in the ring. He thought it was going to be easy.

Before he tells the story, he asks if I know that yawning can be a sign of anxiety. Like all of Shawn's stories, it relates to his answer. Then he says, "I've always yawned before fights and I always just thought it was natural. Come to find out it's a form of anxiety, but I didn't know that at the time."

On the Díaz fight, he recalls, "Coming out to the ring, I had a realization that I hadn't yawned. Remember, I've been yawning since I was in the amateurs—every fight! And once I realized I didn't yawn, I took that as a sign that I didn't care and that whatever was going to happen was going to happen." He made it through the first five rounds relying on techniques. He felt he was giving it his all against an easy opponent, but Díaz was experienced and not going down without a fight. "By the fifth round, I had burned my first and second tanks and was on fumes, and he started to come on strong. And once he starts to come on strong, the mental and emotional battle kicks in."

Every fighter knows about the voices, self-talk, encouragement, or doubt that comes to them in the ring. It's a familiar battle for any fighter. But as he fought, Shawn's voices were reminding him he'd already decided this was his last fight. "They're saying, 'But you don't care anyway. You didn't even yawn coming out to the ring. It doesn't mean that much. This is the last one anyway.' I started to let go. I just started to release and I didn't care." He just wanted to go round after round and get the fight over.

And then something remarkable happened. "I remember being in the corner before the 11th round and I had a thought out of nowhere: 'What are you talking about? You can beat this dude. You are *not* going to *quit.*'" Shawn tapped into something inside himself and finished the fight strong for the last two rounds. "I don't know where the energy came from," he says.

The fight was a draw, but for Shawn, it was a personal breakthrough. "There was a big maturation process through that fight. Afterward, I had to deal with real life, with some personal situations. When I came back to the ring, I was better for making it through the mental battles in that fight. So now when they say 'You're "No stop, no quit," I know I can make it through anything because I made it through that," he says. "I was blessed to get a draw that night—I'll be the first to admit that. But the blessing is that I was able to have another chance to become everything I wanted to become. It was a reset button for me. I was able to pull everything together. I was on my way to getting to where I am now."

It was a pivotal moment in his journey as a champion. "I think if that moment hadn't happened, if that fight hadn't happened, there's no telling where I'd be now. I think that fight happened right on time. I was able to come back a much stronger person and fighter," he says.

Shawn kicked his career into a higher gear. He had several hard fights in 2013, including a Díaz rematch, where he was able to show the world what he could do. The hard work paid off, culminating in his 2013 IBF welterweight title fight against Devon Alexander.

ON WINNING THE TITLE

In October 2013, Shawn challenged IBF welterweight champion Devon Alexander in a title fight in San Antonio, Texas. Shawn came into the fight as a relative unknown, while Alexander was defending his title for the second time. Shawn was the underdog—something he relished. "I remember thinking to myself, 'I'm going to show them. I'm going to show them all. They have no clue what's about to happen,'" he says. Along with the game plan his dad developed, he felt confident going into the fight. "When you've got a perfect game plan, it's just about going out there and executing it."

He doesn't say he was "in the zone" for that fight. He was so focused, he calls it "in the spirit." "The opening bell, I was in the spirit and everything went the way it was supposed to go," he says. He tries to use that fight as a model of a perfect fight from the first bell to the last. "That's how good I felt for that fight."

His message to young boxers today is, "Don't forget why you're there." If a boxer can stay focused on the end result, they're "going to go through anything and anybody who's in your way."

While everyone else saw an unknown fighter, he knew he had it in him to win and was ready for the moment. "I knew I wanted the IBF title. I was fighting for a world title. Everybody said I would be here one day. A lot of people don't believe I'm going to win and the only thing I knew is that I wanted that title."

"Once the bell rings, that's all I'm waiting on. That's the mental state I carry with me, no matter what," he says. "It's like being put in a lion's den. Once they close the gate, there's nothing you can do! Once you get in the ring, why be nervous? I don't think that nervousness is a bad emotion, but I say why get nervous about something that I want?"

He talks about his fights as if they were entertainment, like a true modern-day gladiator would. Victory is always the goal, but in the end, Shawn understands his performances can live beyond his career, becoming the classic fights that other up-and-comers watch. "I'm going to go out there and do everything I need to do to get everything I want," he says.

> **"The belt meant so much to me when my name was called. One of the two greatest moments in my life—having my first son and winning the WBC title. The feeling was the same. I'll never forget it."**
>
> **–Shawn Porter**

ON ADVICE TO HIS YOUNGER SELF

Shawn is introspective about all aspects of his life, including his own fights. He's the consummate student of the sport, including the game plan and mental game. I ask him about the advice he'd give to a young Shawn Porter, but he doesn't want to go back to childhood. He merely wants to go back to a 2014 fight. He was slated to defend his IBF welterweight title fighting UK boxer Kell Brook. Shawn lost that fight by majority decision.

In watching the match, he'd give himself grief about pacing and his game plan. But his lesson is: "Settle down. Understand that there's 12 rounds in the fight and that you can't be locked into one thing for the entire fight."

"In boxing, you need to be able to make adjustments. You have to be able to think and give your opponents something to think about as well. I think that's where I started to mature and change as a fighter," Shawn says.

ON THE WORLD'S TOUGHEST SPORT

During our discussion, we talk about the number of athletes flocking to boxing. Shawn believes the sport is one of the best all-around sports today because of the skills it requires. It demands the most strength, skill, acuity, and athleticism to win. And let's face it, everyone wants to be a boxer, right? "Everyone thinks they can fight. Every guy on the street thinks they can fight. But it's the best sport in the world. It's the hardest thing you could do."

He notes the popularity of boxing on social media—and even MMA fighters now want to box. "The world isn't asking themselves this, but why is everyone going to the sport of boxing? It's because boxing has every element that the other sports don't have. Boxing is the pinnacle of sports," he says.

He also wonders about the new interest in boxing with so many athletes flocking to boxing training gyms to learn the workouts. He thinks folks inside the sport complaining about this influx should ask themselves what it is about the sport that draws people to it. "Everybody wants to do it, wants to see it, wants to be involved with it. Everyone's asking the question 'How do we feel about these guys now wanting to box?'" he says. "But the even bigger question is, 'Why is everyone wanting to box?' It could be *anything* else in the world, but why is it boxing? Nobody is asking themselves why."

TONY JEFFRIES

Boxer, trainer
Status: Active
Weight class: Light heavyweight
Ring name: Jaffa
Hometown: Sunderland, England

HIGHLIGHTS

· Bronze medal at the Beijing Olympics (2008)
· 5-time European medalist
· 9-time British national champion
· 96 amateur fights, 10 professional fights (9-0-1, 6 KOs)
· World-class boxing coach and celebrity fitness trainer
· Owner of Box 'N Burn boxing gym in Los Angeles
· Host of the *Box 'N Life* podcast

Whenever I talk to Tony Jeffries, we always joke about our shared birthdays. (He's a year younger.) As you meet fighters and talk with them in gyms, arenas, and even broadcast studios, you learn to remember the personal details that connect you together. Tony and I met at his gym a few years ago through a mutual sponsor, and I've been a guest on his *Box 'N Life* podcast, where we've discussed nutrition, training, and brain health.

I've always had a great respect for Tony and the work he's done in the ring as a fighter (and trainer) as well as his dynamic approach to sharing the intricate details of the "sweet science" of boxing to the masses. If I didn't know he was a professional, he could easily be cast as a British tough guy in a Guy Ritchie film. With his buzz cut and tattoos, he could pull it off, no doubt. (In fact, he's done a few turns on television and in modeling since he's lived in California.) In real life, though, he's one of the nicest and most gregarious guys you'll ever meet, on top of being a real professional.

From a training perspective, one of the best drills I know is one Tony taught me: a mitts and reaction drill he says is a staple of the Great Britain Boxing Team. It's a light "tap" sparring that starts with your hands at your sides. With each tap, you try to touch your partner's shoulder with your hands. It's a fantastic drill to practice timing, rhythm, and upper-body movement without incurring unnecessary damage. It might be one of the reasons Tony's still so mentally sharp after a lifetime of high-level boxing.

Growing up in the UK, Tony had a different exposure to boxing than many of us had in the US. I ask him what his first memory of the sport was.

"Ever since I learned to walk, my grandad had me in a stance and throwing punches. I started going to the gym when I was 10 years old but didn't expect anything to come of it," he says. He noted how strange it was to be training at the gym as a kid and see professionals who you recognized.

With his first fight at 11 years old, Tony found himself a boxer. After 106 amateur and professional fights, including 56 of them representing Great Britain, he can look back on a strong career. He even has an Olympic bronze medal to show for it.

"You never expect your life to revolve around it, for it to become your identity for the rest of your life, but it has been fantastic. It's had ups and downs, but I wouldn't change it," he says.

ON THE OLYMPIC JOURNEY

When heavyweight Audley Harrison won the gold medal for Great Britain in the Sydney 2000 Olympic games, the British government got serious about funding amateur boxing. The government determined that 22 to 25 was the age range for when Olympic boxers were most likely to win, so they designed a training program with that goal in mind. In 2001, 16-year-old Tony entered an 8-year training program with 50 or so 15- to 17-year-old boxers.

Throughout the program, people came and went, but "only me and two other boxers went the full eight years and went through to the Olympics," he says. And they were paid. "We started off making 500 pounds [$675] every three months, which, at 16, I felt rich because I had more money than all of my friends," Tony says. "Later, I was making 1,000 pounds [$1,350] a month and I'm thinking, 'I'm a full-time boxer.'"

In 2008, Tony qualified for the Beijing Olympics along with six other British boxers. "It was unbelievable. It was a life-changer," he says. "Qualifying seven boxers was an incredible accomplishment since we had only qualified three boxers in the previous eight years," he notes of the British success.

Coming up through a training program had prepared Tony for boxing success. At 16, he was training and living the lifestyle of a professional boxer, but today, he recognizes he still had a lot to learn. "I didn't have a clue what professional was. I didn't know what good eating was. At the time, I would go and weigh in for a fight, then I'd go to McDonald's. [I had] zero knowledge about nutrition. No one told us."

Today, he knows how important nutrition, wellness, physical therapy, and even technology are for the success of a fighter. "Our coaches were old-school. They didn't understand about nutrition, about wrapping my hands properly, so I had injured hands. It was the Wild West."

ON THE HANDS

Hand injuries can be debilitating for a boxer. Your hands are everything. Tony famously struggled with his own hand injuries for years before they forced his retirement from professional boxing in 2012. I ask him about it.

"Even as a kid, I had heavy hands," he says, adding that he always "was a puncher." And, hey, he didn't mind too much because they'd swell up when he was a kid and he'd say to his friends, "Look at me, I'm a fighter. I'm tough." We laugh at the memory. But later on, it became a real concern.

"My hands were always a problem throughout my full career," he says. As he trained, he learned how to wrap his hands properly, but his hands always bothered him. In 2006, he needed surgery, then came back, went to the Olympics, and turned pro.

"I was getting anesthetic injections in my hands before fights," Tony says of the constant injuries. While the pain was a consistent issue, the swelling presented another hurdle as he switched from amateur to professional boxing.

In amateur boxing, there's more padding in the front of the gloves. When Tony was an amateur boxer, his punches also fell on headgear. In 2013, headgear was eliminated by the International Boxing Association (AIBA) for men's amateur boxing, which includes the Olympics. They determined they didn't prevent concussions and other brain injuries. Some consider this decision controversial.

For professionals, the gloves are smaller, with less padding, which caused problems with Tony's swollen hands. "Once I turned professional, hitting rock-hard skulls with smaller gloves, it got to the point that I couldn't zip a top or button my trousers," he recalls. With additional surgeries and recoveries, it was time to retire.

Tony says if he hadn't boxed as an amateur hitting headgear instead of as a professional hitting heads, he would've retired much earlier. He touts them with lengthening his boxing career. "I'm glad the head guards were in. Otherwise, I would have retired a long time ago."

ON RETIREMENT

The damage to fighters' hands can be extensive, requiring trips to the hospital, casts, surgeries, and constant pain. At some point, a fighter decides they want to do just one more bout, then retire. I ask him what deciding to retire was like mentally. For a fighter who'd been living the life of a pro for so long, fighting since he was 11 years old, it was hard to imagine.

"I was 27 for my last surgery," Tony says. "I was waiting for my hands to get better and they just weren't healing. I tried everything." When nothing worked, he decided he'd have to call it a day.

By 2012, Tony and his wife had moved to the US and he started coaching and teaching boxing while recovering from his injuries. He recalls myriad people he thanked, including his dad, who was his manager. He announced his decision to his fans via social media. "I wrote a big status on Facebook and tears are just rolling down my face, thanking people and thinking about people who've helped us, thinking about the journey." He gets a little emotional as he tells the story. "Announcing the retirement was really, really tough." But once he pressed the button to post, "Boom—that was it," he says.

Once he retired, reality set in. He started eating and drinking more. "I got fat, depressed, didn't know what I was going to do." As any recently retired fighter knows, everyone—from the gym to the guy on the street— asks "When's your next fight?" It's all you hear.

Tony found himself constantly explaining he didn't box anymore. It was even worse when people would stop asking. "You go from the boxer in the limelight with the prospect to do great things to an average Joe, which is hard when you've never been a regular Joe—for years."

He was also worried about finances. "I was making good money from my fights," he says, noting he was sometimes making $30,000 for a four- or six-round fight. "I was making good money fighting journeymen."

Realizing he had "zero qualifications but a good business brain," he focused the determination, energy, and hard work he'd put into boxing success into opening a gym and coaching. Obviously excited, he emphatically shares his most important advice: "Life after boxing—it's so easy, mate! So easy!"

I tell him I always think of the movie *Fight Club* and the idea that once you're in a fight, everything else in life has the volume turned down. Once you've been in the ring, everything else in life is easy. He agrees there's still nothing that compares to the experience of winning.

However, he's learned to appreciate retirement—if you can call his extraordinarily busy life and career "retirement." After boxing, he says "life is nice and easy." You're not going through the stress of constantly thinking about training or your opponent or what you're eating. "But at the same time, you never reach the high and that feeling of getting your arm raised, that you beat someone, of being the star of the show," he says.

"That's the hard thing. You miss that ultimate high. I never took drugs, but I imagine it's like taking the best drug ever, then you're addicted to that feeling. It hurts, but when you get over that and understand that, you can move on with your life."

ON DRIVE

We talk about what it takes to win and what gave him the champion's drive, especially when he started competing at such a young age. What pushed him to compete at an elite level before he'd felt the high of having his arm raised or an Olympic medal around his neck? While he says he always had the drive to be better, he was also scared of losing.

"I didn't want to lose, so I worked hard," he says, also noting he was nervous about fighting in the beginning. "I would get the doubts in my mind, thinking, 'Am I good enough to do this? Is this guy too big or too much better?'"

Because he was in a formal training program for the British Olympic team, he learned to pursue shorter-term goals. "I was focused on my next fight. I was focused on beating the guy who was in front of me, not who I might be fighting later."

"A lot of fighters make that mistake," Tony says. "They fail to focus on beating the guy directly in front of them and instead focus on the next fight and the next instead of thinking about the guy they need to beat now."

When he learned to focus on his immediate opponent, he became much more successful. "I would think I've got to train harder than him. I need to do more. You have to be obsessive, which is *so* stressful!"

ON BRANDING

When it comes to building a business, Tony has managed to earn enormous accomplishments in his postprofessional boxing life. He's a successful trainer, working with celebrities and professionals in his gyms. He hosts a successful podcast, featuring key members of the boxing world. And he makes popular videos on YouTube, teaching boxing techniques for nearly half a million followers. Not every boxer is comfortable with the art of self-promotion, but for Tony, the importance of brand-building was something he learned while he was still an amateur boxer.

"I was always really good at building my brand. I was the only guy who had a website back in 2007 and I printed out these autograph cards," he says, describing some of his early strategies. Because he was frequently asked to attend ribbon cuttings and public events, he'd pass out cards with his photo and autograph to everyone who came. "People were like, 'Who are ya?' But it helped to build my brand," he says. "I like to tell fighters now: You have to promote yourself because you can be the most talented fighter in the world, but if no one knows who you are or you're not selling tickets, promoters aren't going to want to use you."

Since 2012, his brand-building has transitioned to learning about graphics and then making videos, even though he was nervous about putting out his first educational video on technique. His YouTube videos teach boxers everything from footwork to combination body punches.

"I was thinking, 'These are my secrets,' so I was really afraid to do it," he says of making his first video. "It was a video on one of my favorite combinations and I'm thinking, 'I don't want people to learn this. I want them to come and train with me,' but I posted it—and it blew up. And I'm thinking, 'Wow, this could be something.'"

And it turned out to be something for sure. "Last month, I made more money on YouTube posting videos than on my 10th professional fight!" he says. "When I retired from boxing, I was thinking, 'How am I ever going to make this kind of money again?' But now I'm doing it and I'm not having to get punched. I'm not waking up every moment thinking about a fight. It's amazing I've reached so many people."

He offers advice to young fighters as they come up. "You need to use these platforms to promote yourself. Keep posting as much as you can to continue to build your name up." Adding, in his cheeky British accent, "It's really changed me life."

"The success has been almost as good as winning a professional fight." And in retrospect? "When I retired from boxing, it was the worst moment ever. Now looking back, it was the best thing that's ever happened to us."

ON ADVICE TO HIS YOUNGER SELF

I ask him what he wished he'd known as he came up through the ranks. He has a simple answer: "Don't worry about what others will think," he says. He discusses how he's seen young fighters get caught up worrying about criticism. It prevents them from growing and having success.

I ask him if he could go back in time and give one piece of advice to a young Tony Jeffries, what would it be? As a content creator, he says he'd have been more dedicated to connecting with his audience and fans. "The more you're in the public eye, the more reach you have and the more you can connect with your fans. If I'd known how to do it when I was still fighting, I would have been a millionaire by now."

And his best advice for future fighters? To be ready for the realities of boxing. "I love Mike Tyson's saying: 'Everybody has a plan until they get punched in the mouth.'"

He notes the rise in "white-collar boxers"—amateur fighters who train but have regular jobs and fight in special bouts. "A lot of my clients for fitness will progress to shoulder and body sparring and say they want to fight. I tell them, 'No, you don't because when you get punched in the face, it's completely different.'"

While he still believes there's no better feeling than winning a fight and having your arm raised by the referee, he counsels future fighters that it's the hardest thing they're ever going to do in life. "If you want to do it, you should, but you've got to get comfortable with getting punched in the face."

He means this figuratively and literally. "If someone really wants to fight, I say, 'Go for it and don't worry about what people are going to say. Don't get to the age where you wish you'd done it. Go for it, experience it, but know it will be the hardest thing you've ever done.'"

JESSICA PENNE

Mixed martial artist
Status: Active
Weight classes: Strawweight, atomweight
Hometown: Newport Beach, California

CHAMPIONSHIPS

· Invicta Fighting Championships atomweight title (2012)

HIGHLIGHTS

· First female Invicta Fighting Championships atomweight champion
· UFC debut on *The Ultimate Fighter* television finale
· Fight of the Night bonus in her UFC debut
· Brazilian jujitsu black belt under Lucas Leite

When I talk to Jessica Penne, she's at training camp, getting ready for her second fight after a four-year layoff. She's scheduled for a bout against Polish champion Karolina Kowalkiewicz just a few days later. (She'd go on to win the match—a big one for her as she works on her comeback to another title shot.)

Because I was also training for an upcoming fight, we talk a bit about the nature of preparing for a fight and how hard it can be. While most combat athletes train year-round, getting ready for a scheduled bout against a specific fighter is an important—but often unseen—part of reaching the championship levels of fight sports.

We also talk about how physically painful it can be to fight. Every little mark on your face on fight night turns into a major bruise the next day. Fighters get used to hospital visits, medical tests, and a lot of pain when they get out of the cage. People who see boxing or MMA from the outside will never understand the mindset.

"It's always been challenging sharing [these feelings] with people because they look at it as an excuse if you share what goes on," Jessica says. In the world of elite training, the most common response to complaints is "Suck it up," which is why many fighters just don't talk about how hard it is. "It's crazy what we put ourselves through, but that's who we are. It's something that I think all fighters share—the ability to keep pushing through."

Overcoming doubt and enduring pain are the common traits professionals share in all fight sports. Jessica embodies these traits as much as any champion today. Over her career, she's become known for her no-quit attitude inside the cage. But she's also had to dig deep to overcome some outside-the-ring troubles. Two different doping allegations left Jessica with long layoffs in her career: one for 26 months and another for 18. Layoffs can be difficult for any fighter, but she used that time to work through some personal issues and improve her relationship with the sport.

ON ALWAYS BEING AN ATHLETE

Jessica has always been a natural athlete. I ask her how she started in combat sports and found her passion in MMA. "I got a fairly late start," she says, "but I'd always been an athlete." Growing up, she competed in soccer, softball, volleyball, and swimming, but something was missing. "I was talented, but I really just didn't have any drive. They just weren't important to me. I did them because I was good at it."

By high school, she started to realize that team sports weren't for her. At the recommendation of a friend, she tried out for the swim team and began competing in backstroke and freestyle. "I found swimming and I was immediately good at it," she says. But most importantly, "I discovered that I really loved competing individually. Training as a team and supporting each other in a team environment but competing individually was very appealing to me."

She started to look for other sports that allowed for individual achievement and found wrestling, but "at the time, they were really not welcoming of females doing wrestling." Today, women's wrestling is an Olympic sport and all-female wrestling teams are popular, but around the year 2000, it wasn't possible. And she wasn't comfortable pushing her way into a sport "that just didn't want me." She moved on but had discovered an interest in combat sports.

When she was 23, she found herself flipping through channels during the Rick Roufus versus Michael McDonald kickboxing match. She saw a commercial for LA Boxing, a cardio–kickboxing gym that was the precursor to UFC, and thought, "'Holy crap, what is that? I'm going to go there,'" she says. "I'd never seen anything like it. So basically I said, 'Hey, I'm here. I want to learn to fight.'"

While she doesn't consider herself a confident athlete, she was talented. She picked up the techniques quickly and several coaches began inviting her to professional fighter training sessions. Eventually, she moved to APEX, the legendary MMA gym, and began scheduling school and work around training. "And I never left," she says. "I finally found that dedication and that drive into a sport that I really had never had before."

I ask her when she first knew she wanted to compete. "I never really thought about it," she says, noting that moving into competition just happened naturally. "Someone just asked me if I wanted to do a 'smoker fight.'" Smoker fights are nonsanctioned, informal—usually illegal—fights held at gyms or other venues. "You basically tape up all the windows, you do it late at night when nobody's there, and you hope the cops don't show up." Fighters are paired up on-site based on who shows up.

That night, they paired her up with another girl. "They kind of eyeballed us and said, 'You're both about the same size. You guys can fight each other.' That was my first fighting experience. I was like, 'Yeah, sign me up. I'll do it again.'" Considering that she'd walked into the gym for an arguably brutal kickboxing match based on an ad, it was a lucky happenstance for her. She wasn't familiar with UFC and had never learned jujitsu.

Ultimately, she never really considered she was on a career path to being a professional athlete. But did she think she was as good as people said? "I don't think I ever really had that thought," she says. "One thing I've lacked in my career is confidence and acknowledgment that this is my profession. People just kept asking me if I wanted to [fight] and I kept saying 'Yes,' and before I knew it, I was a professional fighter."

ON BECOMING A CHAMPION

In 2009, Jessica won the first Bellator female MMA fight. In 2012, she won the first Invicta Fighting Championship world title at atomweight. I ask her what it was like in that championship moment. "It was probably one of the best moments of my life," she says. "It was extremely gratifying and it was the first time that I acknowledged myself as a legit athlete, as a legit fighter. It was a really important moment to me and it was something that I didn't believe I could do until after I did it. It was a really amazing moment."

When self-doubt comes, every fighter has to dig down to find that source of inspiration deep inside. Like many fighters, with careful introspection, Jessica found that her relationship with her sport was really covering up something else. She's had two layoffs in her career, which has given her some time for self-reflection.

"During my long layoff, I had a lot of time to go inward and do some serious work because I was realizing that fighting, competing, training, that everything about this sport was really a Band-Aid to a greater issue, which was anxiety and depression," she says. "It was very therapeutic to always be in the gym. It was a way that I could connect with people because it's always been challenging for me to connect."

Many fighters encounter internal or mental barriers at various points in their careers, and most benefit from professional help to work on them— just like they'd seek out a trainer to help with physical barriers. With that help often comes a deeper understanding of why they connected with the sport in the first place.

"Being in the sport was a positive influence for me. It gave me drive and dedication in all aspects of my life—something I never really had before. But it started to not work for me anymore because my issues were deeper-rooted than just being able to train through them," she says. "So I got to be really thankful and look at the silver lining of my long layoff."

"Everyone must choose one of two pains: the pain of discipline or the pain of regret."

–Jim Rohn

ON THE LAYOFF

The layoff that Jessica refers to was her first suspension for failing a USADA drug test in 2017. The US Anti-Doping Agency (USADA) is the national anti-doping organization (NADO) in the US for major amateur and professional sports. They're also the current administrator for the UFC's anti-doping program. In recent years, the UFC has made a big push to clean up the sport because of the widespread use of performance-enhancing drugs (PEDs) by many competitors.

Jessica failed her test because of the presence of dehydroepiandrosterone (DHEA) in a medication prescribed by her doctor. DHEA is a precursor hormone that can have a number of medicinal uses, but it's a banned substance according to most anti-doping agencies. She was suspended from competition for 18 months, which would launch a series of missteps for the champion. In 2019, she missed weight by two pounds for her match with Jodie Esquibel. However, the morning of the fight, she sprained her ankle and the fight was called off.

Also in 2019, she failed her second USADA test when the results showed metabolites of stanozolol, an anabolic steroid. The failed test came with another two-year ban. She was out of the cage for four years. Any fighter would be devastated. "It still stings a lot," she says. "I've healed a lot from it, there's a lot of pain, and even going into my last fight with Lupita Godinez [in April 2021], there's still a lot of pain and baggage attached to it. There's still some healing to be done about that."

It's a difficult topic and still raw, like an open wound that hasn't started healing. She hasn't had the luxury of distance to give her some perspective. Her thoughts are unique because she's one of the only champions I've spoken with who's actively going through their most difficult career low. "It was an extremely challenging time in my life—financially, personally, physically, mentally, emotionally. It was just an extreme low in my life," she says of the second suspension. "It was really a struggle for quite a while. I focused on the positive as much as I could, but there were serious lows there."

She offers advice for fighters who need to figure a way out of their own tough lows. "What helped me was the mindset that 'This is not happening *to* me—it is happening *for* me.' There is always a positive to learn and grow from in every situation. The only thing I can control is how I respond." She recites it like a mantra—one she's most likely used many times in the past few years. But she knew that controlling her mindset was important because of the depression and anxiety she'd faced for most of her life— so much that she didn't even realize what she was going through.

"It was very challenging at first, but I started acquiring more tools and that really helped me," she says. "Reaching out and expressing my needs and being vulnerable to what I was going through and reaching out to people."

But she had some unexpected positives along the way. "It was really surprising, especially the second time around, how supportive the fans were. Because MMA fans can be brutal," she says about the support she received. "It was really heartwarming and motivating to feel supported by everyone, so that was huge."

ON THE COMEBACK

In March 2021, after a series of delays, cancellations, and a global pandemic, Jessica put a UFC win on her record after four years out of the cage. "It was the longest fight camp of my life!" she jokes. After two opponents dropped out because of injuries and then a cancellation because of COVID-19, she trained for six months, but she was ultimately glad because she'd been out of competition for so long. I ask her if she felt scared or worried re-entering the ring for her comeback. "Competing consistently and having that fight experience is a big tool for any fighter. Being out of the cage for so long brought up a lot of anxiety," she says. "Fear of the unknown—it's the worst. And it gets the best of us. It was extremely challenging, but I felt so loved and supported by my teammates and my cornermen, especially during fight week."

We laugh about the crazy things fighters think about during fight week. Fighters often have fantasies. "Maybe my opponent just won't show up or maybe I'll trip and fall. Or maybe we just skip it and go get a beer," she says. We laugh, but we agree that knowing you have a strong team with you makes all the difference. Thanks to a dedicated manager and team, she was able to make it through, even though she seriously considered retirement.

"I had this story in my head like, 'What if I forget how to fight? What if I don't remember how to do the thing that I pride myself on knowing how to do?' I felt incredibly loved and supported, but I was terrified!" she says. Jessica had to work off the "ring rust" but ultimately won her comeback fight against Godinez. "As a veteran, I pride myself on being able to find a way to win and I think that's where I showed my experience. My fighting spirit is that I can adapt and adjust, and she wasn't making the adjustments."

ON THE FIGHTING SPIRIT

We talk about the fighting spirit—that drive that sets a champion apart. I ask about her about her famous fight with Joanna Jędrzejczyk for the UFC women's strawweight title. Jędrzejczyk was undefeated and dominated Jessica, who took a hellacious beating. But even though her face was a mess, she never stopped fighting back or trying to win. The referee stopped the fight in the third round.

"I never thought about the injuries, my face getting messed up. I've never thought about these things and I think if I really did think about those things, then I shouldn't be in there," she says. "I think that's what separates fighters from other people. I'll do whatever it takes, and whatever the consequences are, I'll deal with those later. But in those moments, that's what I love about this sport. It just really reveals who a person is."

With such a long layoff, any fighter might think about retirement. I ask Jessica if the thought had crossed her mind or if her champion's spirit—her drive to win—sustained her. "In my first layoff, there was no ifs, ands, or buts about it, I was coming back," she says. "But during the second one, it damn near broke me. I thought I was done."

When it comes to advice she'd give a young Jessica Penne, she's a little emotional as she delivers a simple message: "It's gonna be hard. It's gonna challenge you. It's gonna break your heart. But it's gonna be worth it."

During Jessica's time coming up in combat sports, she's seen a lot of changes, especially when it comes to women fighters. I ask her what advice she'd have for young women coming up in the UFC who want to compete at an elite level. She says she hopes they'll embrace every opportunity.

"This is an amazing time for the sport and for females in the sport. Embrace it, take advantage of it. I never dreamed that females would be able to be on the main stage, be a main event. These were really huge dreams to me when I was first coming up. The sport's come a long way. It's an amazing time to be a female in the sport," she says.

JAMES "BUDDY" McGIRT

Boxer, trainer
Status: Active
Weight classes: Welterweight, middleweight
Ring name: Buddy
Hometown: Long Island, New York

CHAMPIONSHIPS

· IBF light middleweight title (1996)
· WBC welterweight title (1991)
· IBF light welterweight title (1988)
· WBC Continental Americas light welterweight title (1985, 1987)

HIGHLIGHTS

· International Boxing Hall of Fame Inductee (2019)
· Trainer of the Year (2002)
· First boxing champion from Long Island, New York
· Has trained Arturo Gatti, Antonio Tarver, Hasim Rahman, Paulie Malignaggi, and Sergey Kovalev

---

B uddy and I share the rare honor of being world boxing champions hailing from Long Island. Long Island certainly isn't known as a hotbed for boxing, but Buddy was the first world champion from Long Island in 1989. I was the second in 2014. Since then, we Long Islanders have been joined by Jamel Herring (2018) and Joe Smith (2021).

Buddy boxed in an earlier era—one before my time—and I was always disappointed that I didn't get to see him fight. However, his second career as a coach has been front and center in my boxing memory. Now through my work as a commentator, I'm lucky to talk to Buddy every few months. The one thing that always stands out? I can honestly say he's one of the most genuinely happy retired champions I've ever met. Boxing can be a cruel mistress, and many boxers leave the ring bitter and disenchanted. Not Buddy. He's solid, well adjusted, and always quick with a story.

I had the chance to talk to Buddy about his humble beginnings and how they helped propel him to his success as a champion as well as a trainer. He's in his 50s but exudes another era. One of classic, old-school boxing, which makes sense. He fought professionally from 1982 to 1997, witnessing changes in the sport that ushered it into the modern era.

ON BEING HOMEGROWN

When I talk with him, he mentions he's just finished a training session. Even retired, he still works with up-and-coming fighters every day, helping prepare them for major fights.

Fights today are typically 8 to 10 rounds or maybe 12. But they used to be longer and much more brutal. Buddy's career saw the end of 15-round fights. (He had two of them.) But in the beginning, he was just a kid in Catholic school. "I tried peewee football, but they always had problems finding a helmet that would fit my head," he says with a laugh.

In those days, he was a regular at the Brentwood recreation center in Brentwood Long Island, or "Brentwood Rec," as it's still known today. It remains one of the only places kids can train for boxing on Long Island.

"They had weightlifting, professional boxing, basketball upstairs, but no kids boxing," Buddy says. But then they announced they were adding kids boxing for ages 12 and up. "I remember it," he says. "It was January 17th, but it was my birthday and I was turning 12." That afternoon, "I walked to the recreation center, signed up for boxing, and here we are!"

I ask him why he chose boxing. "I had a fighter in my family," he says, referring to his cousin, New Jersey fighter Freddie Boynton. (Boynton retired from boxing in 1984 and was recently inducted into the Amateur Boxing Hall of Fame.) "When we were kids, we'd go to his house and he had all these trophies my uncle was always bragging about," he says. "And I said, you know, 'I gotta give my mother something to brag about.'"

Once he started boxing, he knew it was his calling. He loved it from his first day. And by his second day, he knew he wanted to be a trainer.

"Football wasn't for me. I was too small. Even though I played cornerback, I had speed, but I couldn't stay out in that cold weather," he says. "But once I got into boxing, man, the rest is history. I loved it."

He started reading every boxing book he could find, checking them out from his local library. As a fighter myself who's scoured countless libraries for those same books, I know how it feels. For Buddy, as a kid, sometimes that even meant a little innocent destruction.

"I used to go to the Brentwood Library and take out a book called *The Heavyweight Champions* like once every two weeks," he says. "One day, I ripped a picture out. Took it back. They didn't notice it, so every two weeks, I ripped a picture out and took it back." He stops to laugh. "One day, I went looking for the book and it wasn't there. I went to the librarian and she said, 'Are looking for this book?' I said, 'Yeah.' She said, 'I want you to take this book and keep it.' I asked why. She said, 'Because you ripped damn near half the pictures out! So take it, go home, and good luck to you.'" Buddy had been hanging the pictures on the wall of his room. "My mom asked me where I got all these damn pictures from," he says. Instead, he showed her the book. "'Buddy, did you steal this book?' I said, 'No, Ma, they gave it to me.'"

ON THE DREAM

Once he started boxing, Buddy dreamed of becoming a professional fighter and started learning all he could to fuel that dream, fighting as an amateur while he was in high school. After his fourth or fifth amateur fight, he met Jersey Joe Walcott.

He mentioned it to a friend who worked at the rec center and he was impressed. "He said, 'Do you know who you just met?'" At his friend's recommendation, he read up on Walcott, learning his real name was Arnold Raymond Cream. From there, he started reading the life stories of Archie Moore and Sugar Ray Robinson.

"It was always the older [generation of] fighters that drew my attention," Buddy says. "Everybody of course loved [Muhammad] Ali back then, but I just couldn't fight like Ali, but I loved his attitude. I sat in the movie theater and watched the movie *The Greatest* from 10 o'clock in the morning 'til 5 in the afternoon," he says.

It's always been a love affair—just Buddy and boxing. "I used to shadowbox in the basement for hours. My mother used to think I was crazy," he says as he describes making a heavy bag from pillows with stuffing, then hanging it up in the basement. "It was just my dream, man. I wanted it bad."

ON THE DRIVE

For most fighters, the drive to win is a combination of obsession and a love of boxing. Technique and athleticism will get most fighters started, but to be a champion, there's something more—something that particularly motivates them to push through the hard times. When I ask Buddy, he warned me he'd get a "little bit emotional." He had one answer: his mother.

"My mother, God bless. I saw my mother struggle so much," he says. Growing up, his mother was a single parent with six kids. She worked at Pilgrim State Hospital and the paycheck she got every two weeks had to stretch. "We struggled, man," he says as he tears up. As a kid, he watched what she sacrificed in her life—from outings with her friends to new clothes—"to take care of us."

"My ultimate goal was to make my mother not only proud of me, but I wanted my mother to live that life that I felt she deserved. When I first started making money, the first thing I did was buy my mother a car. I got tired of seeing her driving bummy-ass cars and worrying because she worked all day."

He tells the story of being in a Pathmark store with his mother in the 1970s, shopping for his brother's field trip. His mother had picked up some underwear and a bra, but when they reached the register, she didn't have enough money. "So she put her stuff back so my brother could have his stuff to go on a field trip." It was a moment that stuck with him. Even as a 10-year-old, he began to appreciate his mother's sacrifices to they could have what they needed.

"When I won my first championship, I went to J.C. Penney, and I spent like $2,000 on underwear and panties," he says, smiling. When he surprised her with them, she asked what made him buy them for her. When he told her the story, "she started crying because I never forgot."

Buddy lets the lesson sink in for us both while he wipes away a tear. The story is a powerful reminder of the deep emotion that drives the will to win for many fighters. But Buddy is at ease with his emotions and recognizes them as a critical factor in his success. You can almost imagine what he must have tapped into when he had to dig deep to win.

"My mom was everything to me," he says. "My whole career, I wanted her to enjoy my success. I felt my mom deserved that—and more. She raised me to be a man, so I'm always going to be able to take care of me," he says. "But I've got to take care of her while she's here. She deserves the best."

We talk about how his mother felt about his boxing, especially when he was young. "At first, she didn't like it," he says, and she noticed how he couldn't manage to do any chores around the house that didn't relate to training. By the time he was 15, his mother had stopped asking him to cut the grass because it took him so long. "'Just focus on your boxing,' she said," Buddy recalls. "When I was about 15, she said, 'Son, manual labor is not for you. I hope and pray that you make it as a boxer because if you try anything else, you ain't going to do shit.'" Buddy dissolves into laughter, taking off his glasses to wipe his eyes again.

ON THE CHAMPIONSHIP

As it turns out, Buddy did focus on his boxing. He performed well as an amateur and turned professional the year he graduated from high school in 1982. He suffered his first professional loss in 1986 to Frankie Warren in Warren's hometown of Corpus Christi, Texas. But in 1988, his manager called him regarding a fight for the then-vacant IBF light welterweight title. "My manager called me and said, 'Kid, we got a shot at the title.' I said 'Okay, what's the problem?' and he goes, 'We have to go back to Corpus Christi.'" Buddy only said, "Again, what's the problem?"

It felt like the real beginning of something big. "Back in the day, there were big fights on TV every weekend—ABC, NBC, CBS," he says. "I'm like, 'Damn, we're getting that shot.'"

He went to training camp in Secaucus, New Jersey, in January and remembers the cold. It didn't matter. "It was blizzards that year, but 5:30 every morning five days a week, I was up, doing my road work. When I got off the plane in Corpus Christi, Texas, I knew it was my time that day."

Of course, Buddy made an entrance. When they arrived in Texas, it was 100 degrees. "I had a big ass fur coat and it was hot as hell in Corpus Christi," he says. "But once I got there, I knew this guy wasn't beating me."

While some fighters have close relationships with their dads or uncles, for Buddy, it was his mom. "The icing on the cake was when my mother arrived," he says, describing their prefight routine. "My mom would always look at me before a fight. If she would say, 'You look good,' I knew I was in there. But if she said, 'Be careful,' I knew it wasn't gonna be a good day," he says. "When she got to Texas, she just smiled and gave me hug—and I knew: His ass is mine."

ON NUTS & GUTS

Buddy talks about the physical and mental places that a fighter has to go to win, especially in the ring. As individual athletes, some fighters can feel as if they're fighting themselves as well as their opponents. His first championship fight, the rematch with Warren, challenged him at every level.

Warren was relentless in the rematch, forcing a toe-to-toe war. Even though Buddy was getting the better of many exchanges and fighting well at a distance, Warren never stopped pressing. He made Buddy fight for every inch. The pace of the fight was grueling, intended to break the challenger down. Buddy was the more athletic and dynamic of the two, but the pressure wore on him. Warren was a nonstop punching machine, often ending rounds with Buddy pressed against the ropes, fighting for a chance to breathe. However, Buddy's sharp, crisp power-punching won the night. He put the champion Warren down for the first time in his career and won by TKO in the 12th of 15 rounds.

"I'll honestly tell you I'll never forget that fight as long as I live," Buddy says of his first championship bout. "That guy took me to places I never thought I could go mentally. I pushed my body and mind to certain limits that I couldn't do again. You block out everything. You don't hear nothing. You don't want to know what round it is. You don't know who you are fighting. You are just there. And he was on my ass. In our first fight, after round eight, he slowed up. So I'm thinking, we gotta get him through the first five," he says, but Warren was unrelenting. "It's a feeling I can't explain. He hit me everywhere." After it was over, Buddy realized what a physical battle the fight had been. Every part of his body was swollen or damaged.

He believes it's hard to tell people who want to compete at elite levels just how hard it can be. "When you explain to some people, they say, 'Man, you're crazy,'" he says. "You guys have no idea what fighters go through in certain fights. We can't call timeout and have someone fill in for us. It's just us and him. It's 'nuts and guts,' as they used to say." Still, he believes there's nothing like that feeling of being in the ring in a focused physical battle to win. "It's something I'll never forget," he says.

ON THE SECOND CHAMPIONSHIP

In 1991, Buddy got another call—this one to fight South African Simon Brown for the WBC welterweight title. It was a shot at his second title in a second division. If he won, he'd be knocking on the Hall of Fame's door.

"That [fight] was God sent," he says. "We were supposed to fight in September and I wasn't having a good camp. Simon Brown got hurt, so the fight was off." Buddy describes what can feel like a typical series of moves in the fight world today. Promoters and managers constantly shuffle a schedule of fights, which shifts based on the titles, fighters, injuries, and other considerations. Eventually, the fight came together.

"They gave me a choice. They said, 'Buddy, you can fight Glenwood Brown for $200,000 or you can fight Simon Brown for $800,000. Which one do you want?' I said, 'That's basic math.'" We laugh, knowing there really is much more that goes into those kinds of decisions than just the money. Buddy knew Simon Brown was going to be a tough fight. The date was set.

"Simon Brown was 'the big bad wolf,'" Buddy says. He'd watched Brown fight only once, noticing that Brown's opponent outboxed him until Brown stepped on the gas in the sixth round. His opponent had nothing left in the tank. That knowledge helped Buddy formulate his fight strategy. "I knew that when Simon Brown goes here"—he motions with his hand—"you gotta go there"—he motions higher. "I just kept up a faster pace and eventually I got to him," he says.

ON THE INJURY

Buddy ended his career in 1997, after years of dealing with a shoulder injury. He tells the story—an all-too-common one for many boxers. It can feel like a sport where many boxers are like racehorses: only valuable for the number of fights—and purses—they can win. In December 1992, Buddy injured his shoulder while training for his WBC title defense against Genaro Léon. He knew the injury was potentially serious, he says, but his manager asked a doctor to take a look. The doctor and manager conferred in a separate room and came back to report he had tendinitis. He shadowboxed and didn't spar for two weeks before the fight—and he still beat Léon.

Two months later, he was set to defend his title again—this time against Pernell Whitaker. He also went to see a specialist, arranged by his manager, who confirmed the diagnosis and sent him to physical therapy. Eventually, he asked his physical therapist if his shoulder was worse than he was being told. She started to cry, Buddy says. When he asked why, she told him she couldn't say anything or she'd lose her job.

On his way to the weigh-in, his manager asked him if he wanted to pull out of the fight. Feeling it was far too late to quit, Buddy stayed in. He lost the fight and his WBC title. He took his medical scans to another expert in New York, who told him it wasn't tendinitis. "He says, 'It looks like a someone put a hand grenade in your shoulder and exploded it.'" He had the surgery and "then [my manager] tells me I'll never fight again," he says.

To Buddy, it was a personal challenge. "I said to myself, 'They're full of shit. I'm going to come back.'" Six months later, he beat Nick Rupa, starting a string of wins that would lead him to a rematch with Whitaker for the WBC title.

"When I earned the fight with Pernell after beating Pat Coleman, they came in the dressing room to tell me. I started crying," he says, knowing he'd achieved his goal. "The desire to fight left me right there."

His wife asked him why he was crying. His answer was simple. "I said, 'I don't want to fight anymore. I did what they said I couldn't do. I proved them wrong. I just don't have that fire anymore.'"

He decided to go home and think about his decision, but when he got there, he got a letter that pushed him to continue. He needed the money. "I got a letter from my uncle telling me I have to continue to fight. My uncle's name is Uncle Sam." We laugh, but the money he owed for taxes was a serious matter. "Uncle Sam said, 'You owe us this money. How you going to get it back to us?'"

But for Buddy, the desire was gone. "I found out my managers knew that I was injured. The doctors told them, 'Take this fight because the kid's career is over.'" Even with his IRS difficulties, his heart wasn't in it.

He'd eventually file suit against his doctors and lose. He still feels somewhat resentful about his former management. It was an era in boxing where there was a lot of pressure to keep earning—and fighting—even injured. "If they would have come to me and said, 'Hey, kid, your shoulder's screwed up. This is the deal'—and then let me make that choice. But don't tell me I'm okay."

Boxing can be a big-money sport and everyone wants a piece of the action. Fighters today have to be good at the business side, understanding everything from medical decisions to promoter cuts. It's a change from Buddy's era 35 years ago.

"It took a big chunk out of me," he says. "I dedicated all this time to these son of bitches and this is how you do me? You really wanted to screw me out of my money this bad? The attitude was, 'Let's get the best out of this kid while we can.'"

As a sport, boxing can chew up some professionals, but Buddy internalized those lessons and put them to good use. He's one of the most well-adjusted retired fighters in boxing today. He doesn't nurse past resentments and is always ready with a laugh or a story to share his lessons learned. As a trainer, he's coached new boxers on the importance of understanding the business around them.

"I obviously learned from it. I learned big time. It made me a better person as I got older," he says. "But I'm not going to lie: I was mad for a long time, but that's life. What are you going to do?"

ON KNOWING IT WAS TIME

After his second loss to Pernell Whitaker, Buddy continued to fight through 1995 and 1996. His final fight—and loss—was in January 1997 to Darren Maciunski, an old sparring partner. But he still kept going. He accepted an offer for his next fight and went to Colorado Springs to begin training. In Colorado, he found himself on an 8 a.m. run that normally would've started at 5:30 a.m. "I'm running around the lake by the Olympic training center and I just stopped," he says. When his friends asked what was wrong, he knew he'd made his decision. "That's it. I'm going home."

"I walked to the car with my friends, yelling 'You're crazy,' but I went back to the hotel, called my wife, and said, 'I'm coming home.'" His friends swore he'd be back, but Buddy knew he was ready to stop. "I booked my ticket. I left my clothes—I left everything. 'This can stay here,'" he thought. "'It's my past—I'm leaving it.'"

"And I got on the plane and went home, and I have to tell you, that was the longest plane ride of my life because now I'm saying, 'What am I going to do with rest of my life? I'm still young—I'm in my early 30s.'"

He got home and his wife asked him what he was going to do. "I said, 'Give me a few days. I'll figure it out,'" he says. "And the man upstairs helped me, I figured it out, and here I am now."

ON THE NEXT CHAPTER

After a few false starts at office jobs, Buddy decided training was all he wanted to do and decided to go at it "full blast, 200%." By 2002, he was named Trainer of the Year by the Boxing Writers Association of America.

He'd trained amateurs in between professional fights in the late 1980s, but now he knew he wanted to train fighters full time. "Don King hired me as a trainer the night Pernell [Whitaker] fought [Felix] Trinidad. I got my first world champion with Don: Byron Mitchel. We trained for a week before the title fight," he says. Buddy would go on to run Don King's training camp in Florida.

By 2001, Buddy was the head trainer for the late Arturo Gatti when he fought his three historic fights against "Irish" Micky Ward. Each fight was a modern classic with nonstop action and tons of drama. Two of the fights were named Fight of the Year by *The Ring* magazine in 2002 and 2003. HBO named Gatti–Ward I and Gatti–Ward III in its Ten Best Fights of the Decade list.

The ninth round of their first battle will forever be known as one of the most violent and memorable fights in history—so much so that it's known as "Round 9" in direct reference to this fight in most boxing circles. Gatti took a terrific beating and referees were on the verge of stopping the fight.

Good fighters know how important it is to have an experienced coach in the corner to guide them during a fight. Buddy could see Gatti might be in trouble and needed to use his legs in the 10th and final round. He wanted to ensure that Gatti not only had the legs to do it but also the presence of mind to concentrate on the fight. He asked Gatti to stand in the corner and bounce to show him that he still had the legs to do it. Gatti did and went on to box beautifully in the final round, Buddy recalls. Gatti ultimately lost that evening but went on to win the next two fights against Micky Ward. Buddy was the trainer behind the series and behind Gatti's wins.

I ask Buddy what it's like as a coach being so close to a fight of that magnitude and with that intensity. "You can't explain it, man. It's like asking what it's like when you win a title and they put that belt around your waist."

He describes the chaos of the famous ninth round. The doctor was Italian, the referee was Italian, and Gatti was Italian. They were all talking Italian in the corner, he says. "They thought I was stopping the fight, but I was just asking what the hell is going on because I couldn't understand Italian." All three fights have gone down in boxing history as some of the best in the sport, solidifying Buddy's career as a trainer to the sports elite.

ON ADVICE TO HIS YOUNGER SELF

I ask Buddy what advice he'd have today for a younger version of himself at the beginning, but he says he wouldn't change anything. He feels that everything he is today is because of the hard lessons he learned coming up through the ranks.

"Everything that happened to me helps me today, made me who I am, makes me appreciate everything more, understand so much about this game that a lot of people don't know," he says.

Being on the inside gives him a perspective he didn't have as a fighter. And it helps him advocate for fighters when managers push them too hard or too fast. He now knows the business aspects of the sport and also why managers will sometimes push fighters into situations they're not ready for.

"I've had managers tell fighters to get rid of me because they'll be getting a fight and I'll say, 'Are you crazy? He's not ready for this,'" he says. "Then they take the kid elsewhere and the kid [loses and] says, "Buddy, what happened?" and I say, 'You can see what happened.'"

It's made him a strong advocate for smart career management when it comes to fighters as they learn to manage the business. "I've learned so much from my experiences," he says, noting that his former manager was "ballsy," but he learned a lot from him. He taught him to advocate for fighters who're putting themselves on the table for every fight.

MICKEY BEY

Boxer, trainer
Status: Active
Weight class: Lightweight
Ring name: The Spirit
Hometown: Cleveland, Ohio

CHAMPIONSHIPS
· IBF lightweight title (2014)

HIGHLIGHTS
· US Olympic Trials winner (2004)
· Brother of boxer Cortez Bey
· Trainer for Devin Haney

Mickey Bey is one of those special guys in the sport of boxing who everyone seems to know and like. He has a style like the greats of generations past: fast and strong, sure-footed, and moving around the ring with grace and class. He's always in position—always ready to make you miss and make you pay. As I watched him come up through the ranks and become a champion, I've admired his style.

I had the chance to spar with Mickey in preparation for one of my own fights a few years ago. It was one of those sessions where we looked at each other after and nodded, acknowledging the other had the goods—a simple "Okay, you're really good." I also had the opportunity to commentate his title eliminator bout versus undefeated George Kambosos Jr., which Mickey lost by a razor-thin decision. Once you know Mickey, he's a hard guy not to root for. After speaking with him, he cemented that sentiment for me.

We laugh because he says it's his first video call and he's learning the technology. But he's comfortable and at ease talking about his boxing career—and the challenges.

ON A FAMILY LEGACY

I ask Mickey how he got his start in boxing growing up in Cleveland. He grew up with three siblings, including his brother, Cortez, who'd also become a professional boxer. Mickey came on my radar after I fought Henry White Jr., who'd go on to fight Cortez.

"When I was coming up, there's not many things to do in Cleveland, Ohio," says Mickey, who considered himself "one of the lucky people in my neighborhood to have a two-parent household."

Every summer, his parents made sure the kids had activities. His father believed they should "never have a mind that's too idle," and as a result, he played nearly every sport. "I tried everything," he says. "I've done it all."

Boxing ran in the family. "My granddad used to box. He came up with Don King. They grew up together and went to school together," Mickey says. "He was a good fighter. He made it to the national finals of Golden Gloves. It was hard to do that back then, so I guess it was in my blood."

His grandfather died when he was 7 and Mickey started boxing when he was 12 or 13. He was immediately ready to get in the ring to start fighting. "A friend saw an ad in the paper for a boxing gym," he says. The ad had a photo of young fighter. "I thought, 'I think I can beat this cat,' so I went down there. As soon as I went to the gym, I'm trying to spar with the guy that I see in the paper. The trainer is trying to tell me, 'It's not street fighting. You gotta really learn how to box. You gotta learn the basics.'"

"He told me to come three days a week, but I came every single day, even Saturday. He finally put me in with the kid," Mickey says. "I never lost a street fight, but I got whooped. That was my first time getting beat up."

From there, he made the decision he was going to win. "That's what kept me going. The bar is to be able to beat this kid. It didn't take me long, maybe a couple of months, [and] I was beating this guy. And I had some real good teammates. I was sparring with national champions within my first four to six months of boxing."

His parents wanted to encourage him, to keep him off the streets and have something positive to do, so Mickey and Cortez got serious about boxing.

ON HIS EARLY INSPIRATIONS

I ask Mickey which boxers inspired him. "I'm going to tell you a crazy story," he says. He talks about his granddad, who used to box. "My grandmother hated boxing. She didn't want to hear the word 'boxing.'"

His grandfather had an extensive boxing library, and when he passed, his grandmother called Mickey's dad and said, "You might want to come over here in the next hour because I've got the whole thing on the lawn for trash day." Mickey laughs. "My dad went and got it," he says.

In the pile were some finds. "I found a tape that said '[Muhammad] Ali–Sugar Ray Robinson,'" he says. At the time, he didn't know who Sugar Ray Robinson was, but "I popped in the tape to see Ali and I see this other guy, Robinson, and I said, 'Man, Dad, who is this dude?' To me, this guy is even better than Ali." Once he learned Robinson's story, he was hooked. "I was throwing triple hooks in my first few fights."

He grooved on fighters from the old-school era—the likes of Sugar Ray Robinson, Jersey Joe Walcott, Willie Pep, Thomas Hearns, Sugar Ray Leonard, Roberto Durán, Floyd Mayweather, Oscar De La Hoya, James Toney, Mike McCallum, Salvador Sánchez, and Ricardo Lopez.

Mickey is a true boxer/puncher—a style he clearly picks up from Robinson. He has the smoothness that Robinson possessed but also that fluid snap that can do damage. Hearing who his favorite fighters are makes a lot of sense when you see Mickey fight—and when you see him coach.

ON THE MOMENT

We talk about that moment all fighters experience: when they knew boxing would be their path for the future. It's that moment when fighters just know this is the road they should follow. For Mickey, it was his early success as an amateur. "I won at nationals within a year of boxing," he says.

During that first year, Mickey was sparring with Juan McPherson, who was a top amateur fighter, five days a week. (McPherson would go to the Olympics in 2004.) "He was bigger than me and he was super good," and that kind of helped him, Mickey says.

As he practiced, he and the other kids he boxed with didn't have a formal gym, but they had his dad, who was skilled at making connections. "We just had one punching bag in a rec room. We sparred on the floor with chairs around. That's all we did—ran through the neighborhood and hit the bag."

"My dad somehow met Emanuel Steward. [Steward] liked the guys on our team and he couldn't believe we didn't have a gym. He said there's no way we would be on his team in Detroit without a boxing gym. He didn't care how good we were," he says. "So my dad took the challenge. We drove up there and I was the main event against a good fighter that he had. I ended up knocking the guy out and I was only 100 pounds at the time."

Steward, who thought knockouts were better entertainment than going a 12-round fight, invested in the team, opening a gym for them in Cleveland and sponsoring them.

"Finally, we had a ring, a bag, and one of the best gyms in the country," he says. "I trained with Lennox Lewis. I got to learn a lot from Emanuel Steward. And I'm thinking, 'Man, I could make some money from this.'"

Money was a powerful motivator when he began to consider a career in boxing, especially when he thought about what he could do for his hardworking parents. For him, the opportunity to turn pro right out of high school was his chance to make some money and earn a ticket out of Cleveland. "I'm thinking, 'I gotta get us up outta here,'" he says.

But there was something he wanted first: to go to the Olympics. Even with a lot of money on the line, Mickey competed in—and won—the US Olympic Trials in 2004. Meanwhile, Cortez moved to Las Vegas to train with Floyd Mayweather and the Mayweather family. Winning the Olympic Trials set Mickey up for success at the Athens Olympics. But he caught pneumonia in training camp. "We didn't have all of those chances to keep fighting [in qualifiers] like they do now. I went to the last one and lost. I had to take a break." Still, managers had singled him out as a top talent in boxing.

> **"I have always believed and still believe that whatever good or bad fortune may come our way, we can always give it meaning and transform it into something of value."**
> **–Herman Hesse, *Siddhartha***

ON TURNING PROFESSIONAL

Mickey was fortunate to have exposure to a large number of professional boxers early in his career. It gave him a perspective that other fighters didn't have. While money was important, his father and mentors taught him that you sometimes have to choose what's right for you.

"My dad always taught me to never value money. When I was younger, I would get mad when my dad would turn down [work]," he says. He notes that a lot of people, including Don King, offered his dad jobs for "a lot of money," but he turned them down. "As I got older, I understood why he did it because if you take this job, you owe me. People don't do favors for free."

Once he turned professional, Mickey worked with Houston-based boxing promoter James Prince and learned that while he could make money from boxing, he could invest it in business deals and make even more. "I traveled the world with him, and I could see the money he had and the way he helped the community," he says. "When I was young, that's what made me really think—and when I first knew I could actually make money from boxing."

Prince had a plan for Mickey's career, putting him on track to a title in only 11 fights—beating Oscar De La Hoya's record of 12. A plan like that can take years to carefully execute, but Mickey admits he was impatient. He wanted to be in the ring, so he made some management changes.

"It's crazy because in my career, if you look, I have had six to eight years of layoff," he says. "Mind you, I'm still a dedicated person. You would think I was maybe in the club or drinking. I never drank or did none of that a day in my life, but one thing I learned, on my part, the mistake that I made was probably I should have been a little more patient."

He felt his progress toward a title was erratic, but in retrospect, he admits he should have stuck to the original plan. "I think that was my mistake," Mickey says. "And I think that's why I didn't win the title earlier on. Sometimes, as kids, we think we can do, we think we know more."

Every fighter has had to overcome this kind of doubt, listen to a plan, and decide if it's right for them. Mickey talks about how he just wanted to fight everybody all the time. He wanted to be in the ring. But changing direction didn't help his march to a title. "I think that kind of slowed me down a little bit," he says.

Mickey also emphasizes the importance of knowing who you're dealing with and standing up for yourself when it comes to business. At one point, he signed with a major boxing organization but was assigned a manager who'd never been in the business before. Things went downhill bad. "To the point where I could have been the most depressed person in the world. I end up going from supposed to fight for a belt in 10 fights to wait until 10 years later to even fight for a belt," he says.

He learned it was important to know whose word you could trust. Fighters have to know the business and stand up for themselves in everything from who they fight to where their money is going. It's not a business for someone who's too nice or too humble.

Boxing is the best sport in the world, but it's also the worst business in the world. Talent can only take you so far, and there are business and political pitfalls along the way. Not having the right people around to navigate that road and give a young fighter the right advice can spell disaster.

ON WINNING THE TITLE

The title fight finally came in 2014. Mickey would fight Miguel Vasquez for the IBF lightweight title—and he'd win. He thought things might change for his career once he won a belt.

After the Vasquez fight, he had hand surgery and was looking for his next big opportunity. He was ready for a big payday for his title defense, but it evaporated. He was getting better at getting what was his. "Good thing this was the first time in my career having a lawyer," he says. "I told them, 'I'm going to let you all talk to him.'"

He pushed back on the money and ran into the harsh realities of the business of boxing. It's the sad fact that all fighters face sometimes: the unspoken rule that you should take what you're offered and just be grateful that you're getting an opportunity to box. While the industry has changed in some ways as top fighters have learned the business and taken control to a degree, much of the power struggle between promoters, fighters, managers, and media persists. The attitude some fighters still run up against is an old-school attitude. Today, many fighters at the elite levels have also learned to capitalize on fights to leverage additional revenue from other sources.

With an injured hand and problems with the purse, Mickey vacated the title. "Me being quiet and humble, I'm taking all of the hit in the media," he says, which he felt was unfair. "I never complained a day in my life about a payday." His next couple fights were for low money and he felt he was being chastised for not falling in line.

It's a lesson in how complicated deals can be with payments, networks, promoters, and managers. But he made an impression in those fights. "I end up looking good and the networks were saying, 'We've got to get him back on TV,'" he says.

Mickey feels that because he pushed back on the boxing business itself, his road was harder. "It got rocky," he says. "Everybody else was getting rich, and other fighters were making money, and I had to keep fighting for these low payday fights after I won a belt," he says. "And I gotta keep having this stuff come out on the internet to make me look bad because I can't say nothing against this big machine."

ON THE SECOND TITLE FIGHT

Mickey finally took legal action against his manager—and won. But there was a catch: A few weeks earlier, he'd agreed to fight Rances Barthelemy, a then-undefeated Cuban, on short notice for another shot at the IBF lightweight title. He'd go into the fight without any time in training camp and with a last-minute venue change from Las Vegas to Miami. He and his team were left with only one day to hammer out details before the IBF deadline. He'd fight, but he'd lose the bout in a split decision before taking a two-year layoff from boxing.

ON DEDICATION

When it comes to what makes a champion, Mickey talks about the struggle when you're not fighting and money isn't coming in. During his layoff, he had some tough times. Fighters—and the public—hear about large purses in the media, but by the time managers, promoters, and others take their cuts, the amount left for the fighter isn't substantial. Boxing is hard work and an even harder business, and fighters have to understand the realities. "I took a hit sitting out two years," he says. "I was messed up financially. I got eviction papers. I'm not going to sugarcoat it. There were times I was hungry. I was embarrassed, but I had the pride. I didn't even want to look my parents in the face because I'm supposed to be helping them."

Even with his long layoffs, Mickey is dedicated to training and a healthy lifestyle. We sparred a few years ago and he's still damn good. (So good that Coach Andre Rozzier and I wondered why he wasn't getting more fights!) "I'm one of the most dedicated dudes you could meet as far as lifestyle. When I was on the shelf, I had to keep my life [on track]," he says.

ON LIFE AS A TRAINER

Today, Mickey isn't officially retired, but he works as a trainer for a variety of fighters, including WBC lightweight champion Devin Haney. He remembers seeing him box when Haney was only seven years old. "He was a tiny little dude," he says. He saw Haney fight again when he was 12 or 13, and Haney pronounced, 'One day, you're going to be my trainer,'" Mickey says. He was skeptical but laughs at how funny life is. "If it wasn't Devin, I didn't really want to be a trainer. But I knew I would be good at it."

He also works with at least one other young boxer. He's a great fit with kids because he knows the system and what it takes to win. He gets calls from a lot of potential clients to train, but "I don't have the passion for that." He's choosy about the fighters he takes on and looks for the personal connection, for fighters he knows. But he puts 100% into the clients he has.

"I give all trainers more credit now that I've been in this arena. It's the hardest job in boxing other than fighting," Mickey says. "I like the mentorship about it as well. I can help steer young fighters in the [right] way where I know mistakes I made—whether it's business or boxing. I put my all into them in this training."

"I'm willing to do this because my mom was that sort of person. She put everybody before herself," he says. "Whatever you know, you've got to tell them. I'm giving them everything. And they know that. And I think that's why the relationship is good because they can feel it. They know I'm willing to give my all."

As for his own career, he'd still like to go out on his own terms. He wants to finish his time in the ring with a few last fights on top. "I can't go out of the game the way it ended," he says. He's never not shown up. And he's not done by a long shot. "I'm going to go out the right way."

MIKE BAZZEL

Trainer, cornerman, cutman
Status: Active
Ring name: The Mechanic
Hometown: San Mateo, California

HIGHLIGHTS

· Has worked more than 50 world title fights in his career

· Has trained Andre Berto, Andy Vences, Bruno Escalante, Daniel Jacobs, Demetrius Andrade, Edgar Berlanga, George Kambosos Jr., Nonito Donaire, Richard Commey, Sadam Ali, Sergiy Derevyanchenko, Shawn Porter, Vanes Martirosyan, Willie Nelson, and Xander Zayas

---

Mike Bazzel is known as one of the most experienced people in boxing today. He's a successful trainer, coach, and cutman—all positions incredibly important to a championship team. He's also one of the most knowledgeable people in boxing about everything from rules to how to throw a right hand. He lives, eats, and breathes the sport.

I met Mike while I was serving as nutritionist and performance coach for Daniel Jacobs, who was preparing to battle it out with then-undefeated Gennadiy Golovkin (known as "GGG"). After watching Mike work a corner in sparring (and then do padwork immediately after), I jokingly gave him the name "The Mechanic" because that's what he does. He knows how to expertly diagnose and fix problems inside the ring and out. It was only later I'd come to find out that the Charles Bronson movie *The Mechanic* is his favorite film.

Mike is one of the most in-demand trainers today, but he's also an expert cutman. Cutmen handle the superficial medical issues that come up during a fight, like bleeding, bruising, or swelling. In some states, they must be licensed. A good cutman is important. If a fighter can't see or breathe or if other minor injuries aren't dealt with between rounds, the referee can stop a fight—permanently.

In 2020, during the COVID-19 pandemic, Mike was one of the permanent support team members "in the bubble" at the Las Vegas MGM Grand. ESPN's Top Rank Boxing formed a team of trainers and other critical team members to live, eat, and work at the hotel, ensuring they'd stay COVID-free. He was locked down for two months.

ON PRACTICE

Mike prides himself in being an ambassador for what combat sports can be: responsible, professional, and skillful. He's conscious that there are a lot of eyes on everyone in the sport and knows that boxing can be a real cast of characters—at every level. As a trainer and strength coach, Mike's known for his work with Jacobs, Demetrius Andrade, Devin Haney, Andy Vences, Bruno Escalante, and a host of others over the years. As a cutman, he's able to stop the bleeding in 60 seconds between rounds—something that's critically important to a boxer in a fight.

Mike's been on my team for the past three years. His ability to adapt to any situation and to have my back has made him an integral part of the squad. Mike's a believer that boxers have to surround themselves with a strong team—not just on the business side but on the fight side. You have to have a trainer who's quite literally in your corner in every way.

Mike explains that preparing for a fight is broader than just making sure a fighter's in good shape. When a fighter's preparing for a fight, they're dealing with different time zones, promoters, commissions, governing bodies, venues, and environments.

"Boxing is not the NFL or the NBA or Major League Baseball. It's a sport that's governed by many different organizations and many different sanctioning bodies, and it's not easy to find your way through that muck. It's not easy for a fighter or a fighter's team," he says. "Everyone has a certain job. The fighter is the boss, but everyone has a role to play, and everyone plays their role, and that's just what we do. And it's really efficient."

He's been involved in boxing since 1991 but working as a trainer and cutman since 2007. "I held the bucket for years because I was the strength and conditioning guy, and the guys would always want me to go. But in a fight, I didn't really have a role," he says. "How many times have we seen guys in the corners, they don't have a role. You're thinking, 'Why are you here?'"

In a pro boxing match, that 60-second window in between rounds can seem like chaos. Fighters retire to their corners and are surrounded by team members who do everything from remind them of their strategy to treat bruises on their face. In reality, it's a choreographed dance in which each person has a job to do—much like a pit crew changes tires and refuels a race car. Mike's picked up the nuances of success in those critical 60 seconds that can make or break a fight. He believes everything should be focused on the fighter. And when it comes to fixing a cut, wrapping hands, or even where to put the bucket, he says it's one thing: practice.

"I see it all the time," he says. "Just the simplest things" matter in the middle of a fight. In a break between rounds, his focus is 100% on the fighter. He trains cornermen and others on the team to ensure they know what they're doing. "You don't ever want to tell a fighter something that won't help them." Practice is the answer.

He teaches others how to do cuts or wraps. "I can show you some technique, but really, it's practice," he says. "You got to go to the gym and wrap everybody who will [let] you wrap them—every single day." Mike came up through MMA when the sport didn't have in-house cutmen. "Because everyone was coming off the street, saying 'I want to be a fighter' with no experience," the California Amateur Mixed Martial Arts Organization (CAMO) was formed. "It was amateurs—but no headgear. You can't wear headgear in the MMA." Mike took his job seriously and got a lot of practice.

Mike emphasizes how important it is to make sure a boxer's entire corner team is practicing. He notes how many fighters feel a 30-second break between rounds when sparring is good for strength and conditioning, but he feels a full 60 seconds in a sparring round is critical. It's about practice for the whole team, not just the boxer.

"We talk a lot about different types of training, what's beneficial, what's not, what's kind of silly, what's going to help the fighter improve," he says, but he feels some of the best training a boxer can have is making sure their team is functioning smoothly in that time between rounds. "It's a critical time when coaching matters. A fighter doesn't have time to worry about where the bucket is or who has the water. The team has to help the fighter focus on adjustments."

"In all of the top-level fighters, what separates them is the fighter that can make the adjustment in the ring, in the fight. That person who can make that adjustment when things are going bad, they're the ones who are going to pull it off. They're the best fighters in the world right now," he says. But practice is key. "You've got to work on that. That communication between [the fighter] and the coach is so key. If it's not going well in sparring and you guys have not practiced that, how are you going to do it in the fight?"

ON GETTING HIS START IN BOXING

I ask Mike about his first memories of boxing—and ultimately how he became involved in the sport. His family moved from Charleston, South Carolina, to California when he was a kid and he remembers watching boxing with his uncle, a former Marine.

"My uncle was at home a lot. He liked boxing, and at 11, 12, and 13, we would watch it, but it was [Muhammad] Ali—but not the Great Ali. He would say, "That's the best fighter in the world." And I would say, 'Really?'"

Ali was at the end of his career and past his prime. Even a young Mike could see he didn't look like he was in shape. He wasn't impressed with old-school boxing, but he recognized the sport was changing. "I'd see my other cousins in San Diego, and they were younger, and they would watch Roberto Durán," Mike says. "Back in the '70s and '80s, he fought a lot of nontitle fights on TV. You saw him all the time. And I think, 'Wow, that's a completely different thing.'"

By the 1980s, Mike was living on his own and ESPN launched, showing club fighters, journeymen, and pro debuts. He remembers watching Tommy Cordova and Freddie Roach. "In the Bay Area, we had an old-school boxing column by Jack Fiske, a famous boxing writer." Fiske, who covered boxing for more than 40 years for the *San Francisco Chronicle*, would visit gyms, get to know the fighters, and interview trainers.

Fiske gave fans an inside look at the day-to-day struggles of the winners *and* the losers. He gave readers insight into the inside of the sport—the parts people didn't see on ESPN. For Mike, it was a glimpse into the factors that go into winning—and losing.

"It's a whole other world. We've won big and we've lost big," he says. "When you lose and you get these criticisms, that you're going, 'Man, you don't even have any clue what this guy went through to make this fight happen,' you don't even know what they're talking about."

Fiske had written about a fighter named Eric "The Prince" Martin who was teaching boxing in San Francisco. "I was always wanting to do it. I want to try it." Prince trained "regular people," so Mike joined a small group. But he quickly learned that Prince, who was still an active fighter, was training them at a professional level, not for beginners.

"Holy crap, I've never been through any kind of training like that in my life!" Mike says. "He was still fighting! His mindset was, 'Hey, if I can do it, you can do it.'"

Within a few weeks, Mike asked what Prince thought about fighting in the Golden Gloves, but Prince only said, "You want to do it? All right, we're doing it!" Once Mike started sparring and fighting, he found he needed help with boxing instruction. And he began to understand the difference between a coach and a fitness trainer.

"I had no clue," Mike says. "I was getting killed in sparring." After weigh-in problems and weight class changes, he found himself struggling with what he didn't know. "Even now, I draw from experiences from way back. Every mistake I make, I will not make it again." He was beginning to understand he wanted to be in the ring—but not as a fighter. It was the 1980s and the fitness video craze was really taking off. Mike wanted to become a personal trainer and was designing fitness programs and teaching. Even Prince recognized that Mike had great potential for designing strength programs. As he began to expand, he started building connections within the boxing community. He was also seeing a need for coaches to help fighters.

As Mike moved through his career, he expanded into working with other fighters and martial artists focused on practicing every day. As a personal trainer and strength coach, he also became skilled at designing strength programs for athletes tailored to their needs. He later offered a free strength and conditioning program for boxers in the Bay Area five days a week. Fighters began to come from across the US to learn strength and conditioning programs with him. "It was like a little laboratory," he says.

> **"Boxing is the sport to which
> all other athletes aspire."
> –George Foreman**

ON THE VALUE OF TRAINING

Mike sees boxers as athletes unlike those in other sports. He also feels each boxer is a unique athlete. Each body, each fighter, and each set of skills are different. We talk about how boxing is different as a sport for athletes. "I have tremendous respect for what I always call the 'fighter athlete.' That athlete is the most unique athlete in the world. If my role is the strength and conditioning guy, I have a responsibility for that athlete not to screw it up."

Mike looks at strength training as something critical to the rest of a fighter's needs. He also knows that even since the early days of boxing, weight training was something fighters focused on, even though strength and conditioning are considered kind of new today.

"I always look at strength and conditioning as an assist to the training. I'm not taking the place of anything," he says. And while he didn't always see it that way, today he sees it as a critical part of diagnosing what's missing from a skill set and giving a fighter those tools to succeed.

"It's a training method to support your body in the ring. You work with the coach and the trainer and the fighter, and [you] say, "What is it that we need the guy to be better at? What techniques can we use to make that happen?" He also recognizes that they have to make adjustments as they go. "If whatever we try doesn't work in the ring, we have to discard it. Doesn't matter if I believe in it, but if it doesn't work in the ring, you've got to let it go and move on to something else."

Mike works with a lot of fighters as they head into their training camp: the four- to six-week intensive training a fighter goes through prior to a major fight. In training camp, fighters are solely focused on training—all day—as well as nutrition and other fight prep.

He believes the first two weeks are the most important in identifying what the fighter hopes to achieve and how they're going to get it done. And once he designs the plan and techniques, just getting the fighter through camp isn't enough. "You have to apply the techniques, but then you have to apply them in the ring right away. You have to see if they're working in the ring."

Foot placement, body placement, spring, desensitizing, and other tweaks are what they hope to coach a fighter through in camp. But there's very little time to make an athlete more fit. As the coach and trainer, Mike's skilled at quickly assessing where the athlete is physically. We talk about the difference between athletes and the systematic training methods they learn depending on the sport. A boxer won't necessarily be good in basketball. A lot of boxers didn't have a team background with systematic training methods, but boxing is whatever works in the ring.

ON GOING FROM AMATEUR TO PRO

I ask Mike what he's found over the years are the biggest obstacles for fighters from his viewpoint. What are the traits that are most difficult to overcome? He shares something that's not always on a young fighter's radar: the transition from amateur to professional. When you're young, you're quite possibly much better than everyone else you're fighting, but when you turn pro, you're really having to fight for every win. If you're not, you're not getting better.

"If you have a high amateur background, you're fighting guys who are as good as you are. It's hot competition," he says. "When you turn pro, you're building your career, so you're trying to get opponents to get better. You want to see them improve. Pro is a different game. And there are a lot of awkward fighters. It's a very difficult experience for these guys."

He also talks about how coaches and trainers often carefully choose opponents. When building a young pro's career, they're carefully looking for fighters who can help build skills sets. They want to see pros improve as they work their way up the ladder. "The hard thing is that sometimes the opponents fall out. So now we have a guy who's different, more mysterious, but we need the fight for the fighter. Those are hard adjustments mentally for young fighters," he says.

He also talks about another challenge for young fighters: the media. "As they're getting their careers going, the actual interviews are very difficult, especially if you're in the gym training. If you have a gym or coach, that's your sanctuary, that's something that's very sacred to a lot of guys, but then you've got a guy bouncing in wanting to do an interview. It really screws up the training day. You need to do it to promote the fight. If you're rising, you have to do it," Mike says.

"That's another thing that's really tough on a fighter. Some guys are really quiet, don't want to speak. Some guys talk too much. Some guys are very personable and have that great story behind them. That's something the media latches onto, the networks want to see." That's an unfortunate reality today. It's common to see a fighter and say, "That guy's a great fighter, but that guy's a better story."

ON COMMUNICATION

We talk a bit about the pressures athletes are under to not only box their best and win but to also "perform" in front of the media. I mention the media coverage of Naomi Osaka at the 2021 French Open, where she refused to do a press conference, citing her mental health, and was fined $15,000 before withdrawing from the tournament.

How does Mike coach young fighters to prepare for the pressures through the highs and lows? He agrees it's a huge issue today and one that's so important for trainers and coaches to help athletes understand.

"I hate using 'It's 90% mental and 10% physical,' but it's a tremendous strength and patience that you have to have in boxing. It's like learning to adjust in the ring." He likens it to a constant evaluation of where you are and where you want to be, improving as you go. "It's a balance. I don't like those big differences in percentage. Ninety percent is never going to be good—it's too much of one thing."

Fighters have to focus on the physical and mental aspect, and they have to train for both, he says. "Some fighters focus solely on their physical conditioning" because they know how important it is. "If you're not in shape, it's a wrap." Mental preparation is just as important.

In 2019, Mike trained Ukrainian fighter Sergiy Derevyanchenko for his fight with world champion Golovkin. Derevyanchenko was prepared for the fight, but Golovkin dropped him early with a strike behind the head. "It really messed him up—not only the physical knockdown but the mental knockdown. Then he got a nasty cut," Mike says. They also changed the configuration of the corner team, which can throw a fighter off their rhythm. "That was a very tough, high-intensity fight. I've been in amateur fights where a guy was dropped early and came back and won. That's really hard to do! But in a pro fight, it's worse." Derevyanchenko would ultimately lose the fight.

"Not only does [an unexpected knockdown or injury] throw off the fighter's rhythm and pacing, [but] it also eliminates a couple of rounds from the fighter's strategy. In amateur boxing, [a knockdown] means a points loss, but in professional boxing, it's a much more serious matter. A pro boxer has no time to take a round to get your head together," he says.

For trainers, when the fighter who's struggling is new or young or a real prospect, it's tricky. It's a look at how important fight strategy dovetails with career strategy and the importance of knowing how to make adjustments at every level. Communication is key. "I've seen communication break down. I've seen coaches stop talking if a fighter doesn't respond," he says.

From the sidelines, you can notice things that are going wrong. "I don't know why he's fighting on the inside! I don't know why he's not throwing the combinations we've worked on for eight weeks! I don't know!" Mike says. "But as a trainer/coach, it's your job, it's your responsibility to never give up, to keep trying to get the message across to them until the fight is over."

"How many times have you seen the guy stink it up for the entire fight, then in the last round go out and start landing, but [the coaches] never gave up. Every round, the coaches are telling him to do this. It's an intense experience, but finally, it landed. But if you give up, if you quit …" It's clear Mike believes that good trainers and coaches are critically important to the athlete's preparation and success.

He also notes another important difference between amateur and professional fighting. In the amateur world, if you lose, "There's always another tournament. 'You really screwed this one up, but we fight again next weekend.'" In the pro game, you might never fight again. "You lose and it's a wrap, or your promoter might drop you, or you don't even know."

ON THE MENTAL GAME

Professional fighters have to mentally find the will to continue and win. It's something that makes combat sports the ultimate humans-against-themselves endeavor. Mike talks about fighters who've had that moment in the ring where they're sometimes literally fighting for their lives through pain, concussions, and cuts. He's seen "fighters who've gone through the damage where you're thinking, 'Oh my God, I might not live through this! Do I really want to do this? Do I really want to be a fighter?' That's when it's in your head. 'What am I doing?'"

He tells the story of Andy Vences in his last fight against Luis Alberto Lopez, where Vences got "wobbled," "concussed," and cut. "[The fight] was almost stopped, but he was able to pull himself out." But in the corner, Mike could tell he was coherent, that he was "there." Still, as a trainer, he knew the fighter had to find his balance. "I could tell his body was going through things it had never experienced before. His mind was good, but he just had to get his mind to catch up to his body. Once he did, he fought very well in the last part of the fight."

A good trainer knows their fighters, can assess where they are mentally, and what to say to help that fighter focus. A good corner team will keep the fighter calm, work on any cuts, and, most importantly, ensure no one panics. What a coach says in that moment makes a difference. Their language matters. "If I'm saying words like, 'Can you continue? Do you think you can keep going?' the fighter gets in his head: 'Is there a way out of this? There's a way I can be cool and get out of this and no one's going to say anything?'"

He uses the example of a Bruno Escalante fight where Escalante broke his dominant left hand in the middle of the fight. Escalante didn't know if he could continue and his corner team remained silent. In training, he'd worked extensively on training his nondominant hand. He'd often still not use it in fights, but this time, he had no choice. He began working his right in the fight—and finally used what he'd trained for. "But we didn't put anything in his head. Like, 'Oh no! You broke your hand! Are you okay?' It was only, 'Okay, use your right hand.'"

So much of a fighter's training is designed to overcome what the body wants to do naturally. And Mike says that in the corner, the trainer and coach must mentally help a fighter overcome another natural instinct: the mental desire to stop fighting when they're injured. "The trainer's job is to help a fighter find the balance between physical and mental drive. And when crowds are watching, they think the fighter can't feel anything because of adrenaline, but that's not true at all. Getting hit in the ring hurts! Cuts hurt! Everything hurts! If the fighter's getting hurt, then we can make the decision: Let's call this fight," Mike says. "He's hurt, he's not responding, but just because you have damage, if you're still in the fight, that's the whole point. You really want to be a fighter? That's part of it."

Having been a sparring partner for boxers over the years, Mike talks about how different the contact is in boxing than other full-contact sports, like football. "Playing football in high school, we would smack our heads together, but we liked it! But in boxing, it's a different type of trauma," he says. Getting concussed on a regular basis makes the brain want to shut down. It makes you want to sleep. The body works to protect itself."

ON KNOWING WHEN IT'S TIME

Nearly all boxers struggle with knowing when it's the right time to hang up their gloves. The tough part about boxing is that time runs out for most fighters. I ask Mike if he's ever had to coach a boxer through one of their toughest career decisions: when to retire. It's a conversation he's had to have many times.

"There was one where they agreed with it. They were like, 'You know what, I cannot physically prepare like I know I have to.'" But others still have a name and know they can get fights and "make a payday." "You can still do that and still be involved in the game, but you're going to have damage to your body, to your brain," Mike says.

Worse is when a fighter is still physically fast but has lost some abilities in the ring, like seeing punches or defending themselves from getting hit. When that happens, trainers stop fights and sparring matches because real injury is a serious possibility. Mike has had to explain reality to fighters when they've lost this nuanced ability. The message is simply "You're done," he says. "That's enough for you. You can do so many other things. You physically have everything still. Your mind is sharp. But it's time."

Some fighters get it. Others don't. The future for fighters who don't step out means getting tapped to serve as opponents for up-and-coming young fighters. Faced with the decision, others will decide to be "nobody's stepping-stone" and leave while they're on top. Others decide to continue trying to overcome obstacles on their own. If they decide to continue after he's identified untenable problems, Mike has to make the tough decision to part ways.

"Sometimes, physically, fighters have lost a step," he says. "You see it in the gym because they don't have that energy or coordination. That's right there for us. But when you see the guy who still has all the physical speed and can be fast but doesn't have the vision of seeing punches," that's when it's over, he says. Regardless of how the fighter ultimately makes the decision, he sympathizes. "It's a heartbreak, man. It's heartbreaking."

Of course, retiring because of physical or mental issues is different from fighters who hang up their gloves because their career just never took off. Even good fighters sometimes just can't catch a break. "I've been where promoters are just not interested. You know this kid could be something, but he doesn't have the story or he [doesn't] have great knockout power—right now—but get him with someone who could get him in some fights and develop him, but they're just not interested."

ON ADVICE FOR YOUNG FIGHTERS

I ask Mike what advice he has for young kids who want to be professional fighters. "You need a teacher as a trainer. You don't want to go to a place where you can get lost. There are a lot of gyms where you'll kind of get lost. Maybe there's a lot of coaches in there. Find a coach, the trainer that's the teacher, that can teach you how to do this sport, this game."

"Watching people come up, even at pretty good levels, there are a lot of things that fighters just don't know," he says. "Some guys have great skills, but a lot of fighters don't know the importance and the beauty and the effectiveness of learning some of the fundamental weapons in boxing."

As a trainer, Mike is about nuance, honing a boxer's skills beyond just technique and showing them how to actually use them. "There's lots of the art of boxing that's being lost because there are a lot of people involved but not all really great trainers, great teachers."

His advice to young boxers who want to win is to seek out excellence. "There are great teachers, but you've got to find them. When you walk into a gym, you tend to stick to the first person who pays attention to you. You feel loyal to them, but you have to realize and know what you want. It's your career."

Mike says that some amateur trainers have no desire in helping a fighter turn pro and it's important to know if they're going to be able to help you get to where you want to go. If you're coming in as a novice, you need to set goals and recognize that you need a teacher. "You need to come in and try places out, and try the relationships out, and be open to the communication."

He returns to the theme of strong teams, with a reminder that your coach and trainer, your teacher, and, later, your cornermen are all part of your team. They have to support you. "We're talking all the time. We have a lot of meetings. We have a lot of communication. We talk about it. We talk after the fight" about what we need to change or address or eliminate.

"If our communication wasn't there, that falls on me. Every day in training, we need to not just work on our jab, cross, hook, and uppercut, [but] we [also] need to work on our communication. We need to work on the language we need in the fight," he says.

As a trainer, Mike is still learning along with a new generation of trainers who pay a lot of attention to the small details. Those details can make the difference between a boxer becoming an elite talent and a journeyman fighter. "There are so many layers. There's levels to this. You build those layers—just like hard muscle. There's layers to the muscle tissue that make it harder, like iron, but you have to continually add to it," he says. "Sometimes, it's the thinnest of layers that make the big difference. It's not always the big change."

PAULIE MALIGNAGGI

Boxer, analyst
Status: Retired
Weight classes: Welterweight, light welterweight
Ring name: Magic Man
Hometown: Brooklyn, New York

CHAMPIONSHIPS

· WBA welterweight title (2012)
· IBF light welterweight title (2010)

HIGHLIGHTS

· Award-winning fight analyst
· Bare-knuckled boxer
· Owner of multiple businesses

If you've seen a Paulie Malignaggi fight, then you've seen the lead up to a Paulie Malignaggi fight. He has a knack for leaving a lasting impression. Now retired, Paulie put on a show with his fast-talking banter, wild outfits, and crazy hair. But while he was known for his weigh-in getups outside the ring, he also became known for having the goods inside the ring. Even with the brash attitude, he could deliver. He was a showman and a damn good boxer. Today, he's known more frequently as one of the best fight analysts in the business as well as one of the most outspoken.

I vividly remember seeing a fight poster of Paulie's pro debut in my martial arts gym while I was training as a teenager. It was so cool and I just remember thinking, "I want to do that!" A few years later, I'd see him training in the famous Gleason's Gym. I met him briefly and would see him from time to time at fights. He was always friendly, helpful, and quick to give advice about boxing inside and outside the ring. It's one thing about Paulie that has never changed—you'll always find him in the gym giving advice and nuggets of knowledge to anyone who asks.

ON HIS EARLIEST BOXING MEMORY

Paulie was born in the US but moved with his family to Italy as an infant. They moved back to New York a few years later. One of his earliest memories of boxing was watching a promo show hyping pay-per-view sales for the 1988 Mike Tyson–Michael Spinks fight. He was seven years old.

"My English was pretty good at this point, nothing perfect, but I was learning it, and I remember seeing this highlight show on television for Tyson–Spinks," he says. "I'd heard of the mystique of Mike Tyson. The video game had already come out!" (The home version of *Mike Tyson's Punch-Out!!* arcade game debuted in 1987.)

What he remembers most, though, was the excitement. "The host was Larry Holmes and they were breaking down the fight. I don't really understand them very well, and I see highlights of both fighters and records, and I get the gist. This is going to be an amazing fight!" he remembers thinking. "This Mike Tyson, this guy's got a real tough fight in front of him."

Of course, as a seven year old, Paulie didn't understand how promotional television worked. "The whole time, I'm thinking that this fight's going to be on next," he says. "And at the end of the program, it just says, 'Go order.' That's it." Bitterly disappointed, he was sent to bed.

"The next morning, my grandfather has to go get a haircut in the neighborhood, in Brooklyn, and takes me with him to the barbershop. It was an old-school Italian barbershop. And I see the day's newspapers and one of them, that I know now is the *Daily News*, has Spinks on the canvas right under the ropes and says, 'Tyson blows out Spinks in 91 seconds.' And that was my first boxing experience," he says.

Paulie wouldn't come to boxing again until he was in his teens. By the time he was 16, as he puts it, he "misbehaved," getting himself expelled from high school and kicked out of his mother's house. He was living with his grandparents when his uncles decided he needed to do something with himself during the day, "so they put me in a boxing gym," he says. His grandfather wasn't keen on the idea.

"At that point, I was saying, 'I need to do something,'" he says. Finally, Paulie's grandfather agreed to let him box. "That's kinda how it started."

"For the first time in my life, I ended up having something that I focused on and that I was able to concentrate on," he says. "I never did that with school. There was nothing that had really gotten my interest at a point where I was passionate enough about it to willingly do the work, even when no one was telling me to do it."

Finding a passion was a new experience for Paulie. It was the first time he'd done anything just for the sake of doing it. "I'd come home from the gym and go jogging. Nobody's telling me do that." He'd always been a "pretty good" athlete, he says, but never played organized sports, so boxing became the first sport he'd ever had real coaching in. "I just kind of ran with it."

He remembers his first day at the gym his uncles chose for him: the legendary Gleason's. It was Thursday, June 26, 1997, Paulie remembers specifically, two days before Tyson would fight Evander Holyfield for the second time: the fight famous for Tyson's DQ for biting.

"For a week, the gym was full of media and I'm thinking, 'Wow, this gym is great!' My uncles told me this gym had a crazy reputation for having champions come out of it, but this place is nuts!" He was hooked. After that, "this whole experience kind of consumed me."

I point out that it's interesting how the preshow grabbed his attention considering his expertise as a commentator and analyst on television today. "Funny, I didn't catch that until you just mentioned it," he says, laughing. "It's funny how life connects itself and comes full circle sometimes. You don't really notice it at first."

ON INSPIRATIONS

We talk about Larry Holmes on television promoting that early fight and I ask him which fighters inspired him. Who're the ones he watched and looked up to and even fashioned himself after as he pursued boxing as a career?

"Two guys I looked up to because I felt a connection with them: obviously one was Tyson because of the Brooklyn roots and the other was Arturo Gatti because he had the Italian background. His family, similar to mine, moved from Italy to North America. His family chose Montreal; my family chose New York," he says. "We both wound up in boxing in our respective North American regions. We came from the Italian culture of our regions, so I always felt that connection, even though stylistically, I didn't fight like Gatti or Tyson."

When it came to style, "I liked guys more like Meldrick Taylor," he says. "Also guys like Héctor Camacho because of his pizzazz and showmanship. I was always drawn to that, attracted to it."

As he shaped his experience in boxing, he began to think about what kind of boxer he wanted to be and how he wanted to express his personal style.

"When you're a kid and you get in a lot of trouble, you start to feel worthless because people sort of put you in that position after you've messed up so many times. You do it to yourself, but you also start to feel like, man, maybe everybody's right," Paulie says. Boxing gave him confidence he'd never had and self-esteem he'd never felt.

"I looked at guys like [Naseem] Hamed, like Camacho, and they kind of showed you, 'I've arrived. Look at me now,'" he says. "I always saw in myself an opportunity to show people that I can do something, that I can be useful, that I can be somebody that has arrived."

In the amateurs, he had to curb his natural instincts to be a showman. There were rules about attire, and at the time, headgear was required, so the crazy hair didn't come up until later. "When I eventually turned pro and was allowed to wear flashy stuff, I started with the wild, wild outfits and the wild hairdos and the tassels and all that stuff. It was my way of saying, like those guys, 'I've arrived,'" he says.

ON PASSIONATE ENTHUSIASM

Much of Paulie's story with athletics involves his father, who was a pro soccer player in Italy. When Paulie's parents divorced, his mother discouraged him from sports of any kind. Still, Paulie always felt he was meant to be an athlete. Considering his complicated relationships with sports, I ask him about his desire to be competitive and where he went to dig deep for the tough days.

"As a kid, I always had in my imagination that I wanted to be an athlete," he says. But "my mother just wouldn't let me go near sports." He wonders today if he'd have gone in such a bad direction as a teenager if he'd been allowed to play sports as a kid.

"Soccer was always my first passion, but my mother was definitely not going to let me near it after my father!" he says. "I remember watching big games and watching guys score big goals and thinking, 'That must be the best feeling in the world: to score a goal for your country.'"

"When I started boxing, it was the first sport where someone was coaching my athletic talent," he says. He mentions a recent talk he gave to up-and-coming athletes about combat sports. "It's still a sport, it's fighting, it's a separate kind of sport, but athletic DNA still helps you. Natural reflexes, coordination, agility—obviously it needs to be trained, but it helps tremendously. I always had all of that."

But he notes there's something more required for boxing. "You obviously need the right mentality," he says. "You can't be scared, which by that point in my life I had nothing to lose, but the dreams were always there."

He also knew he wanted to live differently than the rest of his family, working at something he loved instead of working only to get by. He does, however, credit his family—especially his grandfather—with showing him the value of hard work and discipline.

"I didn't ever want to be in a 9-to-5 position," he says. "But the old-school Italian mentality is you do it anyway. It doesn't matter if you don't want to do it. You gotta take care of your family. Whether you're a miserable SOB or not, you go to work every day. And I respect that. My grandfather was a really big leader by example, going to work every day at 6 a.m., and his example stuck out to me."

"When I started boxing and I started seeing the principles and foundations that lead you to success, I thought back to that. Repetition is success. Drills are success. My grandfather did it every single day. It didn't matter what the day was, didn't matter how he felt. He was going to work and that's it. That's your bottom line because that's your responsibility to do."

Once Paulie found boxing, which combines athletics and discipline, he knew he'd found his "passionate enthusiasm," as he calls it. "You realize even when you're boxing, you need to do it every single day and you need to do it in a certain way. When there's a passion there, it doesn't feel like work."

He says people ask him how he can get hit every day. "Doesn't it hurt?" Sure, he tells them, it hurts, but he has to tell them that professional boxers don't worry about the pain from taking punches. They're focused on the technique and training to defeat the opponent. People often say to him, "I could never do that."

He finds it hard to explain how he feels differently. "In my mind, you say you could never do that, but I could never do 9-to-5 every day. I just have this passion about what I want to do. Passionate enthusiasm is one of the most important traits and qualities you need to be successful at anything."

ON DISCIPLINE

Paulie recognizes that he didn't have much of a future until his uncles
took him to Gleason's that day. He'd been sitting on the sidelines at his
grandfather's construction job, with everyone in his family keeping an eye
on him. Troubles at his mother's house meant he was sleeping on a couch
at his grandparents' place after he was expelled from school. "With the inner
anger I had at that time of my life and the competitive aspect, it all came
together. I was disgruntled and I was a good athlete. I always wanted to be
in the spotlight and show that I could be successful," he says.

"All of a sudden, everything came together. The whole package presented
itself to me. It was just a matter of doing the work. It was hard work but easy
to do because I wanted to do it. I wanted to come home from the gym and
watch VHS tapes of old fights, and then I'd want to go running, and then
every morning, I'd look forward to going to the gym."

In finding this new drive and purpose, he recognized the lessons he'd
learned from his family along the way, especially those from his grandfather.
"I became the repetition that my grandfather was doing. I always thought
my grandfather was miserable, but for me, I loved doing it every single day.
And he was happy to see me doing it."

He won his first few amateur fights, moving up to the finals in the 1998
Golden Gloves tournament. He remembers dates—March 6, 1998, for
example. "It registers in my mind" as his first amateur match. It was the day
when he had to show everyone what he could do. He won his first fight by
KO in the novice division and quickly moved to the finals of the tournament.

For Paulie, it was a huge confidence-builder. "It was my childhood dream
starting to come together in a different way. I wound up in a sport that
interested me very much. At that time in my life, [boxing] was very key
because it was a place you could bring your anger and channel it."

ON PROVING PEOPLE WRONG

Whether it was because of his family or background or something else, Paulie has always felt like people underestimated him. He's always felt like he had a need to prove people wrong about his fighting ability and he's been able to successfully do it—again and again. I ask him about this need to embrace the underdog mentality—something many fighters use to keep themselves motivated in the ring.

"I'm the kind of person that if too many people are talking too good, I'll mentally slide," he says. "I won't physically slide, but mentally, I'd start to feel like I was the man." A hallmark of champions is that they're self-aware enough to recognize what motivates them. They're masters at believing in themselves but know when to stop believing their own hype.

And even with his flashy prematch theatrics, Paulie learned early on how to stay focused. "If no one was believing in me, I'm not thinking about that," he says. "I'm thinking, 'I'm going to win this fight. I'm going to beat this guy.' And you're not thinking about all the stupid little minute details like how cool you're going look or you want everyone to view you when you walk into the ring. You're focusing on the win."

We talk about the 2012 Vyacheslav Senchenko fight in Ukraine where Paulie won the WBA welterweight title. He had a mental strategy in place regardless of the media coverage, which called him an underdog. "I'm thinking, 'I'm going to get so ready for this fight and box this guy's shoes off,'" he says. Like so many champions, he talks about being in the moment. "I can't remember being in the ring, the entrance, the walk-in. It was all a blur," he says. "I was so zoned in. It was just me and that guy—and that's it. The focus and concentration of everything [are important] when you want to prove people wrong. You don't have a chance to try to feel yourself, feel how cool you are."

Today, he can still dig deep and tap that teenage angst when he needs to. "There's an anger, a motivation, a feeling that just doing it is going to prove them wrong," he says. "You don't have to focus on how cool you look because if you do it, you're going to look cool regardless because you did something they said you couldn't do."

ON THE COTTO FIGHT

Every fighter has to get through brutal matches. There are no easy fights—only varying levels of damage and difficulty every time you step through the ropes. Every fighter wants a challenge, which is why guys like Paulie always seek out the toughest ones. One of those tough challenges was his world title effort versus Puerto Rican legend Miguel Cotto. Early in the fight, Cotto opened up a cut on Paulie's face. Later, Paulie would find his right orbital bone was also fractured. We talk about what he was feeling in the ring.

"I had read Teddy Atlas's book [*Atlas: From the Streets to the Ring: A Son's Struggle to Become a Man*] before the Cotto fight. I had underlined a few lines in that book," he says, noting the parallels between Atlas's life and his own as well as recalling the main message he took with him: "The bottom line was that there are moments in fights that are very, very uncomfortable. There are moments when you feel like you need to get out of this, you gotta go, you don't want to be there, and in those moments, quitting seems like the easiest thing to do, but in reality, continuing is the easiest thing to do. If you quit, you're going to have to live with that decision the next day, the next week, and the next month, and the next year for the rest of your life, wondering what might have happened had you just gotten through that moment."

Paulie sees a fight with its ups and downs as a series of moments. The decisions you make to stay in and continue is a championship philosophy. It's something you think about when you're taking punches—whether you're winning or losing. "It's just a moment. It's not the whole fight." But he always thinks about what he'd regret if he didn't leave it all in the ring. "You'll always wonder what would have happened if you'd have been able to survive that moment and get to that next level. Would you have been able to turn that fight around?" he says. "You'll always have to ask yourself that question." The message from Atlas "stuck on me," he says.

When it came to the Cotto fight, Paulie drew on that philosophy. "It was really important psychology to take into that fight. And there were moments in that fight when I thought of the things I'd read in that book. I just keep telling myself, 'It's a moment, it's a moment … .' And you know what? He's right. There were moments in the fight when it was so uncomfortable, so painful, and you start to question yourself. We're all human beings."

He'd never been cut before or had a broken bone in a fight, but in the first 6 minutes of the 12-round Cotto fight, he had a cut, a broken bone, and a knockdown. "It's moments, moments, moments," Paulie says. At the time, he didn't know how serious his injuries were.

"I heard the noise," he says about the moment when his orbital bone broke, but he didn't know what it was. "But there's so much going on, it's not like, 'Let me analyze this.'" By the last two rounds, he was bleeding profusely, swallowing it because of the placement of his injuries. He'd reached his physical limit, noting that if it had been a 15-round fight, he couldn't have made it.

It was his first career loss and first attempt at a title fight, but he became a hero to the boxing world for his heart and toughness. He didn't realize the reputation he'd earn making it through that fight. "It was an eye-opening experience. It was baptism by fire," he says. "I didn't think about the positives that came out of the fight until weeks later. Because you're mourning the loss for a couple of weeks, but then you start to realize how much positive feedback you're getting."

The loss still stung, but his career was far from over. "There's no moral victory at that stage, but you start to realize people are saying good things about you." The loss cemented his reputation as an elite fighter, earning him prime-time fights and bigger audiences. A year later, he'd win the IBF light welterweight title.

The Cotto fight "changed everything, even career-wise, the way people viewed me. I wasn't just this metrosexual kid anymore," he says, laughing. "People said there's a toughness behind this kid. He might have the hair, he might have the fancy outfits, but he is a fighter through and through."

ON ADVICE TO HIS YOUNGER SELF

I ask him what advice he'd have for a younger version of himself and he echoes a message that many fighters make: He wouldn't want to change the difficulties he went through that made him work so hard for success.

"There are certain decisions in my career I wish I'd not made—but a lot of decisions outside the ring that had to do with my boxing career. Who I may have signed with, who I may have worked with, I'd probably change those things a little bit but, really, maybe not. Maybe the learning experiences from those situations lead to the success I ended up having."

He does, however, have another piece of advice: Don't take what people tell you for granted and maybe don't just necessarily believe everything they tell you. Having grown up in a gym where he was constantly told how good he was as well as how marketable, he feels that it ultimately doesn't matter as much as he thought it did at the time.

Paulie is part of a new generation of fighters who not only had the athletic talent but also the marketability. There was an idea that the qualities he possessed beyond athleticism would get him to a world championship. From multiple languages to his looks and ability to present himself, he was the full package. "I used to think, 'Man, I have everything that I need. I'm so lucky and I'm good at this'—and then you realize it's all BS. None of that actually helps you at all in boxing," he says. "While being bi- or trilingual should help you, being good looking or charismatic should help you, honestly, if you wind up in the hands of people who don't know how to take advantage of it, it's not going to matter anyway. So I realized not to take anything for granted."

When it comes to considering what he would've told himself when he was younger, Paulie finds himself in a philosophical conundrum. If we'd given advice to our younger selves, would we have had the motivations that make us champions today?

"The older version of ourselves is always a bit jaded and the younger version of ourselves is much more enthusiastic, and the enthusiasm leads to the passion you need in order to succeed," he says. "The jaded version of yourself may be more knowledgeable, but it also may kill the enthusiasm of the younger version of yourself that ends up getting to that successful level."

Ultimately, though, he believes the challenges he faced are what made him a winner today. "I feel like I motivate myself a lot on anger. So maybe it made me want to continue to prove people wrong in different ways," he says. "The beauty of being young is that ignorance is bliss. You just have to go through the process yourself."

ON ANGER

Paulie is a thoughtful guy. Over the years, he's considered how his childhood affected him and his success as a boxer. Everyone in his family gets along now, but he acknowledges that there were some tough times growing up as his parents divorced, his father returned to Italy, and his mother remarried. "I'm not a naturally angry person. I wasn't a kid who would fight unless I had to," he says. But circumstances sometimes out of his control contributed to his troubles in school and at home. By the time he was living with his grandparents, sleeping on their couch, he felt the world had labeled him as a bad kid.

"It's much more difficult to try to fit in and find your identity," he says of his moves between suburban New Jersey and urban Brooklyn, calling it "a confusion." As a teenager, he learned hard lessons early. "Feeling where you fit in and anger about circumstances out of your control might seem not fair, but you've got to deal with it. You realize life is hitting you right in the face and that if you don't find solutions, you're going to have a problem."

He knew he was screwing up but never knew how to be successful. "I never blamed anybody else, but I was angry about the fact that I was there. When I started boxing, that was my solution. Now I look back on it and say, 'Maybe if my mother had just let me play sports. Maybe I would have been so much into something that I wouldn't have gotten into so much trouble.' Then again, maybe I would have become a pro at it and I wouldn't have started boxing, so it comes back to what I said before: I wouldn't change anything!"

Changing something in your past alters the outcome of your present. And Paulie is pretty happy about his present. "You take it all as a learning experience, and you appreciate all of the things that went well, and you don't change it because you don't know what side effects the changes might have that maybe you won't like!"

Always eager to prove the naysayers wrong, he tells me about a teacher who told him that if he kept screwing up in school, he'd major in "Would you like fries with that?"

"When I started boxing, when I started doing well, I thought, 'I wonder what that teacher thinks now when he sees me on TV,'" he says.

AUNG LA NSANG

Mixed martial artist
Status: Active
Weight classes: Middleweight, light heavyweight
Ring name: The Burmese Python
Hometown: Myitkyina, Myanmar

CHAMPIONSHIPS
· ONE light heavyweight title (2018)
· ONE middleweight title (2017)

HIGHLIGHTS
· Major star in Myanmar
· King of the Cage and Ring of Combat competitor
· Charities: Street School Initiative, Global Citizen,
and World Wide Fund for Nature

It's rare for a fighter to shoot to fame, fortune, and a title without walking a hard road. Most fighters, like Aung and me, had to struggle on our way to the top. But our roads were different. Today, fighters have to develop a persona, a story, and a style that appeals to fans. Aung La Nsang is one of those fighters. He has a terrific story and a fan-friendly fighting style that makes him a popular pick on any card. More importantly, he has the goods in the ring to back up the hype.

Aung brings his global perspective to the ring and to his own personal life, telling me right away how important fight sports are in other countries. There's just something about fight sports, he says, and we talk about the human-against-human nature of physical combat. Whether it's a fascination with war or simple human nature, combat sports have a unique appeal at home and globally.

Aung likens the appeal to Ancient Rome, where fans were fascinated with gladiators. "The world loves combat sports. And combat sport is here to stay. Ten years from now, a hundred years from now, we still want to have that. You can show a fight to a guy in Michigan, you can show a fight to a guy in Florida, or you can show a fight to a guy in a small village in Myanmar, and they'll be like, 'Wow, this is pretty awesome.' It transcends all types, everybody," he says. "All nations, all cultures. Any civilization has that love for combat sports."

ON MINDSET

Aung isn't naturally an aggressive person. When you meet him, he's almost gentle. He's thoughtful, as is evident with his work in world nature and conservation. He's even been a beekeeper—something that seems to require a person to be centered and, at their core, calm. So it's surprising to think of him in the MMA cage, demonstrating skills as one of the elite champions out there today. "It's a different mindset that I put myself into," he says of the mental state he needs for fighting. "I'm a caring and loving kind of person. If I even say something wrong and hurt somebody, the emotion kind of gets me, so my temperament is very calm and very collected. I just see good things in people. That's what I do."

But for a match, he's able set his natural personality aside or maybe he's just able to tap into something inside himself that he uses in the cage. "You have to kind of separate the two," he says. "When I want to fight, it's like I go all out, you know. I have no regard for my own safety. And I try to finish [KO] people when I fight."

He acknowledges it's taken a long time to learn how to separate his inside-the-ring and outside-the-ring personas. "It's something that I had to separate myself sometimes, you know, when it comes to competing and fighting, and that took many years to get into that kind of mindset."

We talk a little about how he figured out his "Why?" I want to know if it was something always in him. He says it took him some time to learn about why he does what he does.

Learning his "Why?" actually made a difference for him, and he explains how his motivation has changed as he's grown older, gotten married, and had a family. "Before, my 'Why?' was a little bit different. [In the beginning], it's to be under the spotlight, to be fighting in front of people. That was kind of my 'Why?'"

"But that kind of 'Why?' won't get you through the hard times," he says. "When I turned 28, my 'Why?' was a lot different, you know? I had a kid on the way. I had to provide for a family. My 'Why?' was a little bit different, and that's a mindset that changed me and put fire in me when I go out to compete." His "Why?" now is a desire to provide for his family, but it's also "to be the best version of myself," he says.

ON SOMETHING INSIDE

That "Why?" has a lot to do with how he got started in MMA and how he's succeeded in competition. It's something he identified at an early age.

"Since I was a kid, I was passionate about martial arts," he says. "I watched Jet Li movies, the kung fu movies, like all the other kids, and in Burma, you know, when we fight, we punch and we kick. Throwing a punch and a kick was a pretty normal thing for us. It was always inside of us."

While he grew up steeped in the culture of martial arts, he also knew—and understood—boxing. He internalized it. "When I was a kid, I did karate," he says. "I had the choice to do karate or I can play soccer, and I chose to do karate. And then, when it was Christmastime, you know, instead of buying a basketball or instead of buying a soccer ball, my brothers and I would get boxing gloves. So it was like something inside of us."

He had some exposure to American boxing growing up. "I vividly remember watching my uncles" when the Evander Holyfield–Mike Tyson fight was broadcast worldwide. "How crazy," he says when he thinks of the connections growing up. The connections would grow stronger as he moved to the US to pursue a degree in agriculture.

"When I went to college in Michigan, I end up in Berrien Springs, where Muhammad Ali used to live at that time," he says. "So it's like history makes who you are, you know. It's like I grew up wanting to fight and then I got the opportunity finally when I came to the States."

While still pursuing his college degree, he began to train in mixed martial arts, including jujitsu, kickboxing, and Muay Thai boxing. "And I was all over it," he says.

To Aung, his "Why?" today continues to evolve. "Now I understand just being better in my craft is more important to me than fighting in front of people making money or anything like that."

ON GETTING HIS START

Growing up in Burma (now Myanmar), Aung was the fourth of five kids and fortunate to have parents, especially his father, who believed education was the key to success. "Fortunately for us, my dad knew education was very important," he says. Which translated into a really good international school "and that's why I'm pretty much fluent in English."

He says that while they didn't always have a lot of money, they always had access to good education. Today, all his siblings are college graduates and his oldest sister is getting her PhD in engineering. "That's one thing that I'm very thankful that my father did: [He] gave us a good education."

Aung came to the US to study, fully intending to use his education in his own country. He found himself in Michigan at a small Christian school working as a beekeeper. His plan was to get his degree and return to Myanmar as an expert.

"I thought in four years I would be an expert, but a four-year degree doesn't do nothing," he says with a laugh. "But fortunately for me, I found a different passion—and it was mixed martial arts."

ON HARD TIMES & GRIT

By the early 2000s, Aung found that he not only loved this new sport of mixed martial arts, but he was also good at it. What started as a hobby became something he decided to pursue seriously. "In my early 20s, I realized, 'Man, I'm pretty decent,' but if I'm going to pursue this, I have to go all out and I have to pursue it 100%."

The decision was a tough one. The sport was in its infancy and it wasn't clear anyone could make a living at it—even if they were very good. "I went through some hard times, meaning like I pretty much put my other career on hold [to] pursue mixed martial arts," he says. "And as you know, mixed martial arts at that time is still at a very primitive stage."

In mixed martial arts, the pay model is slightly different from boxing. Instead of a prenegotiated purse for the fighters if they win, MMA pays fighters "to show" and "to win." Your payday isn't guaranteed, which makes it a riskier proposition, especially factoring in training and potential injuries.

"You don't make much money," he says of the early years. "You make $500 to show, $500 to win. Even after 10 fights, that's the kind of pay that you get at that time. You can't really provide for a family with that kind of money. You can't you provide for *yourself* with that kind of money."

Aung started his career in 2005 and says he didn't make any decent money until he won the championship in 2017. For 12 years, he worked toward a goal, struggling to get by. "It wasn't easy," he says. "That's over a decade of working toward something."

He watched a lot of fighters come and go—some of whom were tough and had potential. Many of them fell away, lacking the determination to continue at a sport that was—and still is—brutal at the highest levels.

"I've seen so many more talented guys that would train and then fight and then would do good and then they will fall off," he says. "You look at a guy and say, 'Man, this guy's a beast' and then they don't make it because they don't have that grit to keep going and going."

But Aung had that grit. He had that desire to outlast other competitors and to keep training and improving to win. Today, he sees fighters handpick opponents they know they can beat solely to build a winning record. Alternatively, elite fighters choose opponents who drive them to improve. It's how champions are born.

"When you start fighting, your level might be here," he says, putting his hand on an imaginary ladder. "And you might end up fighting a guy down here and that's an easy way, right? But if you start fighting guys here"—he moves his hand to a higher level—"you may lose, but as long as in those times you keep getting better and improving, you'll be able to beat those guys eventually."

We talk about commitment to the craft, to the sport, and that "thing" deep inside that keeps fighters like Aung going. He calls it "grit." I ask him where he thinks his originates. What was the source of that drive? How did he push past the hard times? Now that he's 15 years into his career, I wonder how he's been able to achieve his goals. His answer? Pure, unadulterated love for the sport.

"Well, the love for the sport, the love for the craft," he says.

He talks about his job as a beekeeper in Michigan, which overlapped with the beginnings of his professional MMA career. While he enjoyed his work, he didn't feel the drive to pursue it for the rest of his life.

"I enjoyed being a beekeeper, but there was something missing," he says. "Even as a beekeeper, I would do one or two MMA fights, you know, but during that time, I said, 'Man, if I don't pursue this now, I'm going to lose my chance. I'm going to lose my opportunity.'"

Even loving MMA, though, came with hard times, and for those, he drew strength from those around him who believed in what he was doing. He notes how important it is to have a partner who supports what you want to do—and doesn't second-guess or discourage you when times are tough. "My wife is one of the people that would always encourage me," he says. "Even in the hard times, she would help me and she would believe in me, you know. Having people around you that believe in your goal and push you instead of bringing you down is very important."

ON COMMITMENT AS A PRO

Aung notes that when decided to make MMA his career, he recognized that it takes years to reach an elite level. Commitment is critical because of the time it takes to really learn the skills to win—all while trying to make enough money to live on and train. "The fight life, the sport, is like a marathon," he says. "It takes years to get better, and just making your life sustainable for that marathon, it is very important, you know."

I remind him of his comment that getting a four-year degree doesn't get you anywhere in many professions where you need substantially more education. Fight sports are the same. Four years of training won't get you very far. It takes 10 to 12 years of hard work before you break the surface.

"You need four years in jujitsu, you need four years in some form of striking, you need four years in wrestling to get pretty decent at it, to have an understanding for it," he says, noting he felt one of his deficiencies was wrestling. So three years ago, he moved to Florida to train at a renowned MMA gym to work on his wrestling skills. "If I didn't move down [there], I knew my wrestling wouldn't be able to match people at my level," he says.

Which leads him to his second key to success beyond commitment: treating the sport as a profession. While we think of professional athletes as those who make a living at it, Aung sees his professional approach as something broader. He treats it as his true career, training and studying like he would as a professional in any other area. Having a very professional environment is important to him.

"One thing that changed my career is when I committed and made it as professional as I can be," he says. "A fight is a fight, right? But if you're a professional, you have to set everything in your life so that you can be a professional. Like if you're a professional engineer, you go to work like an engineer—just like that."

> **"If you're a professional MMA fighter, you have to treat it like a profession, treat it like it's your job. So you've got to take care of everything around your life—and I think that's what a lot of the younger guys miss sometimes."**
> **–Aung La Nsang**

He's worked in gyms, teaching classes and training other up-and-coming MMA fighters. He's found that many can't—or won't—commit to this level of professionalism needed to win.

"Some days, they show up and they go super hard, but it's on the days that you don't feel so good, you know, it's on the days that your body is sore that having that professionalism, to show up on time, maybe even come early to stretch out and get ready for the training is a big key. It's a big element that having that professionalism is very important," he says. "And when I started doing that, it changed my career."

ON THE TURNING POINT

I remember watching Aung more than 10 years ago in promoter Lou Neglia's Ring of Combat competitions. He's been fighting for a long time, working his way up to an elite level. Constant improvement is always on his mind. In Ring of Combat 33, he was KO'd in less than 30 seconds by Costas Philippou. I ask him when he decided that he really needed to become a professional fighter and treat this like a career.

"Like, man, it was so embarrassing because I got knocked out in front of my students," Aung says. "I was a coach at a gym, doing coaching full time and kind of training part time. That was the time that I [thought], 'Man, I need to step it up.'" From there, he decided he needed to improve his boxing and work with a striking coach and a boxing coach.

"Mixed martial arts has a lot of elements," he says. "It has the striking part, it has the wrestling part, it has the grappling part. Just to be better with my hands, I had to work with a boxing coach."

Many fighters would've decided a loss like that meant MMA wasn't for them. But instead, Aung used it to gauge what he needed to improve. It's part of what makes him such an impressive champion. He's calm, down-to-earth, and always looking at what he can be doing to get better. To improve his boxing skills, he began working with the Fox brothers, Alantez and Mykal, two boxing title contenders, "training six days a week. That makes a big difference, you know, like putting that time in like that."

"When you're a hobbyist, you probably train like three days a week and that's fine, but when you start training six days a week, it's when you start getting sore and it's like when the pain sets in and then it's like a job," he says. "But if you don't do that, you can't compete at a professional level."

He believes that losing is what drives him to improve. Which is why he believes it's important that fighters keep facing opponents who're as good as they are—or even better. "Losing is what makes me tougher," he says. "It makes me try to fight better, to train harder. After every loss, I try to analyze and be like, 'Why did I lose?' It's always humbling, [but] you always have to re-evaluate."

ON WINNING THE CHAMPIONSHIP

In 2017, Aung got his title shot on short notice against defending champion Vitaly Bigdash. It was a brutal fight that Aung lost by decision. Because of some savvy negotiations for the fight, he was awarded an immediate rematch. Losing again to the champion would've placed him at the bottom of the pack. I ask him how he felt about fighting the man who'd beaten him once already—and with such high stakes on the line.

"I was scared shitless," he admits. "I took the first one on like two weeks' notice. The guy that [Vitaly] was supposed to fight got a staph infection, so they call me up to save the card," Aung says.

"I think it was New Year's or something," he says. "I was with my family, eating and, you know, fat, and I knew I wasn't in shape at all. So when I took that fight, I told them on contract, I said, 'The only way I'm going to take this fight on two weeks' notice is if I get an immediate rematch.' And after that loss, I knew I was gonna get the rematch."

The rematch was essential because Aung got beaten up pretty good in the first fight. "Man, I got cut here, you know, like 12 stitches," he says pointing to the side of his eye. "Eight stitches on this side and like six stitches here," he says, pointing out injury after injury. "It was a mess. He elbowed me and he beat me up real bad," he says, laughing at the memory. But then he turns serious. "So coming into that rematch, I was very dialed in," he says, because he "did everything in [my] power" to be prepared to win. He was teaching at a gym while training for the fight and the schedule was intense.

"Before that fight, I would have to teach classes at 6 a.m. and then I would have to teach classes at 10 a.m. and then I would have to teach classes at 4:30 p.m., all the way to 10 o'clock almost. I would train in between."

His hard work paid off. "When it was time for me to walk out, I was ready," he says. "I was ready to die in there. I did everything in my power to be able to get the win, you know, with all the resources that I had at that time."

He beat Bigdash in their second fight in Myanmar, winning the ONE middleweight championship. "I couldn't believe it. The first shock was like I couldn't believe it, you know. I couldn't believe it because if you watch [the tape], I had a lot of deficiency in the wrestling department. But I almost knocked him out in the first round. I did more damage in the fight."

To Aung, the victory meant even more because the fight was in Myanmar, his home country. The fight was a significant victory for Aung and for his entire nation.

"It's hard for me to explain because it was in Myanmar, right? It was in my home country. And we've never had any sort of champion in anything," he says. "If the Burmese soccer team competes, we know they're most likely going to lose."

"If we go to the SEA [Southeast Asian] Games or these Games in any sports, we usually lose," he says, "and to be able to beat like somebody from Russia like that" was a moment of national pride and importance. He quite literally had the entire country cheering for him. It gave him a sense of personal accomplishment and purpose.

"And to hear everybody cheer and be so happy and to bring alive joy to the whole country was … it's like an indescribable feeling, so happy," he says. "I was so happy that like I'm telling you right now, if I die today, I'm content with my life."

ON FIGHTING BRANDON VERA

I compare Aung to a rock star after his first championship: a national hero in his home country and a bona fide MMA star. And in case there was any doubt, he moved up a weight class to light heavyweight and won his second ONE championship title less than a year later, simultaneously holding two ONE championship titles. He'd successfully defend the light heavyweight title over the next year, leading up to one of his toughest fights, against Brandon Vera in October 2019. I ask him how he accomplished the feat. Overall, it was a perfect kind of professional matchup—one Aung was prepared for and felt good about going into.

"After my middleweight defense in Japan, he called me out," he says. "I've always been a fan of Brandon. As a matter of fact, we trained together. We've had one encounter and he was very nice to me at that time and so I've always admired him as a fan."

Aung knew Vera would be tough but felt it was a fair match. "I really looked forward to it. The whole camp is in a very good mood, even though it felt unreal to be able to fight one of the fighters that I was a big fan of since in my college years."

But he wasn't going to let that stop him from winning when he needed to. "I was going to do whatever it takes to get that win."

Aung would win in a TKO in the second round.

"Like, man, he hurt me good with his elbow, but it wasn't like I was in a mode where I was just going to go forward and try to look for that finish like I usually always do," he says. Aung powered through and finished him.

But the real stars that night were the fans in Tokyo. "You know what's crazy was that usually the Japanese crowd are very quiet, right?" he says. "When I fought him that night, there was a lot of Burmese people there and the Burmese crowd were electric. That's one thing that I miss, fighting for a live audience. The Burmese crowd pumps you up. They have so much energy and you kind of feed off that too."

ON LOSING

Every fighter knows the type of fighter and style of fighting that's their biggest weakness. In 2020, Aung was scheduled to fight Bigdash one more time, but Bigdash pulled out because of COVID-19. Instead, he met Dutch mixed martial artist Reinier de Ridder in the cage. Even though Aung had trained hard to improve his wrestling, Ridder's style focused heavily on wrestling and groundwork, and that would be an issue for Aung.

"His build and his body type—that gives me an issue," he says. "You know, there's always that body type that gives certain people trouble and his kind gave me a lot of trouble just because of the fact that he's a grappler. What do you do with a guy who's much taller than you? You close the distance and that's exactly what he's going to want to do too."

Aung would go on to fight Ridder twice, in 2020 and 2021, and lose both times, giving up his middleweight and light heavyweight championship titles. And while he's philosophical about the lessons from losing, he's also honest about it: Nobody likes to lose.

"Losing for me is, like, I take it as a lesson," he says. But he adds, "They always say you either win or you learn, which I think is bullshit because losing sucks. It's so painful, it hurts so much, but I am working on it."

"There's two ways to go about it when you lose. You know, you can either hide your head in the sand and act like nothing happened or you can try to pinpoint and dissect and try to learn and try to grow from it," he says.

He continues to learn from his losses, using them to chart his next path when it comes to training. "I'm not a complete mixed martial artist because I do have my holes," he says, referring to what he considers gaps in his skill set. For him, it continues to be what he feels is a deficiency in his wrestling and groundwork.

"I fill those holes by knocking people out or, you know, putting that pressure on them, but those holes I needed to address. And now I've been addressing it and I've been working a lot on it. I've been spending more mat time on those certain aspects."

Tackling your weaknesses or facing your fears head-on are principles at the core of his personal philosophy and at the heart of what he believes young fighters should embrace to become champions themselves.

"In anything in our life, that's the way we should approach things. Face your fears head-on," he says. "I don't like wrestling, but to make it more fun, to make it better, I just try to put more time into it, you know, work hard on the technique, break things down a little bit more, and try to get better at it."

As with anything else in his career, he addresses what he perceives as his deficits through training. "We have great, great trainers and a lot of high-level training partners as well, so for me, it's motivating," he says. "It's life. If you don't evolve, if you don't grow, you get left behind."

In this way, he again sees his professional career no differently from professionals in other disciplines. "If you don't get better, time will take over. It doesn't matter what field you're in. You can be in the field of engineering, construction. If you don't catch up with time, you're gonna be left behind."

ON NOT GIVING UP

We talk a little about the sport and how it's changed since Aung started fighting. He notes he's watched it grow and he's watched too many fighters who failed to grow with it get left behind. I ask him if there was ever a time when he felt the sport was leaving him behind or when he might decide to give it up professionally.

"The big moment was in 2015. I just had a kid. I just bought into the gym I was trying to build and help grow, working full time there," he says. "Also, in 2015, I wasn't able to travel because I didn't have [immigration] documents yet and I said to myself, 'Maybe it's time to hang it up.'"

"I was 30 years old, and in our heads, that's our prime, 30 years old, and I'm like, man, when you hit your 30s, it's downhill from there, you know," he says. But then he had a moment to regroup and overcome, facing his fears—this time about age, time, and administrative paperwork.

He changed his mind about turning 30, believing it doesn't have to mean a downhill slide for MMA fights. Still, his life seemed to be encouraging him to retire. "If you have good people around you and you're taking care of your body, I think you can fight longer, but I had a kid. I was, you know, coaching full time and I didn't have my documents. Time is ticking. And I was like, 'Man, maybe it's time to hang it up'—and I almost quit there," he says.

But then he connected with Maryland senator Barbara McCloskey, who helped expedite his documents. By the end of 2015, he had his US citizenship and passport. By the fall of 2016, "I made my first fight in Myanmar." By 2017, he won his first championship.

"So from 2014 to 2016, I didn't have a fight and that's when I almost quit." Aung still kept learning and reflecting and taking away lessons. He taught, he supported fighters as a cornerman, and he even worked.

"Those two years were for me a very good learning experience," he says. "I coached a lot of students. I probably cornered over 100 fights," including WKA and kickboxing nationals. It's still punches and kicks. When you watch and corner 100 fights, your fight IQ gets better."

We talk about how fighters as coaches learn techniques differently. Their vision changes, so they can see nuances other fighters can't see. It was a valuable experience that would contribute to his championship journey.

ON ADVICE TO HIS YOUNGER SELF

With such a structured approach to training and life, I ask him what advice he'd have for a younger version of himself—and also for young fighters out there who might want to be champions. He encourages them to do "whatever you want to do in your heart."

"Hey, if you have a dream, if you have a vision, go all out, don't hold back," he says. "I think a lot of times when we hold back is when we don't commit 100% to something."

He feels if you don't give yourself fully to your dream or goal, "it's going to take you a much longer time and it's going to make you quit. Find a passion and go for it 100%." But, he cautions, "make sure it's sustainable."

"A lot of people have the passion, the fire, and the drive, [but] it's not sustainable. If it's not sustainable, it will just be a flame, but if you want to be a light that can hold up in the dark, you have to have your life situated so it's sustainable, so that you can put effort into it for a long time," he says. "Everything good takes time, you know, but if you're passionate about something, I would go 100%. I would go all-in on it."

He's worked at his gym to carry his philosophy to other fighters who train at elite levels. "Honestly, you have to have good guidance. You have to have good coaching," he says. "You have to have good people around you and I really believe what we have at Sanford MMA is all of the above."

"It's a win-win situation," he says of his run in MMA. "I'm learning from the best guys. I'm training with the best guys. I'm a guy from a little village in Myanmar and I get to do this and follow my passion and my dream."

KELLY PAVLIK

Boxer
Status: Retired
Weight class: Middleweight
Ring name: The Ghost
Hometown: Youngstown, Ohio

CHAMPIONSHIPS

· WBC, WBO, and *The Ring* middleweight unified title (2007)
· WBC and NABF middleweight title (2005)

HIGHLIGHTS

· Trained with Jack Lowe
· US Under-19 amateur champion (1999)
· National Jr. PAL amateur champion (1998)
· National Jr. Golden Gloves amateur champion (1998)

Kelly and I go way back—more than 10 years to when we met at Robert Garcia's training camp in Oxnard, California. Kelly is one of my personal favorite boxers because of his all-action style and KO power in either hand. Kelly always fought with the mentality that fighters "don't get paid overtime." I tell him how my brother and I watched all his fights, including his historic come-from-behind battle with then undisputed and undefeated middleweight champion Jermain Taylor. The fight was in Atlantic City, New Jersey, and the historic Boardwalk Hall was absolutely electric with energy. We've stayed in touch over the years and it's always a pleasure to catch up.

A native of Youngstown, Ohio, where he lived and fought during his career, Kelly is known for his breakout fight against the ever-dangerous Edison Miranda, which he describes as high risk and low reward. Even though he turned professional at 18, "I was always under a lot of pressure since networks didn't want to showcase me or put me on." Kelly was a true working-class talent who had to take on all comers to get recognized.

ON GETTING STARTED

When Kelly was little, his brothers were into sports, so it was natural when he started playing peewee football at around six years old. Later, he played baseball. In the 1980s, every kid was watching karate movies and action films. Kelly wanted to try karate, but martial arts classes were expensive. He tried it but didn't stick with it. Instead, he wanted to try the local boxing gym. His mother was skeptical, but she took him.

The local boxing gym they went to was legendary trainer Jack Lowe's place. On the afternoon Kelly and his mother went to visit, no one was there except one man: boxer Harry Arroyo. "I didn't know who he was at the time," Kelly says. "We asked for Jack, and he said 'Jack's not here,' and he was super nice. When we left, my mom said, 'Do you know who that was? That was Harry Arroyo.'"

In the early 1980s, Arroyo was Youngstown royalty as the IBF world lightweight champion. Kelly dropped martial arts and started training at Jack Lowe's gym. "From that point, I still played baseball, but I really enjoyed boxing."

His parents hoped he might not stick with it. "The first time I sparred, I got my ass whooped and my parents thought, 'Good, he's not going to want to do it anymore.' But the next day, I came home from school and started packing my [gym] bag. My parents said, 'What are you doing?' and I said, 'I'm going back to the gym to whip that kid's butt!'"

Even when he was young, he could identify why he loved boxing. "I loved the brutality of it, but at that age, I'm not sure it was brutality. It was the adrenaline rush of it." No matter the reason, from then on, Kelly was a fighter.

"Do you remember when you were in school and you'd be in study hall?" he asks me, then continues. "I never studied, but I'd have the textbook open with *The Ring* magazine inside and I'd look at it and say, 'One day, I'm going to be right here and I'm going to be ranked fifth or sixth.'"

As Kelly got older, boxing competed with football and baseball for his time. One year, he came off baseball season and then got beaten in a fight. "My dad and my trainer sat me down and said, 'Kelly, we're not telling you to quit the other sports, but we think you should pay a little more attention to boxing. We think you could really do something.'"

"At that point, I was about 15 years old," Kelly says, and that's when he began to get serious about amateur boxing. It's also when he started winning tournaments, like the national Junior Golden Gloves tournament.

ON OVERCOMING OBSTACLES

The next part of Kelly's boxing story almost ended before it started. As an amateur, Kelly lost back-to-back matches in the first round of two national tournaments and began to question if boxing was going to pan out for him. He started wondering whether he had what it took. "I thought about maybe going back to baseball. But we got through it." Eventually, he went to the under-19 division and dominated.

Once he turned professional, Kelly again encountered some obstacles on the way to his championship. From tough opponents to youthful indiscretions (like three arrests, including one for assault) to a stint in rehab for alcohol addiction, Kelly battled through them. We talk about the driving force behind how he overcame challenges and dealt with setbacks.

Although Kelly was signed to the major promotional company Top Rank at the tender of age of 18, he wasn't a household name. Boxers who don't have Olympic gold medals or breakout personalities often find themselves searching for the attention their skills warrant. There's a drive, a force, that keeps fighters going.

"I think about this all the time," Kelly says. "Throughout all of the amateurs, the pros, through everything that went wrong, the setbacks, I was always very competitive with myself."

He describes how that translates to his life today. "I have a drive in anything that I do. The gym I have is a smaller gym, but to me, I still want to make it the best gym," he says of his business in Youngstown.

He feels his difficulties have only served to make him better. In his eyes, it's not only the amount of life experience you have but also how you push through it. "I think individuals that succeed have more trials and tribulations than anyone, and it's the way they keep working through it. They're going to accomplish their goal and achieve what they want to do." This attitude is what keeps him going.

When it comes to his boxing career, he views his own setbacks the same way, even when he couldn't see a way to get through it. He says that working harder and pushing through the moments of self-doubt are "when big things would happen." Today, he finds there's a lot of good that came from that kind of discipline, so "it kind of became a habit."

We talk about the moment that the best boxers have—that moment when he knew he could be a champion. "When those times came, you dug deep and you'd say, 'You ain't done, man. You can do this.'" And as he admits, after major losses, anyone could think "maybe this isn't for me."

For Kelly, boxing success wasn't just winning in the ring but making boxing financially sustainable. As he turned professional and moved up the rankings, things started moving quickly, but he still wanted his version of success. "Once you crack the top 20 or 15 of the rankings, you start thinking, 'This is getting real.' It was probably three years into my pro career before I realized I could make a living at it."

ON THE FIGHTER'S EGO

We talk about how a fighter calms the negative voices in their head—the ones that pop up after a win and put the weight of expectations on your shoulders and make you put pressure on yourself to keep winning. I ask him how he handles that voice that sometimes tells you what you can't do.

His basic message is that losing is no fun. He learned it the hard way. "You're coming out of the amateurs, and you're doing well and everyone knows you're a fighter, and you leave school for a week for a tournament, and you come back early, and everyone knows you lost," he says. "Everyone has the ego, but when you go out there, it's just you."

Kelly talks about the luxury other athletes have—one that fighters don't. Public pressure can be hard for a boxer used to competing in the ring against a single opponent. "When you come back from a loss at football camp, you say, 'Yeah, my quarterback sucked. The running back fumbled the ball on the two-yard line.'" But solitary athletes have no one to blame. "When you come home from a loss in boxing, you have no one to point a finger at. You got beat."

For a newly professional athlete, that public pressure can be rough, especially in your hometown. It can be a dangerous position for a budding young star. As a local hero, there can be a lot of traps—from picking up old habits to hanging out with the wrong crowd.

The shift from amateur to the professional level also makes a difference, especially once you win a championship. "It's an ego thing," Kelly notes. "You're defending your world title. There's the pressure of having a city on your back," he says. "And you've got 6,000 people in the arena and 20,000 watching on pay-per-view or premium television. The pressure is huge."

What you say or do in public matters and there's no room for behaving badly. "Every aspect of being in that situation is tough," he says. "You're a role model. Your whole life changes."

ON MENTAL HEALTH

These days, there's a lot of discussion about the health of fighters and the unique challenges boxers have. There's the physical health aspect— everything from nutrition to brain health because of hard hits to the head— and the mental aspect of the sport. Social media, interviews, promoters, other fighters, and the media add to the pressure and scrutiny boxers are under every day. I ask Kelly what advice he'd give a young fighter on how to handle the fans and the pressure.

"You know how everyone says, 'Don't pay attention to what they say [about you]!' Come on, man! You're human," Kelly says. "No matter how many people say 'Don't pay attention,' it bothers you, especially when someone questions your manhood and what you're doing with your career. It's frustrating. There are times you just want to unleash with a serpent tongue, but I held back."

Kelly thinks the sports media is even more critical now than it was 5 to 10 years ago, when he was at the height of his pro career. "It's harsh now. No fighter is good [in their own eyes]—they're overrated according to some of these guys."

He feels it's disingenuous to tell young fighters to just ignore social media or the press. "The only advice I could give is to try to stay away as much as possible, but I would never tell anyone to not let it bother them." Then he adds, "And you can make them eat their words. Sometimes it made me work that much harder."

ON TRAINING

When it comes to training for a fight, there are many ways to do it. I wanted to know what kind of gym guy he was and how that helped him prepare to win. Did he enjoy training or did he hate it?

"I'm going to be brutally honest: I hated training and I loved it—if that makes any sense. When I retired, I was so happy and I'd see people running in the park and I'd say, 'What idiots! What's wrong with them!?!'"

He describes training with the legendary Jack Lowe, who'd follow him on a run "drinking coffee and eating a doughnut" but cutting him no slack. "Every time had to be faster than the one before."

"I trained six to seven hours a day and I really put the work in. If you don't have the energy to pull the trigger in the seventh round, if you don't have the conditioning, the strength, the fast twitch work, the endurance, you won't make it through the fight," Kelly says.

Making weight was another kind of training. "The scale is one of the biggest opponents we have before a fight," he says.

But still, it was worth it. "When I got home after six to seven hours of training and I was tired, it felt good. I do miss that at times."

Kelly was known for his two-handed punching style. He was a powerful fighter and an endurance guy, known for breaking down opponents and knocking them out late in the fight. It's a style most boxers don't find sustainable for an entire career. Because boxing is so demanding on the body, he acknowledges his style of fighting wasn't conducive to him staying in the sport for a long time.

"I didn't retire early because I didn't want to train," he says. "Boxing, it's not a longevity sport." He notes that depending on styles, some guys can fight into their 40s, but with his style of fighting, "I wasn't made to be in the sport for a long time. I took a lot of shots."

Kelly asks me about my own biggest fear in the ring and I say it's getting tired. That's why I train so hard. "The guy in front of me is trying to kill me, and if I'm weak, I can't defend myself," I tell him.

Kelly agrees, sharing the same fear from his boxing days. "I would have nightmares that I'd be in fights and not be able to do anything. Like the guy was rocking me and I couldn't do anything to defend myself."

He still keeps himself active and healthy, having slimmed down a bit, and speculates he might even enjoy jogging again knowing it's not his job.

ON HIS WAY TO THE CHAMPIONSHIP

In 2007, Kelly upset Edison Miranda, winning by TKO and earning a shot at a title fight. It was a big win, especially because he knew how dangerous Miranda was. "I thought I wasn't meant to get a title shot," Kelly says. "Miranda was the bogeyman. His reputation wasn't fiction and I had to fight him before [I could get] the title fight. No one was giving me a good chance. Everyone said, 'Just go around that guy,' so when I drew that fight, I was thinking, 'Screw him and how he thinks about my power, my output.' I don't think anyone expected me to knock him out."

Following the Miranda fight, Kelly would knock out Jermain Taylor for the WBC, WBO, and *The Ring* middleweight championship—a unified title. (He'd defeat Taylor a second time the following year to retain the title.) Analysts knew it would be a brawl with two explosive punchers in the ring.

I ask him about the Taylor title fight. By the second round, Kelly was struggling after a knockdown. I wanted to know what it was that drove him to get up and come back to win.

"[Veteran referee] Steve Smoger came in the locker room before the fight very adamant about the rules. He grabs me by my robe and goes, 'If you get knocked down and you show me you're there mentally, I will not stop the fight.' There's two types of knockdowns," Kelly explains. "One where you're totally out of it [mentally] but your legs are good. Then there are the ones where you're there mentally. I could tell you who I saw in the second row, but my legs just weren't there."

Somehow, he found it in himself to get up. "That thing that Smoger told me stuck in my head. I grabbed Taylor and was hitting him in the ribs, not to hurt him but to signal to Smoger that I was still in the fight."

Kelly believes that sort of awareness in the ring is one of the things that come with experience. "If I didn't have 26 or 27 fights going into it, I probably wouldn't have done anything that I did," he says. "It's amazing how fast your brain works when you're in that ring. You have to think about what move you're going to do next. You're trying to counterpunch. If you get hurt, you're trying to put on the poker face. Time really does slow down there."

ON THE SERGIO MARTÍNEZ FIGHT

Kelly successfully defended his titles until 2010, when he suffered one of his only two career losses: to Argentinian boxer Sergio Martínez. (Both of his losses would come at the hands of future first-round Hall of Famers, as he lost to Bernard Hopkins in 2008.) Known for his quick style, Martínez was a tough matchup for the hard-punching Kelly.

Additionally, Kelly had battled with his weight before the bout. Even though he was an endurance guy, he was physically tired toward the end of the fight, but he maintained his mindset. He never stopped and never went down.

"Still, it was brutal to be tired in front of a guy like Martínez," Kelly says. "In the ninth round, I hit a wall due to the battle with the scale leading up to the fight. I could not pull the trigger. I just didn't have it. It's frustrating because I wasn't breathing heavy. But it was my body saying, 'Listen, homie, I don't know what you think I can do.'"

In retrospect, Kelly can look at what he might have done differently. "I don't regret the fight with him, but I do think, 'What if things were different in that fight?' What if I'd come in two pounds overweight and said, 'Screw it, I'm moving up.' I sucked it up and he was the better man that week. Still, at the end of the day, I have two losses to two all-time greats."

ON RETIREMENT

Kelly retired when he was only 30 years old but with a robust 40-2 record. I ask him how he knew it was time and what was going through his mind. Considering his hard-punching style, his career was longer than many people predicted. He weighed brain health and financial security, but ultimately, he was ready to move on.

"I always talked about retiring early probably because the training was so hard," he says. "I promised my wife I wouldn't fight much past 30. And I had my kid before winning the title and things got real. I always observed people around me and there were some pros you could see stuck around too long. I didn't want to be like that. When I won the world title, I was always looking to the next financial security fight. I was always looking to fight my way out."

After his loss to Martínez in 2010 and a rib injury, Kelly took some time off (including a stint in rehab for alcohol addiction). He was working to get his career back on track and left home to train at Robert Garcia's camp in Oxnard. "I was getting that hunger back again," he says. But a comeback fight with Andre Ward fell apart after Ward injured his shoulder.

"When the Andre Ward fight didn't materialize, I was done," Kelly says. "I just didn't have it in the tank for another two months of training camp. At that point, is it worth it? I had the money in the bank, I had the three world title belts, and I had two babies at home." He decided to retire.

ON ADVICE TO HIS YOUNGER SELF

Kelly credits his dad and his wife as the reasons he can be where he is: retired and with investments. His advice is to make sure you're surrounded with people who have your best interests at heart. "You have to be strong. You have to get through it and make the right decisions because your life does change."

He notes that if you want to party and hang out at bars, remember that someone's always watching. "If you're a rock star, a rap star, or a movie star, it's a lot more lenient lifestyle. If you're an athlete, especially a boxer, make one or two mistakes and you're written off."

While he feels he tried to be careful, he wanted to enjoy life too. "I didn't ignore people when they told me to look out for certain things or to watch out for specific pitfalls. I listened to them, but you don't know," he says. "Life is about living it, experiencing it, and making mistakes—and that's how you learn. I don't think I did anything that bad, but I did stupid, immature, petty things a handful of times too many."

"Everyone is going to run into setbacks. They're going to have things they shouldn't have done," he says on his sometimes rocky past. "I would warn them as much as possible, but young kids coming up are going to do what they want to do, so hopefully when they make that mistake, they have a good consultant or someone who says, 'You see what just happened? Let's change it.'"

"I worked my ass off all throughout my career and I think the numbers show I took the sport seriously, but with kids, they're going to have to learn, but maybe you have some kids who listen and say, 'I'm going to take all the advice this guy is giving me and walk that straight road.' And that's the best thing you could hope for."

But if he had to give a young Kelly Pavlik advice all those years ago? "I'd put his ass in a bubble and push him around to keep him out of trouble!"

ABNER MARES

Boxer, analyst
Status: Active
Weight classes: Bantamweight, super bantamweight, featherweight
Hometown: Hawaiian Gardens, California

CHAMPIONSHIPS
· WBA featherweight title (2016)
· WBC featherweight title (2013)
· WBC super bantamweight title (2012)
· IBF bantamweight title (2011)

HIGHLIGHTS
· Competed at the Athens Olympics (2004)
· Hosts the *On the Hook with Abner Mares* podcast

I've long been a fan of boxer Abner Mares, but my first real interaction with him was when he invited me to appear on his podcast as a guest. He's a boxing analyst and fight commentator, so he's obviously very well spoken, but he did homework prior to our talk. He came off as fun and light but also extremely professional and prepared. It's something that mirrors his approach to boxing. He might seem like a very nice guy, but when it's time to go to work, he's a stone-cold professional. It's clear he's there to do a job.

Listening to Abner's humble beginnings in the sport was incredibly eye-opening to me. He's had a unique beginning to his boxing journey— fundamentally different from any fighter I know and defined by the fact he was never interested in boxing when he started. He's a family man, a dedicated professional, and a complex individual with deep layers. He's shaped by his entry into boxing as well as his deep family ties and responsibilities.

ON THE BEGINNING

Abner grew up in a large Mexican family surrounded by boxing. He was the fourth of 11 kids and boxing was always there. His father, his older brother, and his older sister all boxed, although none of them turned professional. It was just around him every day. So much so that Abner wasn't really a fan. It was never anything he wanted to do.

But his father didn't really give him a choice. "Boxing was always part of my life. Always there," he says. "When something's there every day, when you see something every day, it's boring—and I didn't like it. I didn't want to be a boxer. To be honest, I really got forced into this sport and I thank my dad to this day. He made me become a boxer. I didn't like it. I didn't want to be part of it. I just wanted to do different things. I wanted to play soccer or, short as I am, I liked basketball as well! I was a kid, but early on, at seven years old, for your father to say, 'Hey, you're going to practice boxing. You're going to shadowbox.' I just didn't want to."

ON THE DRIVE

Training is hard. Training camp is hard. Sparring is hard. I ask him what his drive was, especially without a love of boxing and a real desire to even do it. I wanted to know what was at the center of how he pushed past difficult times without the passion. Abner credits talent for his early success. To him, he never had to push through hardships. He was just good. "I went to tournaments and I won. I didn't pay any mind to it," he says. It's not something you'd expect to hear from an Olympic boxer, but, of course, there's more to the story.

Abner talks about how he started training at seven years old, but even then, he still got into trouble. When he was 14, his father saw him heading toward a rough path in life and sent him to Mexico to train. "He said, 'You're going to practice the sport here because you're good at it, son,'" Abner says. His father had connections to Mexican boxing officials and arranged for a sparring session with a top amateur boxer. "I beat the hell out of him," Abner says. "They say, 'Hey, this kid is staying here.'" And his Mexican fight career was off and running.

Once in Mexico, he talked with the head of the boxing committee in Mexico City, who gave him an idea of what his talent could mean. "He told me, 'You have a great talent. You can take it to the Olympics and represent your country. After that, you can become a professional and make money for your family and support them.' Boom—it hit something different," he says. "Now he got me thinking."

His father hadn't made a very strong case for him being a boxer. "I guess my dad didn't know how to talk me into the sport," he says. "We never really had that talk to make me understand why he saw a potential in me and that I could make something of this talent." Once he sat down with the professionals in Mexico, he understood.

He stayed in Mexico City for the next few years, medaling in a huge number of international tournaments—from the Pan American Games to the World Junior Championships. He came up in the amateur rankings, then went to the Athens Olympics in 2004. "And lost in my very first fight," he says, chagrined.

"I got robbed in a good fight and it took a lot from me," he says. "I was demolished. I lost motivation." But he took heart in the fact that his fight was famous on TV. Boxing legend Julio César Chávez was the on-air commentator and "my fight became famous because Chávez cursed on national TV."

Abner found his passion for the sport in the belief that his talent had a purpose. It was bigger than he was and there was a reason he was a success. Once he understood the idea that something was going to come from what he was doing, he found his motivation.

"We're not just doing things because we want to do them. There is something in return, there is something that's going to come out of it, there's something that's going to make us bigger," he says. "All of the prep work— the reading, the fighting, the homework, the training—there's something that is going to come from that. Once you realize that, you get the drive, you get the energy, you get the satisfaction."

ON TURNING PRO

By the time he was 19, he turned pro, and with his heavy amateur fight experience, the transition wasn't as difficult as Abner thought it would be. "Of course, there are the jitters and no headgear and smaller gloves— what's that gonna be like? But once you get your first fight in, it's like the same thing. It was an easy transition for me," he says. Most fighters making their pro debut start at the four-round bout length, but because of his vast amateur experience, Abner went right to the six-round distance.

I tell Abner how entertaining I always thought his style was. He's fought the top of his divisions over the years and always seemed to be in dogfights. I ask him where he digs deep in those kinds of trench warfare battles that made him famous.

His motivation and drive have changed over the years, especially with a family. He married at 18 and is still married with two "beautiful kids," he says. "You have different stages of your life, different goals." When he got married and had a baby on the way, "my drive changed drastically."

"Now I'm not just fighting for myself. I'm fighting for a wife and I'm fighting for a kid," he says of his career start at 19. "Boom—it changes your whole mentality. Now I'm fighting for them." For Abner, his desire to succeed in boxing was "to become someone in life, to provide something for my family and my kids. If I have the talent to provide them with a good lifestyle, so be it."

Before, his goals had been conquering world titles and making a name in the sport. But the idea of providing a good living for his family was appealing. "In Mexico, we call boxing 'the poor man's sport'" because anyone can get a pair of gloves and hit the bag, and if you've got the talent, boxing will take you to the big leagues and big money. He's brutally honest that his drive for his big fights was to get out of poverty.

Because of his experience, Abner fought brutal opponents early on. By his 14th fight, he beat Isidro Garcia for the WBO-NABO bantamweight title in 2007. By 2010, he faced Yonnhy Pérez for the IBF bantamweight world title. (They'd fight to a draw, even though most press people felt Abner won.) Immediately after the Pérez fight, he fought in Showtime's single-elimination bantamweight tournament in 2011. In the first round, he beat Vic Darchinyan to win the IBO bantamweight world title.

"I was the youngest guy in that tournament, with guys like Vic Darchinyan, Joseph Agbeko, Yonnhy Pérez. Honestly, everyone was saying Abner's going to be out in the first round," he says, laughing.

ON THE EYE

We talk about some of the who's who of tough opponents Abner has faced over the years. "Anselmo Moreno, one of the best pure boxers I've ever faced," he says. "I had to dig deep in that fight to get another world title."

I tell him I watched him live in 2013 when he fought Daniel Ponce De León in Las Vegas for the WBC featherweight title. De León was a super tough but slightly awkward guy who could really punch. He tells me there was a lot happening behind the scenes for that fight, which all had to come together for his win.

Prior to the fight, Abner had suffered a detached retina—one of two major eye injuries in his career. The New York Boxing Commission won't sanction fights where eye injuries are involved, so the fight was moved to Las Vegas. "Mentally, I had to be ready. I was [mentally] defeated. 'Man, what if I get hurt?'" he says. "So many things going through your mind."

He had it repaired, but it's been an ongoing issue. In 2018, he was forced to withdraw from his proposed bout with Gervonta "Tank" Davis, a budding superstar with dynamite in his fists. It was set to be one of the biggest fights of his career—and with a great payday. "Because in the back of my head, I knew it might be my last fight. If I don't get cleared, they're going to red-flag me. That's it. I told me wife, 'Babe, let me just get in this fight,'" he says.

He'd been cleared by his doctor but felt some discomfort in training camp. His wife pushed him to go for a second opinion. He wanted to wait until after the fight, but his wife said, "'You might go blind. You're crazy. Think about us. Think about your children.'"

"That's when you know you've got a real one—you've got a real wife," he says. "Any other woman would say, 'Go ahead, cash out, go get that money.'" He knows how lucky he is to have a wife behind him who cares about their family and his health.

Abner was quoted in the lead-up as saying, "I'll go blind. I don't care. Let me fight!" It's a controversial declaration and I ask him about it. I want to know how he prioritizes fighting, the sacrifices, and his family.

"Let me tell you: It must've sounded stupid then, but I remember telling my eye doctor, 'Let me fight this one fight. I don't care if I go blind.' And the doctor got really mad and he said, 'Abner, you're stupid. I'm never gonna let you fight like this,'" Abner says. "But that was how bad I wanted to fight. I really wanted to fight to fight Gervonta. I know I could beat this guy. I know I could win. I trained really hard this week. I was pretty much done with camp, but things happen for a reason."

ON A CHANCE OPPORTUNITY

Some of the best fighters have had a little bit of luck—and Abner is no different. "Opportunities open all the time," he says. "You've just got to be patient and have faith in God and faith in yourself. Don't give up. Keep grinding, training, interviews here and there."

In 2020, just such an opportunity came up for him to move into broadcasting. After a television appearance on *Inside PBC Boxing* (Premier Boxing Champions) on Fox with Shawn Porter, he got a call from Stephen Espinoza at Showtime Sports. He thought Espinoza might be calling him offering him a fight, but it was for a commentary job instead.

Abner had a number of thoughts going through his head, especially because he'd dyed his hair pink during his boxing layoff. "The first thing I thought about was about my dad and my family and the basics: 'Do not let go of an opportunity. Take advantage of opportunities,'" he says. "If I say 'No,' I may not get this opportunity again. So I said, 'Yeah, yeah, of course. When do you need me?'"

But he had to come clean: "'Just one little detail: I have pink hair.'" Fortunately, Espinoza laughed. "He says, 'With your personality, you can pull it off. You're good. We'll see you out here.'" He did the show as a test run, then another, and then they offered him a job.

I tell Abner how impressed I am that he's able to make these career changes so fluidly and recognize what drives him. His desire ultimately doesn't change, but his goals might. He's driven and he prepares for commentating the way he does for fights. He relates it to the lesson he learned when he was 18. "Drive changes every time, every day, with different circumstances," he says.

I find this fascinating considering he started boxing without a love or passion for the sport. We talk a little about how much preparation is involved in calling fights and what it takes to be ready for a broadcast.

"People behind the screen watching and listening think it's easy. It's not easy, man," he says with a laugh, pointing to a huge briefing book on his desk. "They say, 'Man, you got an easy job 'cuz you know this shit. You box!' But you have no idea how much studying and homework I have to do. I don't know all these fighters and their backgrounds. I know boxing, but I need to know their story too. It's a lot of homework, but I take it with the same desire, same passion, as wanting to become good at it. If I was good at boxing, well, guess what, now I'm going to be good at commentating."

ON HIS FUTURE IN BOXING

I have to ask him the obvious question—the one that's on my mind, especially after his long layoff: Do you want to fight again?

You can tell this is a question he's answered before and you can tell that he's not done with his championship journey. "I do. I do, but the desire changes now," he says. He feels he's accomplished many of his goals. He's won multiple championships in different divisions and he's made his money. "I'm stable. My family is good. I got a good job," he says. "People ask, 'Why would you want to fight again?' I don't have to."

But any fighter understands what he's saying. "I'm not doing it for the money," he says, to be clear. "I want to go out on my shield. I want to give the people one more fight. I want to give myself one more fight. People think of Abner as the fighter that got injured. I want people to see me fight again—the Abner that won that last fight against that tough fighter. I want to come back. I know I still have a lot left in me. I have a lot left to give."

He notes that Anthony Dirrell is 37 years old and still fighting undercards. I point out that I'll turn 38 in March 2022. "It sounds wrong when you say 'If he can do it, I can do it,'" he says. "But if you really put your work, your heart, your mind to it, when you look at these good fighters, it's like, 'Man, why are these guys so good?' If you look at most of these great fighters, they really eat, sleep, drink boxing as a sport."

ON HIS LAYOFF & THE MEDIA

One torn retina is very often a career-ending injury in boxing, let alone two. While he was able to defy the odds and return in 2013, making a comeback from that kind of injury is nearly unheard of. Abner and I wanted to be in the ring our entire careers, but we've had similar layoff issues outside our control. I know how hard layoffs were for me. I ask him how he's been dealing with his time off.

"It was hard, man," he says, serious. "Asking why is this happening to me again. Another eye surgery again. Any type of surgery is hard, but an eye is different. I had to be facedown for a week because of the procedure. Not being able to run or train for a month. Not being able to lift anything heavy."

Abner also got lot of backlash in the media and from fans after he withdrew from the Davis fight. When a fight is called off, pundits love to speculate and they nearly always get it wrong. He had to deal with the blowback on top of the surgery. "You're getting so much bullshit," he says, frustrated just remembering it. "I was getting so much backlash. 'Abner is scared. Abner didn't want to fight Tank. Abner is a pussy. Abner faked this.'"

He's mystified why anyone would think he'd fake a torn retina. Other injuries would be so much easier if he'd wanted to get out of the fight. "I could say I pulled my hamstring. Twisted my ankle. Anything but my eye."

Some commentators speculated he was scared, which makes it clear they have no idea what drives fighters to get in the ring. "Something that I've been doing my whole life and I was in my prime," he says." I just fought Léo Santa Cruz. I'm proud I was first person to call Tank out. Nobody wanted to fight him then. I saw there was an opportunity to beat this young kid. Not seasoned, not mature at the time, not centered. I wanted to take advantage of that opportunity and exploit him on that."

Abner's still working through medical clearances to find out if he'll ever be able to fight professionally again. It's a different kind of fight. "I am still overcoming. I still haven't fought. I'm still going over it," he says. "I'm waiting to see if I get the clearance or not. It's not all sweet on the other side. You may see me on my social media smiling—and my passion is boxing. And I really want to do one more fight."

Knowing firsthand the challenges of a layoff, I ask what got him through the hard times. "Honestly, I'm not too sure I've gotten through it yet. I'm still dealing with it," he says. "I'm not gonna lie, during the first year, I kind of picked up drinking," he says. "My first year was so tough. I had no fight. I had nothing. What am going to do? I can't be on TV because I had an eye patch. My eye was messed up. As a man, I just felt so insecure. Just dealing with so much."

We talk about overcoming the challenges and the importance of seeking outside help. I share that during one of my layoffs, I sought professional help for bouts of depression. When your life has been professional boxing and you're off because of circumstances outside your control, the insecurity can set in. Once I started fighting again, I got help again. It's been a big part of my mental preparation.

Abner agrees—and he's sought help—but his clearance to box remains an uncertainty. "I had my wife pushing me [to get help]. But it's something that's hard to get through. I still haven't gotten my clearance. There's still an insecurity in me. I'm scared."

ON ADVICE TO HIS YOUNGER SELF

I ask him what I've asked nearly all the champions: If they could go back in time and give advice to a younger version of themselves, what would they say? Abner thinks for a minute.

"I'd say, 'Damn! I'm proud of you!' Look what I'm doing. Look what I've accomplished. I'm a high school dropout from the 9th or 10th grade. I don't really have the education. I get along with my kids so well. They say, 'Dad, you're a high school dropout, but Dad, I'm so proud of you!' Everyone from the neighborhood says, 'Champ, I'm proud of you!' and I say, 'Guess what—I'm proud myself!'"

We talk about how some failed boxers are bitter, while others can't let go. I tell Abner I love talking to guys who're happy with what they've accomplished. Talking to other people like that makes me happy.

"We tend to not realize what happiness really is. Some people think it's being rich and successful, being famous. For them, that's being happy. For others, happiness is just being healthy and little things like having a roof," he says. "Once you realize that you're really blessed, be happy. Be thankful."

SERGIO MORA

Boxer, analyst
Status: Retired
Weight classes: Light middleweight, middleweight
Ring name: The Latin Snake
Hometown: East Los Angeles, California

CHAMPIONSHIPS
· WBC light middleweight title (2008)

HIGHLIGHTS
· First winner of NBC's *The Contender* (2005)

The Contender was a prime-time reality TV series showcasing young boxing talent that first aired in 2005. The fighters lived together and trained to fight one another in a tournament to win $1 million. As they got to be friends (or enemies), they never knew who they'd draw in each round. As one could imagine, it provided ample opportunities for TV drama.

The series was a huge deal for young fight fans like me. It legitimized boxing by airing it on mainstream national television for the first time in more than a decade. It also gave young, hungry fighters a huge chance to skip the line and get national exposure early in their careers. And there was the $1 million payday for the tournament winner. Aside from the obvious benefits to the fighters themselves, it was a great way to let the public see how boxers prepare for fights and the significant difficulties associated with working up the rankings.

I was a fan of many of the fighters who were favored to win the tournament. Sergio Mora, who starred in the first season, was a bit of a dark horse because he wasn't as well known as some of the show's favorites. His aggressive personality and brash confidence made him a standout character immediately. As he knocked off the higher-ranked members of the show, it became apparent that "The Latin Snake" wasn't someone to underestimate. Sergio went on to win the tournament— a precursor to his dream of winning a world title.

Sergio has since retired and become a highly respected boxing analyst. We've worked together on many occasions and he served as the analyst for several of my fights over the years. Aside from sharing a love for cigars, we also have a number of similarities in our upbringing and growth in the sport—mainly big brothers who beat the crap out of us!

ON HOW IT ALL STARTED

When I ask Sergio how he got his start, he laughs and tells me to do an internet search for "Sergio Mora backyard BBQ boxing." Of course, I already know what I'll find: stories about how he and his friends used to film each other boxing in their backyards with friends.

"We were like the Little Rascals of East LA, where everyone thinks they could fight," he says, laughing. "And I was the youngest. I was the smallest, but I was a little badass at 13 years old."

Maybe it was because he was the youngest, but it made him the toughest too. "I remember we'd throw on the gloves and I knocked one guy out and the next guy and the next guy. I KO'd three guys within like 30 minutes," he says. "I didn't even know what I was doing. I was literally just fighting. I wasn't boxing, but that's what gave me the confidence," he says. "I can knock out bigger, stronger, older fighters. Maybe I should take this serious, so my friend's dad, who was there watching us, took me to a gym the following day and that's how it started."

He credits his older brother, who, like a lot of our older brothers, simply beat us up on a regular basis. "I was just naturally good at fighting, to tell the truth," he says. "And I think that my older brother had a lot to do with it. He was a brutal older brother, man," he says. "I'm not talking about getting punched in the arm," he says, to be clear. "My brother *kicked* me in the head! Whether I liked it or not, he molded me into a tough person and to be able to take more pain than normal."

I tell him I can relate because I had a similar older brother. Both our brothers were five years older and I tell him that mine was a tough street fighter. He kicked my ass—and not just punches on the arm. We'd go to blows! I was getting punched in my face all through my upbringing. I tell Sergio that my brother used to make me street fight—not unlike Sergio's backyard BBQ boxing matches growing up.

Sergio remembers being afraid to fight, but his brother would make him. And when friends would punch him, he had to punch back. "My brother pushed me into these situations to fight and defend myself, and I would literally get punched in the face and just stand still not doing anything because I didn't want to fight. It wasn't in me to fight." Still, he learned to fight back and credits his older brother, who was known as a "bully beater": the guy who beat up the bullies. "Everyone in my neighborhood respected my brother—everyone at school and high school and middle school. But I wasn't that bad," he says, grinning.

ON EARLY INFLUENCES

I ask him how he got his start in boxing and who inspired him when he finally got into a boxing gym. Sergio's family grew up watching Mexican boxer Julio César Chávez, but I wondered who else he'd watched as he developed his own style.

While he ultimately wouldn't settle on Chávez's style, he loved what Chávez could do in the ring. "He's really a great fighter," he says. "The first fighter where I saw what he did to the masses. He pulled nonfans in and [I could see] how he made a brutal sport beautiful. He brought a whole country together and didn't even speak English, and Americans loved him."

Chávez would show a young Sergio what an athlete could do inside and outside the ring, but "once I actually did start watching boxing, Sugar Ray Leonard and Roberto Durán were my favorites."

"You know, I love the flashing the speed of Sugar Ray Leonard, how he looked like a pretty boy," he says. "He would come into the ring winking. He was the golden boy from the Olympics. But then, you had Roberto Durán, who was all tough guy. As a guy from the street, you know, I looked up to meanness, not prettiness, so it was a mixture of both of them."

He found that as he got into boxing and began to study their styles, he understood them even better. "I realized if I fight like Durán, my career is not going to last, but if I stick and move and try to fight pretty, I might have something, so Sugar was really my inspiration," Sergio says.

I ask him what gave him that early drive to work hard and overcome obstacles—and to keep fighting and improving in the boxing gym. I ask him what he tapped into in a controlled boxing environment when he was training and preparing for real fights. Everyone has those tough moments, but I'm interested in how he moved past them. Again, Sergio credits his brother—or, at least, his desire to prove to everyone he could fight. He also feels it was pride—and a fierce competitiveness.

"It was maybe the little brother syndrome. I wanted to impress my brother. I wanted to impress the people that were older than me. I wanted to maybe prove something to myself ultimately," he says. "It was just basically not backing down from a physical challenge and not backing down from a fight."

He experienced many of the competitive feelings that all fighters have when they step in the ring. "If I get a bloody nose, I want to bloody my opponent's nose. If I got beat up one day, I'm going to come back and want to do better the next day, so there was this inner competitiveness of wanting to prove it to myself and prove it to the people around me," he says.

And with that competitiveness and desire to learn and win came the ability to stick with boxing. Sergio was fortunate that as he stuck with it, he improved and learned he was pretty good. His attitude was, "Just give me another shot and another shot, and finally, when you do start kicking these guys' asses, you realize, okay, well, that's going to move me on to the next challenge, and then basically you just go from one challenge to the next to the next, and then you realize you're better than most and you make a career out of it."

I wonder when he understood he could actually be a professional boxer and make a living. When did he know it was what he wanted to do? He knows it must have been fate because most young boxers don't have all the pieces fall into place so easily. But he knew he had it in him to succeed pretty early on. "Everything lined up perfectly. Like fate had it worked perfectly for me," Sergio says. "You know there's other fighters that always say, 'Well, I never had support. I never had people helping me. I never had money.' Boxing's not for everyone, but I could do it."

In those days, young boxers started sparring in just a few weeks, "which is a no-no nowadays," Sergio notes. "I was sparring a guy that'd been there for over a year and he was the bully of the gym. He didn't kick my ass, so I held my own my first session. Second day, I did a little bit better, and by the third session, I was beating him up. That felt good, being the bully-beater."

He describes the idea that every gym has an "alpha," and once you can beat everyone in your own gym, you branch out to others to see who else you can beat. "It just feels good to go from your gym to your city to your state to the regionals to the national level," he says.

ON *THE CONTENDER* SERIES

By 2000, Sergio turned professional and had a fast start right out of the gate. With a 10-0 record, he signed on as a contestant for the first season of NBC's reality show *The Contender* in 2005. It was a huge opportunity and Sergio knew there were a lot of eyes on him. On the show, he had the opportunity to meet and train with one of his heroes: Sugar Ray Leonard. I ask him how the whole thing came about.

Sergio was training for a fight on NBC when he heard about the show. Knowing they were looking for young, talented fighters to work with Leonard, he was thinking, "Wait a minute. 'Young, undefeated, fighter coming up, has a great story to tell.' That's me! Where do I sign up!"

He was sparring with Fernando Vargas at the time and Vargas took a group of fighters to audition. "He cut the line," Sergio says. "I remember it was a long line to get there and we went to the front of the line." They sparred in front of Sylvester Stallone and some of the producers, and Sergio clearly impressed them. "And the rest is history," he says, noting that getting that sort of exposure early "opened all the doors that the professional game wasn't opening at the time."

I want to know more about the pressures of a reality show, especially when you're taken out of your element. You're in a competition but taken away from your training routine and coaches, plus you're forced to live with cameras constantly rolling. It seems like a tremendous amount of pressure. Professional athletes don't always excel when they're taken out of their normal and natural environments. I'm good at knowing what I know, I tell Sergio. I ask him what helped him get past that and win.

"It's funny you say that, man, because I loved being sequestered," he says. "We were isolated, like in quarantine before quarantine was even heard of because of the cameras." However, he didn't love every aspect of it. "We were fighting and training and living with the guys that were potentially put in front of us to fight," he says. "I didn't like that situation, having to train in front of the guys I'm going to fight, but I loved everything else."

He laughs, marveling at what an amazing experience it was for a kid from East LA. "I loved the food, I loved the attention, I loved the great equipment! I mean, brand-new equipment. We would have massages, we had access to Jacuzzies, we had a cook, we had a barber, real training, and recovery!"

He appreciates that he was young and had no obligations at home, which made it easier for him—along with his friend Alfonso Gómez, another East LA kid who was a contestant on the show. The other contestants were adults with adult connections. For them, the isolation was harder.

"I missed my trainer," he says. "But the other people, they're parents, so they miss their kids. They're married, so they miss their wives. They had some attachment that they were missing." He had no attachments. "We're like on vacation doing what we love, so I think that was a big positive for us, not having kids, not having a family, not having responsibility."

For him, it was "paradise, doing something that we love and potentially make a million bucks. So it was a win, win, win, win for us," he says. "We were guys who grew up with nothing and were given everything."

Some of the contestants on that first season went on to become successful professional fighters. Ishe Smith, his quarterfinal opponent, would go on to win a world title. Jesse Brinkley, his semifinal contender, was a tough fighter and an experienced journeyman. And Peter Manfredo Jr., his opponent in the final bout, was a favorite to win. Sergio was most definitely an underdog fighting an opponent with a lot more experience. He'd defeat Manfredo in a unanimous decision to win the show's prize money, then defeat Manfredo a second time in a rematch eight months later.

I ask him about coming in as the underdog and moving up through the ranks, beating fighters who were better known with more experience. I also wanted to learn how it felt knowing that winning would be life-changing professionally and personally.

"Destiny. Destiny got involved there," he says. "Everyone wants to just talk about hard work, but no, there's destiny too, man." Sergio had fought Manfredo in the amateurs and knew he was a tough fighter. He'd also sparred with Smith before they were both cast. He felt destiny had a hand in all of it.

With Smith, "we sparred in Las Vegas," Sergio says. "I remember he hit me with the right hand and rocked me. I'm like, 'Damn, this guy, he hurt me.' Jesse Brinkley, that's the guy I was worried about. I faced the toughest opponents, but if you're going to win a tournament, you have to go through the toughest. There's no easy way to winning. I fought the best and I won the tournament for good reason."

ON WINNING A WORLD TITLE

In 2008, Sergio fought Vernon Forrest for the WBC light middleweight title. Forrest was one of the greats of that generation and had held the title for a year. Sergio was a 4-1 underdog going into the fight. For Sergio, it was a potentially huge win. I always love to hear what was going through a champion's mind when they hear "And the *new* … ."

Sergio says he'd sparred with Forrest once. "He wanted to kill me and he hated me in sparring," he says of the sparring match about a year before they fought. "I did well against him. I want to say I got the better of Vernon Forrest, but I was in super great shape and I think that maybe he was just starting camp. But whatever the reason, I did well."

"My trainer was like, 'Do you know what you just did?' so that gave me the confidence," he says. He knew he had what it would take. He was going into a championship fight with a 20-0 record against a great fighter and he knew he'd worked hard for it. "It was all lined up to do something great," he says. "And that's what I live for and that's what I wanted, and maybe I didn't want to do it against Vernon Forrest, but the opportunity came up and I couldn't pass it up."

Sergio would go on to defeat Forrest in June, winning the WBC light middleweight championship, with Forrest going on to say he'd underestimated Sergio's abilities. They had a rematch in September and Forrest defeated Sergio, winning his title back and showing why he'd been such a dominant fighter for so long.

ON CUTTING WEIGHT

Sergio had trouble making weight for the September 2008 rematch against Forrest and he wouldn't fight again until 2010. After a win against Calvin Green, he faced Sugar Shane Mosley and had weight troubles again. (The Mosley fight would end in a controversial split decision draw.) Six months later, he'd lose his first of two fights against Brian Vera.

Most people don't know how complicated and difficult it is for fighters to make a contracted weight before a fight. If a fighter comes in even a pound or two over, they face fines and other penalties, including fight cancellation and title forfeiture. It's serious business.

Today, fighters use specific nutrition regimens and training strategies designed to help them lose weight while still maintaining the energy to train. But fight week can still be a brutal time to try to lose that last couple pounds of water weight. Some fighters have more issues than others, but cutting weight is something that every fighter has a plan for but dreads.

Sergio is honest about his problems with his weight, acknowledging they cost him a championship. But he's also clear that once he got his weight under control, it helped him keep his career alive. "Now that my fighting days are over, I can be 100% honest and say that I wasn't disciplined," he says about his weight swings between fights.

He says a lot of it had to do with how easy boxing and training came to him. "I was so naturally gifted and so naturally disciplined once camp started that those six to eight weeks in camp, I would train my ass off," he says. "But guess what I would do the three, four months that I was out of camp? I would indulge. And let's just keep it at that."

His ability to indulge meant he could gain 30 to 35 pounds in between fights. And because of his six-foot frame and body type, the weight gain wasn't noticeable. He didn't look fat, "so it's not like people were looking at me saying, 'Hey, man, you need to get in the gym.'"

He learned a hard lesson when the Forrest rematch was scheduled just three months after the first fight. He'd gained more than 30 pounds. "They gave me five and a half weeks to train, and I lost 28 pounds in five weeks," he says. He lost eight pounds on the day of the weigh-in, but "I had nothing," he says of his empty tank. He learned a valuable lesson. "That's the discipline of being a professional, and after that fight, after I lost my title, I never went past 15 pounds ever again."

Today, as nutrition experts, we professional athletes have to fine-tune our bodies in training and between fights. Huge swings in weight simply aren't healthy. But even 10 years ago, athletes were learning the hard way. Sergio got serious about his weight in between fights and it made a difference.

"That's the reason I think I extended my career another 10 years after that because of not blowing up and ballooning and fluctuating in weight," he says. "But it took me losing a title and leaving a lot of money on the table to finally get disciplined and realize that this is a something you've got to take serious—your health *and* your weight."

I ask him how he cut eight pounds on weigh-in day. "I almost fainted. I remember my trainer almost couldn't bear watching because I almost fainted in the sauna," he says, laughing. One popular technique is dehydration to the point where you can't even sweat anymore. "You know how it is when the sweatsuit's not working anymore and you have no sweat left, there's only one thing to do—and that's the sauna. It was just the worst."

While sometimes cutting a couple pounds on weigh-in day is necessary, it's not realistic to think you can cut significant weight the day before a fight and then still perform in the ring. "I don't recommend it to any fighter," he says. "I mean, maybe the last pound, the last two pounds in the sauna. I just think there's a right way and wrong way of making weight."

In terms of preparing for a professional fight, weight is just something you have to plan for, like any other physical aspect of your fight, he says. "The fight is won and lost on the scale and in the gym. And if you already go into a big fight thinking about, 'Yeah, I made weight the wrong way—maybe I left it in the gym. I don't feel as strong. Maybe I need to take these early rounds easy to see how my body is going to react,' you've already lost in your mind. You're already behind for half the fight."

ON DANIEL JACOBS

In 2015 and 2016, Sergio would fight Daniel Jacobs for the WBA middleweight title twice—and lose both times. While Sergio had come up to the regular middleweight weight class, Jacobs still seemed like a substantially larger guy, especially when Sergio got in the ring with him for the first time. I've worked with Jacobs personally and he's a physically big guy for a middleweight. They looked like they were in different weight classes. I ask Sergio about his mindset going into his matches with Jacobs.

"I remember when I got into the ring with him, my trainer behind me must not have thought I could hear him because he says, "Holy shit. Look how *big* he is!" he says. But Sergio is very clear: "I was so ready and prepared and confident and strong. And I knew that he was struggling making weight."

Sergio alludes to the fact he knew Jacobs was struggling with weight because he recognized the signs from experience. "He didn't show to the press conference. I knew he was making weight." Even still, Sergio felt he had an opportunity to win. "I had to take the fight to him, but it was an opportunity I couldn't pass at that point in my career. I was 37 years old. They offered me, you know, good money and it was for a world title. I couldn't say 'No.'"

The fight was an edge-of-your-seat shoot-out, with both fighters trading knockdowns. It was over, though, when Sergio tore a ligament in his ankle. "I was already in a bad position, and he stepped over me and pushed me down, and I just heard a little snap," he says. "When I got up, I put pressure on it and I said, 'Something's not right here. It's not broken, but something's not right.'" A referee will stop a fight if a fighter can't walk or can't see. Sergio signaled he was injured and the fight was stopped. "I remember I kind of looked at the referee, and he goes 'What?' and I said 'I can't walk,' and he waved [the fight] off."

He faced Jacobs again 13 months later, and the second time around, he didn't feel as good going into the fight. He'd lose again. "I knew that second time around, he was just too big," he says. "I just hoped it was quick and painless." But it wasn't. Sergio would go down three times before the referee stopped the fight in the seventh round.

ON HIS LAST FIGHT

No fighter wants to end their career with two tough losses, especially in championship title fights. But there's always the drive to win another title, to make a comeback. Sergio would take 18 months off and come back to fight Alfredo Angulo in April 2018. I ask him if he knew it would be his last fight or if he made the decision to retire later.

"For the Angulo fight, I didn't know what I had left, so I just wanted to get back to my winning ways and I wanted to get another big shot at another big fight," he says. He had a plan with his promoter that with another one or two big wins, he could have another shot at a title.

Sergio had always prided himself with his footwork. "I made a career out of being fast with my legs," he says. "I took pride in the speed of my footwork, of my angles, of just being able to embarrass guys with movement."

But he experienced something else with Angulo, who's known for his slower, more thoughtful approach. "I was peppering Angulo, thinking, 'I could stop him.' And then the fourth round came around and I had no legs. [Angulo] is painfully slow and I was slowing down with him, and that was a scary feeling," Sergio says.

By the later rounds of the fight, he was bargaining with himself. "I remember the sixth, seventh, eighth round, thinking, 'If I get out of this, this is my last fight.'" He realized that in his head, he was done. "In my head, I'm already thinking, '*If* I get out of this.'"

From there, he was just praying for each round to end. "Please let the fight be over, let me win, and I'm done. This is my last fight." In the end, he won in a split decision, but he knew he'd made an important choice.

"I knew it was a wrap," he says. "I got no more legs. I'm done. I don't want to fight anymore."

ON REALIZING YOUR STRENGTHS

We talk about how hard it is to make the decision to retire. It takes a lot of strength, pride, and courage to acknowledge that you can't physically keep up anymore. Then it's hard to follow through. We both know fighters who should be done, but they can't say "No" to the money, the attention, or the quest. Sergio was smart enough and courageous enough to understand when he was done. We talk about how fighters can learn from his experience and listen to that voice that says, "It's time."

Sergio believes you have to realize your strengths. "Most guys that fight past their prime, either they've got power, they've got size, or they've got a lot of experience," he says. "That can actually get them through the later stages of their career, but when you just rely on your legs, speed, and footwork, I don't have that anymore. What am I gonna beat these guys with?"

He says it's not heart that gives fighters courage for the next stage of their career—it's smarts. "It takes a lot of brains, intelligence, knowing you're just going to get hurt. You got money in the bank. You know you did well. What are you doing this for? Let's see if we can transition this to something else."

Sergio has made a great example of how to continue a successful career in boxing doing something else. He now works full time as one of the best boxing analysts in the business. We joke that it's something we have in common in addition to both having older brothers who used to beat us up. I ask him what the change has been like and what challenges he's found in this new stage of his career.

It all comes back to brains—and that legendary Sergio Mora confidence. "We know who we can be, we take calculated risks, we strive for greatness, and we put in the work," he says about how we both view working as commentators. "But it all comes down to making the right decisions."

Sergio would say that work ethic would also be part of what makes for a good transition. Making the right decisions and having a good head on your shoulders make a bright future for anyone.

ON ADVICE TO HIS YOUNGER SELF

I ask Sergio a question that's fascinated me throughout all these interviews: What advice would he give his younger self if he could go back in time? Many boxers say they wouldn't change a thing, but Sergio is more pragmatic. He has a fast answer when I ask what he'd tell that 13-year-old kid boxing in the backyard.

"Go to college. Get an education. Because putting all your eggs in this basket?" he says, tapping his desk. "Chances are you're not going to make it."

He acknowledges what a large role *The Contender* played in his early career. "I got lucky with a reality show. If that reality show didn't come around, I wouldn't be in the position I'm in," he says. "I'm not prideful enough to say I could have found another way. No, I got lucky."

He recognizes that having boxing talent would've given him some opportunities, but he also knows that an education would've made some kind of difference in his life. "So I would tell myself, 'Box, but don't put everything into boxing. Just get an education and, you know, get some skills.'" He laments that he doesn't even know how to work a computer. We laugh, but he's clear in his message. "If boxing didn't work out, what was I going to do with my life? So that's what I would tell myself when I was kicking my friends' asses," he says with a laugh. "Yeah, you're a tough guy. Yeah, you could probably make some money here, but why don't we learn to use the computer too?"

ALICIA NAPOLEON

Boxer
Status: Active
Weight classes: Super middleweight, middleweight
Ring name: The Empress
Hometown: Long Island, Lindenhurst, New York

CHAMPIONSHIPS
· WBA super middleweight title (2018)
· WBC silver super welterweight title (2016)

HIGHLIGHTS
· Co-owner of the Overthrow Gym in NYC

Alicia made her pro boxing debut shortly after I won my world title in 2014. I saw her fight live at the B.B. King's in NYC and I immediately took notice. Her entrance was electric and she had a flair that you rarely see in women's boxing. She won via a first-round TKO that night, showcasing her aggressive and ruthless stopping power—another rarity in women's boxing. And one more reason I'm a fan? She's also from Long Island.

She smiles big any chance she gets, but come fight time, she has a take-no-prisoners approach. She's never afraid to take a few shots so she can dish out her own. Over the years, we've seen each other at one gym or another. I've always enjoyed talking about how we Long Islanders deserve more recognition on the world stage.

I talk to her while she multitasks, feeding the newest addition to her training team: her daughter, Alina. It's fitting because Alicia has been such an advocate for equality in sports for women. We chat about boxing, the will to win, family, and careers. She's a New Yorker (no doubt about that!) and a boxer and a mom—all with the same spirit and attitude. She's an accomplished fighter, singer, artist, and supporter of women in sports. On top of all that, she's a champion.

ON THE BEGINNING

Alicia tells me about her love of entertaining. Before boxing, it was music. "I didn't know I was going to become a fighter," she says. "I originally wanted to become a professional singer and a performer. I ended up being a performer—but on a different stage, which is awesome."

She loved sports growing up, but her first love was baseball. It was the sport that helped her realize how much she loved being an athlete. But she began to realize something wasn't right. "I loved it so much. I wanted to be a professional baseball player when I grew up. I think that's what really started my fight for equality."

She started to notice that the opportunities for women as professional athletes were different—and it didn't seem fair. "I really did not comprehend why women did not have the opportunities men had," she says. "At five years old, it was crushing to hear that I couldn't be something I wanted to be."

As she gravitated toward other sports, she tried everything from cheerleading to ballet to karate. "I loved the contact sports," she says. She found wrestling and she joined the team.

"I did it because I overheard a coach talking about how girls shouldn't be on the wrestling team. The coach was mad that a girl tried to sign up and I did it purposely because I'm like, 'It's not fair. We should have a chance too.' So I signed up to try out for the wrestling team," she says, flashing her trademark smile as she tells the story.

"They made the girls take a physical fitness test that the boys didn't even have to do to prove that we were strong enough," Alicia says. "So we did it. I got a standing ovation!"

She still keeps in touch with her former coach. "My coach loves me now and he follows me in boxing and he's like, 'She was on my wrestling team,' but he doesn't know that I know what he said." She takes great pride in this early triumph, as she should. It was the first of many fights for equality— and born of the attitude typical to many athletes today: Sports should be open to anyone who's good, regardless of gender.

"I just always liked the physical and mental challenge," she says of most sports. "And I always like to do things that women aren't known to do. I just always believed in equality and being able to do what you love, and your dreams shouldn't be shut down for nothing or no one."

She has a strong belief that women can be beautiful while still being tough and working hard. "I shouldn't have to fit in a box just because I'm a girl," she says. "I love being a woman, and I love being feminine and girly, and I love being an athlete, and I love kicking butt."

Having seen Alicia fight in person, I can vouch for the fact that she can kick butt. I call her "beauty and the beast" because she has a flashy and aggressive style, but she also has something that many female fighters don't have: power. She's looking for KOs and has the goods to deliver. I talk to her about her fighting style and ask her when boxing became part of the picture for her. "I always liked boxing since I was really little," she says. "I remember seeing [Mike] Tyson on TV and, you know, my grandfather and my father watching the fights. And, you know, living out on eastern Long Island, there was no boxing."

Still, it was something she wanted to do and some friends knew where she could go. "I remember sitting at lunch with a group of friends and I remember saying 'Oh my gosh, I want to box so bad. I wish I could box,'" she says. One of her guy friends knew of a boxing gym a few towns over. She discovered Memorial Boxing Club during her senior year of high school and started training with well-known Long Island coach Mike Murphy.

There were several trainers at the gym, including "an older woman, Maria, who was helping me," she remembers. "I couldn't even jump rope!"

It was her first lesson in boxing: Even though you're an athlete in another sport, boxing involves different physical demands and a specific kind of fitness. You don't have to be a great athlete to be a great boxer, but Alicia is a great athlete and that stands out from a lot of the other women in her weight class. She caught up quickly.

Murphy soon had her sparring with another girl who was already competing at top amateur levels. Alicia had never been in the ring before. She realized it was a test—that he wanted to see what she had. She showed him heart.

"She gave me a bloody nose and we just went at it, and I just remember [thinking], 'Oh my God, I can't quit. I don't care how hard this girl hits me, I just want to kill her. I just want to just go hard and go all the way,'" Alicia says. "I'll never forget that experience. It was awesome. It was liberating."

She credits Murphy with that realization. "He knew and I knew that I could do this and I was built for this." She was 18. From there, she went on to fight in the Golden Gloves. She remembers her first fight. "It was a dog-eat-dog fight—and boy did I just blow my steam the first two rounds and died out the last two," she says, smiling at the memory. "And everybody was just, 'Holy crap, we've never seen so much heart in that ring'—and that's all everybody would always say."

She had to learn how important heart was in boxing and why it mattered that she had so much. "I really didn't understand that because it's hard to understand that. You just are who you are," Alicia says. "You don't think anything of it, but now being in the sport for going on 16 to 17 years, I understand what heart means. I can recognize it now—who has it and who doesn't have it."

She recognizes the value in those early lessons, even though she lost that first fight. "It's just cool what you learn over the years and learn about yourself," she says. But the spirit inside her was there. "It just made me want to do better." And like many fighters, she was scared.

Some fighters worry about getting hit. Others worry about a knockdown. But they all experience fear when getting in the ring for the first time. "It was scary stepping in the ring because I was so scared about losing," she says. "I didn't want to be humiliated. That was my fear—of being humiliated. I never had a fear of getting hurt; I couldn't care less. I felt invincible."

She talks about how she tapped into her inner confidence. It's one of the reasons she loves boxing. "I was scared to be defeated and embarrassed, so I just wanted to keep going and going and going and going until I just beat that fear," she says.

Alicia stuck to it and kept progressing. As she fought, she discovered how to turn her fear into motivation. From her experience as an athlete, she knew she could tap into more. "I overcame it and was able to channel it. I really wanted to find my confidence in myself and in my ability, and that's one of the things I love about the sport." She credits boxing for helping her find that confidence and belief in herself.

ON RAGE

I ask her about an interview I read where she talks about tapping into her rage. It seems like a constructive way to deal with a destructive emotion— but also risky. Boxers need control, and those who rely on too much rage and anger have to learn to channel it. Boxing wins fights, not anger. "Since I was a kid, anything bad, anything ugly, anything that hurt me, anything that made me upset, I always found an outlet to transform it into something beautiful," Alicia says. This includes her art, poetry, singing, or sports.

She says she was a "bigger girl" in school. "I had curves," she says, with "a lot of flavor and body." So whether she was dealing with body image issues, kids in school, or even arguments with her parents, she learned how to channel her emotions. "I would transform it," she says of her negative emotions. "I would take it and make something beautiful out of it."

Alicia describes her family as "full blooded Italians." She grew up with an extended Sicilian family, which meant that grandparents and other relatives were sometimes quick to offer their own advice about a girl's body, mind, and role in life. When it came to grandparents from different cultures and different generations, they sometimes showed their love with criticism, teasing, and put-downs. She often heard that her legs were too big, she was chubby, or she wasn't smart enough to succeed.

By the time she was 14—a tough age for any girl—her parents were going through a divorce. "They went through a really hard time, my parents, and when your home crumbles like that, it's really hard to feel any sort of stability, safety, love," she says. She has an amazing empathy for her parents, especially her mother, who battled through some difficult times. "I really stepped in and had to take care of my siblings as if I was their parent for many years." It made boxing the perfect outlet for her pent-up emotional energy.

ON BOXING AS THERAPY

Alicia talks about boxing as a way to release her negative feelings when a poem or painting didn't work. "Boxing was a release for me. It was therapy," she says. "When I found the gym, it was better because I could just try to break the bag or take it out in a sparring match or whatever or do something positive."

"I really needed to get physical and boxing was definitely my therapy. And a place for me to transform all that doubt, fear, rejection, brokenness. I mean the horrible things that kids were saying, school, and the feeling like you're never good enough, you're not pretty enough, you're not popular enough. It was just a place that I could find some internal healing," she says of finding boxing. "I wanted to beat my way out of that dark feeling and find my worthiness in the sport."

It's taken a lot of time and hard work, but she feels like her journey in boxing has helped her heal, especially once she turned professional. She has a place where she's recognized for doing something she loves—and that she's really good at!

"I found the place where I finally could love myself," Alicia says. She gets a little emotional talking about the incredible journey she's been on. Her baby has fallen asleep in her arms. "I love boxing. It's my life and I miss it so much being a mom," she says of her layoff. Her daughter was born in 2021. "I feel like I came full circle for myself in this sport. I can't wait to get back in the ring and come full circle and do it all over again at a better, higher level."

We talk about the pressures that many fighters have faced growing up and how that's transformed itself into excellence. Outsiders think it's a refuge for kids to keep them off the streets, but in reality, it's a refuge for kids and adults of all ages and all levels. As adults, we use fight sports as outlets to express emotions and overcome pain. Everything takes discipline and sacrifice, but fighters sometimes tend to make things hard just so they can overcome.

ON GOING PRO

I ask her about turning professional. It's not a decision that's right for everyone—or one that fighters make lightly. It can be a big adjustment for someone who's been successful at the amateur level.

"I was trying to find myself for a long time. Like, 'Who am I? What do I want to do,'" she says. She was in school studying fashion. She was also actively recording and trying to make a singing career happen. But she encountered the same body image issues in fashion that she had growing up.

"I hit so many brick walls," she says. "'You're not skinny enough. You need to work on new things.' Mainly, I didn't fit the mold with my body," especially in the early 2000s, when a thin body type was popular. Not to mention the US singing tour that fell apart when her tour manager walked off with the money she raised.

She was still boxing—but not seriously—and she'd found she didn't love fighting in the amateurs. With 27 amateur fights, she'd made a name for herself but was starting to feel restricted by the rules. "In the amateurs, I never felt that I fit in it. It didn't feel like me," she says. "I mean, it's important to be an amateur because you really learn the sport, you learn the ring, you learn how it feels to be under pressure."

But at 27, she knew she needed to make a choice about her future—and she decided to turn pro. "I needed to make a decision. Either I'm going to continue this sport and I'm going to take it further and I'm going to really try to go all the way," she says, or else she needed to go another direction. "So I just jumped. I took a leap of faith."

It was one that paid off. "And I know nobody really believed in me either, but I knew there was something inside of me. I knew I could do it. I just knew I could be something—and be something big."

ON THE FUNDAMENTALS

Alicia had been working with coach Danny Nicholas, whom she credits with teaching her the essential techniques. "He was a godsend because if it wasn't for him, I would not know the fundamentals of boxing the way I do," she says. "The most important part of any champion are the fundamentals. If you don't have the fundamentals correctly, you have nothing."

As she committed to a professional career, she worked with Nicholas to learn the techniques before he turned her over to coach Leon Taylor to learn the higher-level skills of professional boxing. It was invaluable training.

She notes that working with a higher-level trainer would've been impossible before she had the knowledge Nicholas gave her. "I can comprehend everything he wants to instill in me now, which is such a great feeling," Alicia says. "It's like the blinders and the blindfold was taken off of me, and I could see in the ring, and I could understand what's happening, and I could think now."

She still thinks about her decision to leave the fashion world and give up her singing career, but she's glad she fell in love with boxing. "I was just at a point in my life where I know that I'm not going to work in the fashion industry. Music's not going the way I wanted to go, and I had to make a choice between music and boxing," she says. "At the end of the day, I chose boxing, and I chose to really work on that craft and put 110% into it. I'm really focused to become great."

ON WOMEN IN BOXING

We talk a little about women in boxing. They're becoming more recognized every year, with international and national networks featuring women's bouts more frequently. We talk about women leading the charge, like Heather Hardy, Katie Taylor, and herself. "I just jumped without really knowing what was going to happen," she says. "I saw an opportunity for women before it even happened. I just had a feeling like it was going to shift."

Boxing as a sport for women is poised to really take off, which makes Alicia's planned comeback even more exciting. "I hope nobody forgot about me," she says.

Alicia's trademarks are her style and performance. She knows how to handle herself in front of a crowd and present herself with a flair at everything from weigh-ins to fight night. She's known for her hairstyles and boxing kit, which she designs herself.

"That's one of the biggest reasons why I wanted to turn pro—because I felt I had my own platform. I was my own soloist. I could be me. I could come out in the outfits and the hair. I could flourish and be me," she says. She credits trainer Danny Nicholas again. "He really helped me believe in the star quality that I had deep inside me. God sent him to water that seed in that season. He was the only one that saw the greatness in me and he really pulled it out, so I owe a lot to him and I want people to know that about Danny."

"Being a strong, fearless woman makes me feel beautiful."

–Alicia Napoleon

ON LOSING

We talk about winning and losing—and why losing can be so important for moving forward. So I have to ask her about her 2016 loss to Tori Nelson. Both fighters were undefeated at the time. "I was extremely confident and I'm ready to take on any challenge, like any other authentic fighter," she says.

But there were the sorts of problems on fight night that any fighter has to work to overcome. A long card with amateur and professional fights, an unheated warehouse, and a late schedule meant she didn't fight until nearly 1 a.m. "I'm starving. I went out there with no cheers. If anything, probably boos because I'm visiting her territory," she says.

"I come out to my music in my outfit and I'm dancing. I shake off the boos and the crowd, and I had my family and friends there. I always have some people with me, but then, you know, Tori comes out with like her 120 belts," she says with a laugh, noting that it seemed like at least that many.

"I knew, like, they thought I was just some flashy girl that was all show who didn't have anything to back it up, but they were surprised because after I got out of that ring, all her fans gave me respect." She lost, but she held her own. There were a couple punches that were hard to recover from, but she never went down. "I'm tough. You can hit me with everything. My heart will outweigh any punch. And I fought her tooth and nail as best I could, and we went all 10 rounds," she says.

After the Nelson fight, she moved on from Nicholas and began training with Taylor. Trainers go through the same pressures fighters do and knowing how to make a move is always difficult. But Alicia knew it was time: She'd learned the fundamentals and was ready to work toward her own world championship. She credits Nicholas with believing in her, even when she struggled to believe in herself as a fighter.

"Isn't it so cool how in this sport people are able to recognize your greatness before you even notice what you had?" she says. "So many people would have so much to say about me, but I had to find it for myself. I had to believe what they saw, even though, like, I felt it—I just I couldn't see it yet."

ON BECOMING WORLD CHAMPION

In 2018, Alicia defeated Femke Hermans for the WBA super middleweight title in a 10-round unanimous decision. Hermans was an undefeated and hungry contender from Belgium who made the long trip to Brooklyn, New York, to try to upset the hometown favorite. "I feel like the lead-up is always more powerful than the victory for some reason," she says.

Alicia tells a story of a pastor praying over her when she was 18 years old. "He told me if I follow my heart that God is going to bless me tremendously. That the world will hear my voice and my name will be in lights," she says. "And when I walked into that arena with my name all over the arena and lights, I said, 'Wow, this is part of that prophecy, but it's just the beginning because I know God has more.'"

Alicia is a woman of faith and feels, like many fighters, that God has a plan for her. "I just felt the Holy Spirit with me and it was just so beautiful to see," she says of the moment. "I'm such a competitive person, and that victory, it was so like, 'Okay, this is the beginning now. This is the first of many. It was like, for a split second, I enjoyed it and then I was like, 'What's next? Who's next?'"

We talk about the emotional release that comes after a major fight. Win or lose, male or female, many fighters find themselves in tears the hours or days after a bout. There's so much work and energy that goes into a fight that it's as if the body or mind has to release it somehow. "I did break down and cry though," she says. "After I walked into the locker room with my husband and when everybody was gone, it was just me and him, I just broke down like a baby."

Alicia would go on to defend her title three times, including a major bout against Hannah Rankin, which was also the first female world championship fight at the Nassau Coliseum in Uniondale, New York. She immediately notes that it's one of her favorite fights. She's lived up to the title of "world" champion and has consistently fought women from all over the world. This was a classic US-versus-UK matchup and both women came to win.

She feels the fight was one of the highlights of her career and is still disappointed that local television affiliates that frequently televise boxing chose not to show the match. "Two world champions, two females, first females in the Coliseum, a local Long Islander—it just doesn't make sense to me," she says.

For her, it was one of those fights that fighters dream about—the match where the discipline, the training, the energy, and a little magic all come together in the ring.

"That was the fight where everything transitioned," she says. "You saw all the training and discipline. I was the sharpest. I was perfect that night and I beat Hannah," she says. She stops, still amazed. "Like, beautifully. It was like a dance. The whole night was a flow—the whole night. It was like I fought in slow motion. I saw everything."

And then there was the fight with Elin Cederroos. Alicia would lose to Cederroos and give up her world championship title in what could have been considered a Fight of the Year candidate. Both women fought with heart, following the ebbs and flows in momentum throughout. When it came down to the scoring, the difference was a knockdown scored by Cederroos in the second round.

Alicia showed heart and grit and everything else it takes to be a champion. While she'd ultimately lose, she showed her skill set, power, and toughness. I tell her that even though it was a loss, it's my favorite fight of hers. She agrees. "Besides Hannah, it's my favorite fight too!" she says, laughing.

Alicia notes how much taller Cederroos was. "She was so big!" she says. "I didn't even realize. I'm only five-five. I'm not that big. She was at least six feet tall. She was a monster! She was solid. Like, her punches didn't hurt me. She was just strong and a little awkward because she was so big."

But she has no regrets about the fight. "If I won that fight, my baby wouldn't be here," she says with her infant daughter still napping in her arms. I ask her why she felt the timing was right.

After the Cederroos fight, she kept calling her manager, asking, "'What's going on? Can I fight? Is there something I can get ready for? I gotta get back in the ring. I've got to get my belts back.' Ideally, I wanted to finish out my career and do as much as I could and then settle down and have her in my late 30s," she says.

But the COVID-19 pandemic changed everything. "Once I saw that we had a pandemic, I was like, 'All right, listen. I lost my belts. Everything shut down. The world is shut down. The sport is shut down. I'm just going to have my baby and enjoy it,'" she says. "I'm going to enjoy resting because I never rest. I'm always hustle, hustle, hustle, hustle. I don't sleep. This is God opening the door for me to have my family. And this is the time I just felt it's time for my baby to come."

ON ADVICE TO HER YOUNGER SELF

Alicia has a way of turning negatives into positives. Losing her title before a major pandemic would be the worst timing for most fighters, but she turned it into an opportunity. With so many unknowns in life and in boxing, she took the leap and she's happy she did. I ask her what advice she might have for her younger self.

"I would go back and tell her 'Listen, kiddo, it's nothing to worry about. You're going to be all right. Believe it or not, you're going to be a world champion,'" she says. "But I feel like if I would tell myself that I might not work as hard." I tell her this is a dilemma many fighters who've answered this question contemplate.

"Maybe I wouldn't tell her she'd be a world champion but just say, 'Listen, you're gonna be fine. Just keep doing what you're doing and keep that faith. And just keep working toward going all the way because all your dreams are going to come. Just don't quit,'" she says.

She adds, "I would tell her, 'You're on the right track. There's many times in life you feel like you're not on the right track.'"

FREDDIE ROACH

Boxing trainer for boxers and MMA pros, former boxer
Status: Active
Weight classes: Super bantamweight, featherweight, super featherweight, lightweight
Ring names: The Choir Boy, Baby Face
Hometown: Los Angeles, California

CHAMPIONSHIPS

· New England featherweight champion (1969)

HIGHLIGHTS

· Trained eight-division world champion Manny Pacquiao, world champion Miguel Cotto, Julio César Chávez Jr., Amir Kahn, and many more
· Seven-time Boxing Writers Association of America Trainer of the Year (2003, 2006, 2008, 2009, 2010, 2013, 2014)
· WBC Lifetime Achievement Award (2008)
· USA Boxing Hall of Famer as fighter, trainer, and manager (2021)
· Member of the International Boxing Hall of Fame, California Boxing Hall of Fame, and Nevada Boxing Hall of Fame
· Named an honorary Philippines citizenship (2009)

Freddie and I go back to 2014, when I defeated his fighter, Ruslan Provodnikov, and then lost to another of his charges, Manny Pacquiao, in back-to-back fights. Needless to say, we spent a lot of time around each other that year. Freddie is a trainer, but he's also a former fighter and forever competitor. He takes his boxers' fights very seriously. In recent years, he and I have stayed in touch and our paths have crossed on more than a few occasions. These interactions are much different—and have been much more pleasant—than when we were building fights on the opposite end of the ring.

He's a wealth of boxing knowledge and loves to share stories from his long career in the sweet science. I'm always excited to hear another tale from the great Freddie Roach. More than anyone I've ever known, he has an immense love for the sport of boxing. I was thrilled when Freddie responded to my interview request. I've been a fan of his for a long time. It was a poignant interview because he now has his ups and downs with Parkinson's disease. He's still working every day, sporting his trademark thick-rimmed glasses. We talk while he's at his gym, and while his speech is sometimes difficult, his mind is sharp. He's still one of the best strategists in boxing.

Before he was one of the best-known trainers in boxing, Freddie was a professional prizefighter with a respectable record. And while he gave his all to win a title in his career, he found his real calling as a trainer. As a fighter, he was trained by Hall of Famer Eddie Futch, and when he started training fighters, he started out under Futch.

When he struck out on his own, he became known as the coach behind some of boxing's greats, like Manny Pacquiao, Miguel Cotto, Virgil Hill, Mike Tyson, and many more. While he never had his own arm raised for a championship bout, he's the man behind dozens and dozens of world champions—all points of pride for Freddie.

Freddie is an engaging, funny guy with a lifetime of boxing stories and experiences that he shares with fighters, gym clients, and other trainers every day. We talk about his own boxing journey as a fighter, what a difficult sport boxing is, and why training matters. "Boxing is a very difficult sport," he says. "It's a really hard sport and it's one that I think few people choose, but when you choose this sport, expect to give 1,000% every day. You have to work your ass off to make it."

ON HIS OWN BOXING DREAMS

We talk a little bit about how he got started in boxing. His own boxing career was quite robust in its own right. He fought in 53 fights between 1978 and 1986, finishing with a record of 40-13-0.

"I wanted to win a world championship so badly," he says. "My life has been my career and I trained as hard as I could," he says. "I gave everything I could and then, finally, I decided I wasn't going to be there. You know, it was just the level was a little bit too high for me. I got to fight a couple of really good fighters," he says, smiling.

One of his most notable fights was in 1985 against two-time world champion Bobby Chacon. "It was really a charm to be able to fight Bobby Chacon, one of my idols growing up as a kid. And doing okay with him but not good enough to win the fight," Freddie says.

After working for years to make a title happen, he realized it was time to call it a day. "At some point in my life, I chose to retire because I wasn't getting any better and I thought that, you know, I'm very open to maybe training people." He went to his own trainer, Eddie Futch, and asked him if he could work with him training fighters. "It worked out well," Freddie says. "He taught me a lot about the boxing game and he taught me a lot about the training game, and there's a world of difference there."

ON THE TRAINING GAME

I tell Freddie that trainer Buddy McGirt surprised me when he said he'd known from the beginning of his boxing career that he wanted to be a trainer. I ask Freddie if he ever felt the same way and thought during his fight career that he'd become a trainer.

"Not really. The first year of retirement was not good. It was kind of a rough year," he says. "You know, just finding out, like, what am I gonna do with my life? Where am I going to be? Eddie was such a good guy to me. He taught me a lot about the sport, so I thought he was one of the best guys to go to and then he had a very good stable of fighters."

Freddie began training fighters Virgil Hill and Marlon Starling—
"really crafty guys"—and he discovered he was good at it.

"I started doing mitts with all the fighters," he says. "Eddie was getting
a little bit older and they didn't do mitts too much back in his era anyway.
When he did mitts with you, it was like one punch at a time and just work on
the technique of that one punch over and over. Then mitts kind of went into
combinations that you have and things you put together and things that you
maybe can invent a little bit as being a trainer."

After serving as Eddie's assistant and winning a couple world titles,
he knew he'd found his home in boxing. "Then I said, 'This is where I fit.'
I'm a better trainer than I was a fighter," he says. "I wish I could have
fought like that, but it just wasn't my style."

We talk a little about Freddie's days as a boxer and his style. He says he
had a tough time settling down and was never able to get better at it. "I liked
to fight in action fights—and fight hard. Sometimes I wish I'd settled down
and just boxed a little more because I could box if I wanted to, but when the
first punch landed, the fight begins!"

His style was all action—the-take-one-to-give-one style. So much so that
he became known as a "bleeder"—that guy who's constantly taking punches
and gets busted open. "Someone said one night, 'You know, Freddie Roach is
bleeding again.' And they said, 'Oh, what else is new?' I just didn't want that
reputation," he says. "It was my 27th pro fight that I started to cut, but the
thing is, before that, I wasn't such a bleeder back then. The thing is, as time
goes and we get older and maybe a little bit slower, we get the scar tissue,
and once the scar tissue gets there, it's never gone."

ON TEMPERAMENT

I ask about a fighter's temperament and how much control the trainer has
over raw talent. Can a trainer coach a fighter into changing their mindset in
the ring? I ask him if he could tell when he saw young fighters if they'd be
able to develop and change.

"Sometimes you got what you got, but a lot of times, you can change them, but it does take awhile and, you know, slowly mold them into what they do best as a boxer and not just as a puncher." But as a former competitor and as a trainer, Freddie knows it's every fighter's dream to get the chance to fight for a world title. "I wanted to fight for the world title and I was close with Bobby Chacon and [Héctor] Camacho, but being in your [Chris's] shoes is where I wanted to be," he says.

Once he moved into training, he embraced his new role in boxing. "I just decided that maybe it wasn't made for me. I'm just not going to get there, so going into training was a really good move for me and working with all these fighters was great," he says. After five years of working with Futch, he decided to go out on his own. "The only bad thing about working for Eddie Futch was he didn't pay you that well," Freddie says with a laugh. "He paid me in knowledge and that's what the key was."

When he knew it was time, he had a couple fighters who broke off with him and he began training them on his own. One of his fighters was Virgil Hill, who'd win the WBA light heavyweight title in 1987 and successfully defend it 10 times, holding it until 1991.

"It was really, really great because winning a world title with a fighter, giving him the design for the fight of how he can become world champion in that fight," he says of a fourth-round TKO against Leslie Stewart, makes all the training worthwhile. Freddie notes that not only was Hill "just a very good student" but that he's also a trainer now in Los Angeles.

ON NATURAL TALENT VERSUS LEARNED SKILL

We talk a bit about natural talent versus learned skill and the father–son relationship. Freddie was trained by his own father and has seen a number of talented boxers train their kids for boxing. He's smart enough to know that many of these young fighters can be successful, but he also knows they have to approach boxing differently. He sometimes has to teach them how to work harder at different skills than their champion fathers did. Instead of channeling natural talent, he has to teach them how to be great boxers.

"Whenever you have a father–son relationship, it is very difficult," he says. He's had to say, "'Okay, your dad was born to fight. Your dad is one of those special people. He just knows how to go out there and he knows how to fight, but me and you, we have to work at this. This is our job. We have to work at getting better,'" he says. The message usually sinks in. Then they can "work harder and, you know, just not take things for granted."

ON THE EARLY YEARS

As we talk about fighters who're "born to work" versus guys who really have to work at things, we talk about drive and mentors. In my search to get to the heart of what really drives boxers to get in the ring and win, I ask Freddie what his own motivation was. What made him push past the hard times and dig a little deeper to succeed?

"My dad, he was my first trainer and he knew that he couldn't take me any further, so we took a trip out to Las Vegas. And he started introducing me to the trainers," he says of his formative years in boxing. "Finally, we met Eddie Futch and he seemed like the right guy. My dad liked his style very much." It was the beginning of a lifelong relationship.

"You know, it's funny because my dad, he stayed seven days with me out in Las Vegas," Freddie says. "And then he had to go home and take care of the family because he had six kids at home." Freddie was on his own and boxing became his focus.

"My dad was a tree surgeon, and I majored in horticulture in school, and I always thought I was going to be a tree surgeon for the rest of my life," he says. "But when I moved out west and Eddie started developing me, he made me a better fighter and a better boxer. I was really, really surprised how much better I was getting, and, you know, when you have a knowledgeable guy like that, the key is to listen. They have knowledge. Make sense of what they say."

He progressed as a boxer and Eddie became his mentor as well as his trainer. "Everything started clicking together," Freddie says. He talks about the training experience for a new guy in the gym. "I found my home. I found out what I can do here."

That experience changed when he retired from boxing. "That first year off was a little bit rough—just like not knowing what to do," he says. "Like going to the gym and I'd start training and then just think, 'No, I better go home.'" He wanted what so many fighters want: just one more shot—just one more time in the ring. "But mentally, I knew that I couldn't, you know. It just wasn't there anymore."

He smiles. "Being a trainer was so much more fun and it worked out really well for me!" Today, he has a gym in LA that he calls his home because he's there so often. "I'm really grateful that I have this place to go every day."

> **"Work hard and good things happen. Work is what it takes to get to the top. There's no other way around it. There's no shortcuts, that's for sure. Work hard, enjoy those wins, and keep fighting for them."**
>
> **–Freddie Roach**

ON MAKING THE DECISION TO RETIRE

Every fighter gets injuries and trains to fight through them, but some injuries make fighters start to think about the next part of their career—and life. It takes a special dedication to fight eight or more rounds with a broken hand, fractured orbital bone, or broken ribs. So I want to hear about his 1981 fight against Mario Chavez, where he broke his hand in the second round, went 10 rounds, and won on a split decision. The fight was significant to Freddie because he'd been guaranteed a shot at a title fight if he won.

"I saw the right hand opening and I let it go as hard as I could. He saw it coming and just took his head down a little bit." He hit Chavez "higher on the forehead." He broke his hand but went on to fight with that injured hand and win the fight. "It was hard to not throw because it didn't hurt when I landed," he says. He had surgery on the hand and was out for a while, missing a shot at a title fight. By the time he was ready to return, he'd moved up in weight class. "I was out for about a year and I put too much weight on. I went from 122 to 130 and it just was too big a jump at the time," he says.

The change up in weight class is a hard one to make. We talk about how much harder guys hit that are even five to seven pounds heavier than you are. Force increases exponentially. We also talk about the pressure he was under to retire. Or, rather, the conversations that friends were having with him, encouraging him to consider it. "I'd got it in my head that I wasn't getting any better," he says.

He remembers one long discussion he had with Eddie Futch at the gym. And the idea that he had a way out by becoming Eddie's #1 assistant. "That was the key right there, I think. Without Eddie involved, I wouldn't be here today," Freddie says.

Still, he remembers how hard it was to make the decision to walk away. "There's that part of the heart that said 'I can still do this,'" he says. "And then I lost three out of my last four fights. And I thought, 'Hmmm, maybe he was right.'" We laugh over the fact that fighters are a stubborn bunch. For Freddie, it became obvious when he found he was training a fighter for a card while he was also fighting the main event. "And it was like, 'What am I doing here? Am I training or am I fighting? Which way do I go?'"

"I finally came to my senses and I did retire and went strictly into training fighters," he says. "And it was so much fun!"

Freddie reminds fighters of one of the most fundamental lessons: Do what you love. If you have a love of the sport, then work at it, but once it's not fun anymore or fulfilling, it's time to take a step back. He considers himself lucky to have found something he loves even more than boxing: training fighters. And he's very, very good at it.

"Bringing the best out of those guys was just what I wanted to do and where we are today worked out very well," he says. "And as each champion came, and more came, and more came, I said, 'This is where I belong,' you know, and it was a good choice."

We talk about past interviews and I mention there's a quote I love from a recent HBO *Real Sports* segment where Freddie said, "I hope I work 'til I die." I ask him if he still feels the same way. "Yes, definitely," he replies quickly. "This is what I do. It's what I love. I come to the gym six days a week and nothing is more important than getting the fighter ready for the fight."

Even with a string of world champion fighters in his stable, he's still appreciative of the Virgil Hills of the world because they "have believed in me and trusted me." He notes, though, that the trainer has to be a fit. Hill and others "tested the waters, you know," he says about how important it is for a fighter and trainer to click. "Getting these guys to listen to you and getting the combinations down and then learning how to do mitts really well and be good at that also."

Freddie learned from his fighters along way, picking up tips and techniques from fighters who'd trained or fought in other countries. "I think Virgil Hill taught me a little bit about catching because he had been to different countries and so forth." But ultimately, he loved working with the fighters one-on-one with the mitts. "It was really just me and them working together, and it worked out really well for me," he says.

ON ADVICE TO HIS YOUNGER SELF

As I've conducted these interviews, one of the more interesting questions I've asked every fighter is what they'd say if they could give advice to themselves when they were just getting started. Some wouldn't change a thing, while others would put themselves on a different path.

I ask Freddie what advice he'd have for his younger self knowing what he knows now about the game, the sport, and everything. "I would have told him to box more and not fight so much," he says with a smile. "I was a better boxer and I knew I could box a little bit, but once I got hit, the fight was on. I kind of wish I could have used my ability to box more."

We laugh about that fundamental lesson—the difference between boxing and fighting. I tell him I learned it from Robert Garcia between rounds of a sparring session. I remember Garcia telling me very calmly "not to worry about if it was exciting—to just box." I learned "when you box, you win."

Freddie says that he also tends to stay quiet in his corner but then give targeted advice. "I'm quiet in the corner because I don't believe in yelling at fighters," he says. "And when they come back to the corner, I can talk to them. I don't want the yelling to get everyone excited."

It's good advice on keeping everything calm and focused for the fighter to think things through. "I want him to calm down so he can follow through with the game plan," he says. "And sometimes when Eddie couldn't make the fight and a new assistant was in the corner and he'd be yelling at me and I turned to him and told him shut up." This is Freddie's clear, confident approach as a trainer.

ON TRAINING MANNY PACQUIAO

We talk about one of Freddie's most famous fighters: the legendary Manny Pacquiao, who recently announced he's running for president in his home country of the Philippines. I ask Freddie about Pacquiao's retirement and what role he feels a trainer plays in helping guide a fighter through that decision.

"My role is just to stand behind the fighter," Freddie says, noting that it was Pacquiao's decision and they didn't really know what he'd decide to do when it came to retirement. "The thing is, we weren't exactly sure which [option] he was going to choose because he does love boxing—and boxing was his biggest sport for a long, long time. But you know, he's at that point where maybe politics might be a little safer place for him."

Pacquiao finished his career as an eight-division world champion and as a first-ballot Hall of Famer. "He's a good politician. He does good things for his country," Freddie says.

I ask him if he's had to have conversations with other fighters in the gym about when he thinks it's time to hang it up and what happens when he sees them still holding on. Has he had to coach a fighter like Eddie did with him?

"That talk you might have isn't always the best talk in the world, but it has to be truthful. You have to see where they're at in their career, and if they have a little more, maybe you go on, and if they don't, then you know it's over," Freddie says.

He makes it clear that as a trainer, he does "whatever I can do to help them" and sometimes that means offering them the same kind of way out that Eddie Futch offered him: a chance to become a trainer.

"There are probably about 10 fighters here that I used to train that train fighters here now," he says, referring to his gym. "They work here at the gym, and it works out well because we have similar ideas on fighting and how to train certain styles."

And having a stable of name fighters helps clients who come into the gym too. "I was telling a guy the other day, 'Do you know Justin Juuko?' and he says, 'Didn't he fight [Floyd] Mayweather?' and I say, 'Yeah, he did. Justin, when did you fight Mayweather?'" he says. It's a great example of how boxing can connect people together. "So [Justin] started talking to the new customer and now he has a new customer. And it works out really well."

GLOSSARY

AIBA
International Boxing Association

CAMO
California Amateur Mixed Martial Arts

DQ
disqualified

IBF
International Boxing Federation

ISKA
International Sport Karate Association

KO
knockout

MMA
mixed martial arts

NABF
North American Boxing Federation

NABO
North American Boxing Organization

PBC
Premier Boxing Champions

TKO
technical knockout

UBA
Universal Boxing Alliance

UBF
Universal Boxing Federation

UFC
Ultimate Fighting Championship

USBA
United States Boxing Association

WBA
World Boxing Association

WBC
World Boxing Council

WBO
World Boxing Organization

WKA
World Kickboxing Association

INDEX

ACKNOWLEDGMENTS

I'd like to thank DK Publishing for allowing me the platform to put my words into print and to continue my dream of being an author. This book was a labor of love. Love of the sport and love of the individuals who put their lives on the line for the sake of passion. The book encapsulates many of the thoughts and principles that paved the way for all the success in my life. It's also given me the opportunity to relive some of the greatest moments of my career and put my feelings on paper to share with the world.

Everything worthwhile I've ever accomplished in my life has been difficult. This project was no different. This project had so many layers and was close to not getting done on a number of occasions. I'd like to send a huge thank you to Christopher Stolle, who believed in the book from day one. Without him going to bat for me time and time again, this book wouldn't be here today.

I'd also like to send a very special thank you to my new friend and colleague, Renee Wilmeth. She helped me every step of the way with this book: from keeping me organized, to instilling confidence in my writing, to motivating and pushing me, and, lastly, to making sure my thoughts were put into the correct words. Without her tireless efforts and competitive attitude, this book would be on the editing room floor right now.

Lastly, I'd like to thank all the incredible people who contributed to this book. Without the courage to share their epic stories of victory and defeat, this book is nothing. This work is based on love for a sport that doesn't love anyone back. Each story in here is based on a deep passion and drive to achieve greatness. Thank you for allowing me to share your stories.

ABOUT THE AUTHOR

CHRIS ALGIERI is a professional boxer and kickboxer who's held the World Boxing Organization (WBO) junior welterweight boxing title, the International Sport Karate Association (ISKA) world welterweight kickboxing title, and the World Kickboxing Association (WKA) world super welterweight kickboxing title during his more than 15-year professional career.

Chris has appeared on HBO, NBC, Showtime, Spike, and ESPN as a fighter and commentator. He's currently working toward another world boxing title to accomplish his goal of being a multiple-time world champion in two different sports.

Chris established himself as the "Pride of Huntington," fighting in Long Island, New York—just miles from his hometown of Greenlawn—at The Paramount in Huntington, selling out the venue nine consecutive times. In 2014, he defeated defending champion Ruslan Provodnikov for the WBO junior welterweight title—considered by *The Ring* magazine as the Upset of the Year.

This victory led to the biggest fight of his life: In only his 21st professional boxing match, Chris moved up to the welterweight division to fight Manny Pacquiao for the WBO title. Although he lost that fight, he gained a lot of respect in going 12 rounds with the future Hall of Famer.

He's since won the WBO super lightweight international title with a thrilling war at the famed Madison Square Garden, stopping his opponent over eight rounds.

Outside the ring, Chris graduated from Stony Brook University with honors in May 2007 with a bachelor's of science in health care management and then went on to receive his master's degree from the New York Institute of Technology. He's certified as a sports nutritionist (CISSN) through the International Society of Sport Nutrition (ISSN).

Chris has gained worldwide recognition as a professional boxing analyst during live boxing events broadcast by ESPN+ and DAZN apps.